Growing 101 Herbs That Heal

gardening techniques, recipes, and remedies

Tammi Hartung

Medical Herbalist

STOREY
BOOKS

Schoolhouse Road
Pownal, Vermont 05261

The mission of Storey Communications is to serve our customers by publishing practical information that encourages personal independence in harmony with the environment.

This book is intended to educate and expand one's concepts of how to deal with a crisis. It is not intended to take the place of courses in first aid or to replace medical care when needed.

Edited by Deborah Balmuth and Robin Catalano
Cover, text design, and production by Mark Tomasi
Production assistance by Susan Bernier and Jennifer Jepson Smith
Cover photographs by Giles Prett
Interior photographs by Giles Prett, except pages 3, 6, 45, 135, 153–60, 162–65, 167, 168 (right), 169–80, 181 (right), 182–94 (left), 195–210, 212–14, 216–19, 221–26, and 228–38 © by Martin Wall; pages 166, 181, 194, and 211 © by Brother Alfred Brousseau, F.S.C. (elib.cs.berkeley.edu/flora/photos); page 168 by Denver Botanic Gardens; page 161 by Jim Manhart; page 220 by Panayoti Kelaidis; and pages 172 and 215 by Bruce Curtis
Illustrations by Brigita Fuhrmann, except pages 90, 91, 92 (top), 93, 94 (bottom left), and 95 (bottom) by Kurt Musfeldt
Indexed by Peggy Holloway, Holloway Indexing Services
Professional review by Kathleen McKeon
Photo location and styling assistance by Mariam Massaro, Wise Way Herbals, Worthington, MA; and Lilian R. Jackman, Wilder Hill Gardens, Conway, MA

Printed in the United States by R.R. Donnelley
10 9 8 7 6 5 4 3 2 1

Library of Congress Cataloging-in-Publication Data

Hartung, Tammi, 1961–
    Growing 101 herbs that heal / Tammi Hartung.
        p. cm.
    Includes bibliographical references.
    ISBN 1-58017-215-6 (pb : alk. paper)
    1. Herb gardening. 2. Herbs—Therapeutic use. I. Title: Growing one hundred and one herbs that heal. II. Title.
    SB351.H5 H3235   2000
    635'.7—dc21
                                                                99-052839
                                                                CIP

contents

Dedicated with love to my husband, Chris, and my daughter, M'lissa;

To the Green Nation, my greatest teachers;

For Rosemary, who showed me the magic of dreams.

Foreword

A garden is a sacred place where plants and people meet, where the richly woven relationship unfolds. Surrounded by plant medicines that are strong yet gentle, this relationship is new to many of us, yet it is as ancient as the earth itself. Gardening — tending the earth — helps us remember our connection to nature as our fingers reach deep into the rich, moist soil. Like the garden itself, our relationship with the plants continues to change and mature. What we plant reflects our inner interests and dreams; wild or tended, they are always unique. We give a part of ourselves and in return receive many gifts. When we work together with the cycles of nature, we cultivate beauty as well as compassion and wisdom within each of us. A life infused with the simple pleasures of working in the garden is a good life.

Medicinal gardens are places to learn about plant wisdom, to taste and smell. They are outdoor classrooms where we learn to use plants for healing. In our gardens, we discover, as our ancestors did, how to bring plants from the wild into cultivation. At this time we are blessed that people are returning to the earth for their healing. Herbal medicine has become increasingly popular, and for good reason. As an herbalist and plant lover, I celebrate this renaissance of herbal medicine, yet like many of us, I am deeply concerned about what is happening to our wild plant populations.

The wild lands of North America supply many countries with the plants needed to make medicines. Many are prized for their roots, and our most cherished native plants are quickly disappearing from the wild. There is a growing tradition among herbalists and plant people to protect our wild plants. One of the easiest and most rewarding ways to do this is to begin growing these plants in gardens and on organic farms. It is vital that we not wait any longer to begin. It is truly the best hope for the future of these plant medicines we have come to love.

Many farmers and gardeners around the country have expressed genuine interest in cultivating organic medicinal plants; the time is right for this type of growing effort. Many farmers have found this opportunity to be both economically sound and incredibly rewarding. I believe we will see these farms and gardens become natural repositories for both seed and information, as well as places to study and learn about the life cycles of many medicinal plant species. What could be better than turning a passion for herbs and growing into a blossoming business opportunity?

We are very fortunate at this time that the information regarding cultivation of medicinal plants is being researched and shared. Whether you are a commercial grower or simply a curious herb gardener, you will be sure to find wise and helpful guidance for growing and using herbs for pleasure and livelihood inside this book.

SHELLEY TORGOVE
Clinical Herbalist; Member, American Herbal
Products Association and United Plant Savers
Denver, Colorado

Preface

This is the passionate story about the work that Chris and I do at Desert Canyon Farm & Learning Center, work that facilitates relationships between plants and people.

Today's society is about production and convenience — people trying to accomplish too much in each 24-hour day. This book is about offering alternative choices, teaching people to slow down and notice the health-giving gifts of the plants. It is about sharing knowledge of growing and preparing botanicals, and using them for cooking and medicine.

Our wild medicinal plants are disappearing at a fast pace. We must start conserving and stop harvesting wild plants for commercial purposes. We must use organic farming methods in place of commercial wildcrafting. Growing medicinal gardens is as important as it is magical. In this way, we will nurture the earth that nurtures us.

As an herb grower, I have found two major roadblocks: first, a lack of understanding of how to successfully grow many medicinal plants; second, people who know how to grow these plants but refuse to share their knowledge. This book now offers medicinal plant growing information for the home gardener.

Cultivate plant relationships in your life. Become inspired to prepare and use your own remedies. Cook delicious medicinal meals. And have fun! Think a bit like a plant instead of a person, and offer quiet, sincere words of thanks to the plants — for they are our greatest teachers.

This is my work, play, rest, and spirituality. I am blessed by the Green Plant Nation and honored to write this book.

Acknowledgments

This book is the result of an interest that began 36 years ago with a leaf herbarium school project.

My deepest thanks goes to my great-aunt Ruth and my great-grandfather, each of whom shared with me a love of plants and the land. They started me on my life's journey.

My husband, Chris, and daughter, M'lissa, have helped me in every possible way, taking on extra responsibilities that allowed me to focus on writing. They offered countless hugs and love, which made this book change from idea to reality.

My family also offered great support. They cooked, cleaned, taxied M'lissa, proofread, and coaxed a rebellious printer into meeting deadlines — all with smiles, love, and endless energy.

My teacher and dearest friend, Rosemary Gladstar, has given love, wisdom, encouragement, and friendship. Thank you, Rosemary — you are one of my brightest shining stars.

Grateful thanks to colleagues, friends, and clients, all of whom encouraged and offered expertise. My appreciation goes to Shelley Torgove for a beautiful foreword. Thanks also to my apprentices and students for your cheerfulness, even though I was weeks behind on grading your homework. Nelly and M'lissa, your computer notes were magical.

Everyone at Storey has been wonderful, offering support, guidance, and huge amounts of work. A special thanks to my editors, Deborah Balmuth and Robin Catalano.

It is impossible to thank everyone who has inspired this book or helped me develop skills as a medical herbalist and grower, but know that each of you holds a special place in my heart.

an introduction to growing medicinal plants

 Gardening with medicinal plants is intriguing to many of us. The reasons are numerous, ranging from enjoying a first-hand experience of growing our own botanical medicines to using the garden for its extra income potential. In addition, many of us have realized that the act of gardening can be therapeutic, providing not only physical exercise but also the opportunity for contemplation. Still, as enjoyable and important as these reasons are, I ask you to look beyond them to a much bigger picture. I challenge you to consider how growing your own medicinal garden can improve the earth.

Remembering Our Roots

The tradition of humans using plants for our own needs is an integral part of our historical role in living as a part of the world. It brings to the forefront of our consciousness a very important concept: It is not our intended purpose to control the world but rather to exist in partnership with all other living creatures on this planet. My question to you is simply this: Have you thought about how much positive impact you can have on Earth by simply growing a medicinal garden?

Let me share a story with you, one that you will most likely recognize.

In the beginnings of humankind, we honored our relationship with the green nation. We used plants for food and for medicine, to make clothing and practical utensils, and as an integral part of our spiritual traditions. We carefully gathered and thanked each plant in anticipation of how we would use it. Later, we began to learn to cultivate some of the plants we used, primarily those we used for food. Other plants, such as those used for medicines, we still gathered from the wild. As time passed, the larger percentage of the plants we used were cultivated as food sources. However, we have continued to harvest our medicine plants, mainly from wild places.

Medicinal Plants for the Present and the Future

As we now begin a new millennium, the medicinal use of plants has been reclaimed by many individuals. Around the globe, people continue to recognize and use plants for their medicinal benefits to health and well-being. In 1998, the World Health Organization claimed that 80 percent of the world's people still relied on medicinal plants to treat illness and disease. The market for botanical medicines at a retail level reached $4 billion in 1998 and continues to increase. While all this news is great for people, it isn't so fantastic if you're a wild medicinal plant.

In 1997 the World Conservation Union (comprising the Smithsonian Institution, the World Wildlife Fund, The Nature Conservancy, the Royal Botanical Gardens at Kew, and ten other governmental and independent research and conservation groups) stated that 12.5 percent of the world's 34,000 plants are threatened with immediate extinction. In the United States, 29 percent of the 16,000 plant species existing in the nation are at risk of extinction. A very large percentage of these plants are used medicinally.

So, you may want to know what is causing this problem. There are many factors that contribute to the survival or extinction of a plant. The plant's very own gene pool plays a large role in its ability to survive. The community of other plants and animals in which it grows also holds incredible influence. And there are still other factors such as climate, development, logging, livestock grazing, recreational activities, and, of course, wildcrafting (the practice of harvesting plants from wild places).

As the demand for botanical medicine continues to increase, more and more plant material is needed to make the products people are using for their health needs. Resources for acquiring this plant material have traditionally been through the avenue of wildcrafting. I wildcrafted on a commercial level for more than 12 years, and I have worked as a plant sourcing person ("buyer") for manufacturers for many years. During the course of that work I have watched the quantities required to make their products go from small amounts — as little as five pounds — to thousands of pounds annually.

The big issue in all of this is sustainability. Is harvesting our medicinal plants in this fashion a sustainable practice? Of course not! Can we

The popularity of endangered medicinal plants, such as passionflower, continues to soar. Organic cultivation of these plants is becoming more and more critical.

Let's Start in the Garden

We must immediately begin cultivating the medicinal plants we choose to use for our health and well-being. Where do we start? Well, it begins in the most simple yet complicated place, a place of pure magic and positive energy: our gardens.

We have the perfect opportunity to work positively on behalf of the plants we use simply by growing them. Cultivating the plants we choose to use for our medicines relieves the burden on the wild plant communities. Most importantly, we need to start growing all the species that are currently at risk or endangered. We must also begin growing the plants that are holding their own — maintaining their population numbers — before they, too, become endangered. There used to be literally tons of echinacea growing on the prairies not so long ago. This is one of the plants we are most concerned about, because it has been wildcrafted nearly to extinction.

In the past we did not know very much about how to cultivate many of these "wild" plants. However, many of them have turned out to be very easy to grow, like *Echinacea purpurea*. Others, like *Echinacea angustifolia* and false unicorn root, are true wild spirits of the plant kingdom and do not easily lend themselves to cultivation. My suspicions about these recalcitrant cultivatees have been confirmed — it's not really that they mind being cultivated, it's just that they want a little respect in the process.

With study and practice, we have learned that a little care and understanding will enable us to successfully raise hard-to-grow plants, even on a commercial scale. These are the plants that will teach us patience and careful observation. These are the gifts of a true gardener, are they not? The plants remind us that nature as a whole is still in charge and our role is to be part of the process, not

afford to continue harvesting wild plants for commercial purposes? Of course not! Then should we stop using these plants for medicinal and other purposes altogether? Of course not! But what can we do about this situation?

 ## The Importance of Organic Gardening

If I'm going to use a plant for medicine, I want to know that it is not going to be full of chemicals that do not promote health or, worse yet, that may actually contribute to harming my body. I also must know that the earth has not been compromised or contaminated. Gardening organically, without using harmful substances that poison the earth and our bodies, is essential.

the controller of the process. Many medicinal gardens have become our classrooms and laboratories where we can learn from the plants.

Nourishing Our Bodies and Our Earth

As we plant our gardens, we must grow them in a nurturing and honoring way. We must learn to grow these plants organically, free from synthetic chemicals. This means using great discrimination in what types of fertilizers we choose and finding the best and least harmful ways to control pests, diseases, and weed problems. We must learn how to nurture the soil, use water in a conservative way, and take advantage of companion/complementary planting.

As we create garden schemes and designs, we must learn to think a little bit more like the plant and a little less like a person. I challenge you to think about where each plant might grow in nature, where might be the ideal place of its own choosing. Would the plant choose a shady place near a stream, or would it find a sunny, gravelly slope more to its liking? What will the seed need in order to sprout? Maybe it will need a harsh winter or perhaps it must land in a dark place, like under a fallen leaf, before it can find the right circumstances to germinate. If we learn the individual personality of each plant, we can then decide how best to incorporate them into our gardens.

We sometimes forget about the usefulness of popular garden herbs like calendula, but even the most common herb can be used medicinally in a variety of ways.

Desert Canyon Farm
& Learning Center

Our farm, Desert Canyon Farm & Learning Center, sits at the base of the mountains in the high desert of southern Colorado. Chris and I decided four years ago, after 16 years of working for others, it was time to stop managing arboretums, garden centers, and herbal manufacturing facilities for other people and do something on our own. We planted 34 different medicinal plants in our field that first spring and put up a greenhouse the following fall. The school was born with a few public workshops and a two-year herbal apprenticeship program. We were in business.

Our strategy is to remain diversified in what we do, with a common theme running through all of our projects. We field-grow medicinal herbs, perennial bare roots (young perennials that are dug up and delivered to nurseries, where they will be repotted and grown), and we do some seed production. The greenhouse holds our field plugs and provides us with income from potted herbs, unusual perennials, and specialty vegetables. The school runs year-round; the entire farm serves as indoor and outdoor classrooms. I also travel extensively, teaching and doing consulting work, and I maintain my private clinical practice as a medical herbalist. Seldom does a day pass when the farm isn't as busy as a beehive.

When we arrived, no one knew what to think of us, those crazy herb growers up on the hill. One gentleman, who works in the prison industry here, reminded us as he was introducing himself that a neighbor of ours was "busted for having pot in his barn." Chris smiled and said, "Well, the only thing you will find in our barn is catnip." Last summer we became proactive about educating the law enforcement groups in this county about chaste berry. Because chaste berry leaves have a shape similar to that of marijuana leaves, some kids on the school bus thought we were growing illegal drugs! We invited everyone out for a field class, and it was great fun. Even the greenhouse heater repairman participated!

Chris and I still find time to sit on our porch and enjoy the chiminia, a southwestern outdoor fireplace, in the evenings or take in a soak at the local hot springs. Chris makes time to play as a jazz musician and I relax by stitching quilts and doing embroidery. Of course, having a teenager in the house means that life is always surprising and lively too. Some friends of ours (also growers in northern Colorado) have said many times that work is only worth the lifestyle it gives you in return. They are very right; as the busy spring comes around each year or we are struggling to keep going during the harvest season, we look up at the sunlight on Mount Cooper and all is well.

The fields at Desert Canyon Farm are beautiful and the gardens and pond are alive with the Earth's creatures. We take in the positive energy of students all around us or the neighbor stopping by to seek help in identifying a plant from his yard. We reflect on the fact that we have come a long way from when we arrived in Canon City as just a couple of "crazy herb farmers."

Gardening for the Soul

Whether you garden for pleasure or to add to your livelihood, growing medicinal plants is a very important and enjoyable task. It may be a way for you to improve your health — through both the physical act of gardening and the medicinal benefits of the plants — or to offer healing remedies to your family and friends. The act of gardening itself is therapeutic and healing. It most certainly will be an opportunity for you to nurture the piece of the earth where you live and to relieve some of the pressure on plants living in wild places. It is a chance for you to make a grassroots statement about how important it is to have organically grown plants in your foods and medicines (and anything else that is made from plants).

Gardening may also be an avenue for you to do some research on how to grow these plants. This might prove very helpful to organizations that are involved in promoting the survival of plant species all over the world, such as The Nature Conservancy and United Plant Savers (see Resources for more information). Regardless of the reasons you may have for growing medicinal plants, a garden of this nature will most certainly add beauty and magic to your personal space and daily life.

Picking and Choosing

I'm often asked how one should decide which herbs to grow in a medicinal garden. There are many different ways to choose. You

The beauty of the garden space heals the spirit and soul, just as the plants offer healing to the body. The design of your garden can be as simple as a set of containers or as elaborate as a formally laid-out field.

might decide to plant a garden based on personal health issues. Or perhaps you'd like to develop a new product line of herbal remedies and want to grow all of your own raw materials. My suggestion is always that you begin with plants for which you have a personal liking, plants you think you might use the most.

In choosing the plants for this book, I wanted to share those that I am especially fond of but also plants that are broadly useful in medicines and fun to grow. Why 101 of them? Well, I think it's fun to have a lot of choices in my life and I'm hoping that my enthusiasm for variety will be contagious. Be prepared: As you read and use this book, you will probably fall in love with many of these plants. Keep in mind, however, that this is just the tip of the iceberg. There are thousands of herbs you could consider growing as you travel on your gardening journey.

I also wanted to give consideration to plants for which it isn't easy to find growing information. My own learning experience has often been one of frustration as I realized that there was not much information available on how to design a garden, propagate, and organically grow and maintain medicinal plants. But I have learned to turn my frustration into an adventure. Now it is my hope that I can save you some of that frustration and encourage you to become adventurous in your medicinal gardening experiences.

Enjoy the journey!

 United Plant Savers

United Plant Savers is a nonprofit organization that strives to save wild medicinal plants through education, research, and encouraging organic cultivation. You can contact United Plant Savers at P.O. Box 98, East Barre, VT 05649.

Turning Your Garden into a Business

Often I am told, "It must be wonderful to have an organic farm" and "I wish I worked in a greenhouse." Sometimes people ask questions like, "If I wanted to raise herbs, how would I do that?" and "To whom should I sell my herbs?" This is where I can answer those questions and give you a few tips — and a big reality check.

Q. *What is farming really like?*
A. Many folks have a very romanticized impression of what it's like to earn a living raising herbs. Don't get me wrong — there are some pretty incredible benefits to raising and selling herbs, but it's not easy and it does take an amazing amount of ongoing research, continuous brainstorming, and never-ending stamina. It also means being willing to spend most of your time on your knees pulling weeds, working six or seven days a week for three-quarters of the year, and being on call 24 hours a day to baby-sit a greenhouse the entire year.

Despite the time, energy, and work involved, my husband and I don't have an employer to answer to, we live in the place of our own choosing, we have wonderful community support from our neighbors, and we make a contribution to the well-being and quality of life of others through the plants we grow. But most important, we take care of this beautiful small piece of Earth and do our best to work in a harmonious relationship with all that exists here in a positive way.

Q. *How do I get started?*
A. The key is to create something realistic to begin with and try it out. Then go from there, and remember to be flexible. Being in business for yourself is a fluid situation that must change with

markets and circumstances. It may be just right for you, but it might not.

Every serious grower needs to start with a business plan and, unless you are quite wealthy, a business loan. Call the Small Business Administration in your area and ask for the packet on putting together a business plan. Do not cut corners on your business plan contents, but do be precise and to the point in your presentation. It does not need to be fancy, but it does need to be complete.

If you will be asking a bank for a loan, there is a lot of information you must provide. You will be asked about your expertise and qualifications to build a successful business of this kind. To answer this question, include your résumé with references. You will also need to provide other in-depth information. Your bank will be able to give you more details.

If you have any letters of commitment or interest from potential customers, you should include them, too.

After you have polished up your business plan, begin looking for a loan officer who is open-minded to alternative types of businesses. We talked to many loan officers who just shook their heads and wished us well before we found one who was willing to work with us.

Q. Why garden organically?

A. If you plan to sell medicinal herbs, in any way, from your garden or farm, becoming certified organic is worth some serious consideration. Here are some great reasons to go organic:

- ▸ Fostering consumer confidence
- ▸ Complying with the standards of herbalism
- ▸ Protecting raw materials, especially endangered plants
- ▸ Taking responsibility for the Earth

If you are interested in becoming certified organic, you should contact your state Department of Agriculture or county extension service to find out what certifying agency to call. Each state has a slightly different certifying procedure, even though the standards are usually similar. The "fine print" is important, so ask for a regulations packet before proceeding.

Q. How do I locate my market?

A. There are so many possibilities for generating income through growing medicinal herbs, including:

- ▸ Selling at local farmer's markets
- ▸ Supplying local restaurants whose chefs are interested in incorporating medicinal herbs into their cuisine
- ▸ Selling to regional herbalists who would like to buy plant material to prepare botanical medicines
- ▸ Supplying herbal manufacturers who would be happy to support a local supplier
- ▸ Creating your own line of products. (If you do make your own products, you will need to meet all appropriate regulations for packaging and labeling; see chapter 8 for more information.)

If you are going to provide raw materials, either fresh or dried, begin learning from manufacturers and industry groups which plants are of strongest interest and which plants have already saturated the market. Join local grower organizations for support and resource information. The Internet is a great place to look for organizations, up-to-date growing topics, and medicinal plant information. Also, learn what is popular in your region if you wish to do business at a farmer's market or with local restaurants.

Q. Should I sell fresh or dried herbs?

A. Dried herbs. The market for dried medicinal herbs is very good and broader than the market for fresh medicinals. More manufacturers use dried plant material in their products. However, producing dried herbs requires some type of drying facility. You must be able to dry the herbs completely, and then be able to store them out of direct light and away from moisture in an insect- and animal-proof environment that is free of dust and other contaminants.

Fresh herbs. Some fresh herbs will command a greater price than dried, and vice versa. The market for fresh herbs is considerably smaller and the competition is greater. Remember that providing fresh herbs to customers means that they must be picked and handled very carefully to prevent bruising or damage. Fresh herbs must be shipped within 24 hours of harvest, otherwise makers of high-quality products will not accept them. You must have some way to keep the herbs cool until they are shipped. In addition, packaging and shipping fresh herbs is much more difficult and costly than for dried herbs.

Q. *How do I work with a raw materials buyer?*
A. It is important that you cultivate a positive relationship with your raw materials buyer and try to meet his or her needs as much as reasonably possible. You should also be able to clearly convey your needs as a supplier. Stay in close contact with your customer, but don't become a pest. Send complete information about the herbs you will be selling the next season by January at the latest; November or December is even better. Include pertinent plant information and your purchasing, shipping, and delivery terms. Encourage customers to place their orders by January or February to facilitate your seeding and planting schedule. You should expect the buyer to provide you with his plant-receiving requirements when the order is placed; ask if they're not given. Be willing to work with the buyer to make reasonable changes, but don't commit to things that you cannot accomplish.

 A Guide to Using This Book

This book has been arranged to make it easy and fun to read. You will find information that speaks of my own experiences and those of others. The step-by-step adventure begins with planning and designing your garden (chapter 2). An in-depth look at maintaining healthy soils (chapter 3) follows. Then you'll discover how to propagate different herbs (chapter 4), and to incorporate them into your garden.

Of course, no gardening book would be complete without instructions for maintaining a healthy garden, so you'll find that information in chapter 5. Be sure to read chapter 6 carefully for general insight into organic insect and disease management.

I want to inspire you to harvest and use your plants, so I've provided a detailed harvesting guide in chapter 7 as well as easy-to-follow directions for the kitchen "pharmacy" (chapter 8), where you will prepare your own medicinal remedies. Since I am a firm believer in promoting good health through our foods, I've added chapter 9, which includes delectable recipes for cooking with medicinal herbs.

I would like you to have the opportunity to get to know 101 different medicinal herbs, so I have profiled each one of them in chapter 10, A Gardener's *Materia Medica.* Come back to this section whenever you want to understand or experiment with a specific herb and need to know a lot about it individually.

If you need some guidance on where to buy seeds or a gardening item, or if you need further information on a particular subject, simply turn to the back of the book. This is where you'll find information on resources such as gardening supply companies and professional organizations. There is also a reading list that contains my favorite plant books so that you can explore individual subjects further. ❦

Two

selecting the plants and designing your garden

As all gardeners — seasoned and beginner — know, the next best thing to actually planting the garden is designing and planning it. This is certainly one of my favorite parts of the process. Still, as creative as designing and planning are, there are some guidelines to consider that will make the project come together in a much smoother fashion. ❧

Discovering Your Garden Personality

The first question you must answer is a personal one. What type of garden personality are you? Do you like a very formal garden? Maybe you are a practical-garden personality, or perhaps you are a wild-garden type.

It is also possible that the garden space has some personality traits that will need to be considered. Do you want this garden to be easily accessible from the kitchen? You might like to plant a scented medicinal garden beneath a bathroom or bedroom window. Perhaps you would prefer to grow your plant medicines in containers on a deck or balcony.

Usually the more formal the garden is, the more time will be required to care for it. I always recommend a bit of soul-searching before designing a garden. It will bring you little pleasure if you design a garden for yourself that fits another's garden personality. (If you are asked to design a garden for someone else, you should keep your own personality to yourself and be sensitive to the other person's preferences.) This is also the most appropriate time to do a reality check with yourself. Ask yourself these crucial but sometimes difficult questions: "Just how much time do I plan to spend caring for this garden? Is that a reasonable expectation for the type of garden I hope to plant and the lifestyle I am currently leading?" The answers to these questions will be different at various times in your life. The garden you plant today may be very different from the one you plant five years from now.

For people who have a very busy lifestyle or limited space, a container garden may be the perfect solution.

Siting the Garden

In order to design your garden, you must first determine where in your yard the garden will be. Sit quietly for a moment and observe the potential areas. Consider these questions:

▶ What existing features are in the area? Are there buildings or fences, trees, shrubs, or maybe a stream?

▶ What will border the garden space — a patio, lawn, woodland?

▶ What type of light does each area get? Is it totally shady, in full sun, a bit of both?

▶ Do you plan to plant in beds or rows or containers?

▶ Is the existing soil decent or will you need to prepare it more extensively?

▶ Is the location visually pleasing, or is it most important that it just be a practical space?

I find it's always wise to answer these questions as best I can while I'm sitting *in* the proposed garden space, where I can see and feel the situation. I take as many notes as possible about all that I am seeing. These are very helpful to me during the design process.

Planning for Easy Access

Whether you are establishing a brand-new garden or integrating medicinal plants into an existing bed, easy access is key. Several factors will need to be considered at this point. First and foremost, is the garden in a place where you can work in it easily and harvest from it on a whim if you want to? So many times I've listened to the same story: that a garden was planted and it turned out to be quite lovely, "but I just never seem to really use any of the herbs. They're just not handy." Being able to pop into the garden to pick some basil or heartsease flowers allows you to use fresh basil in your spaghetti sauce and to serve

a salad dressed with beautiful edible flowers. Ease of harvesting medicinal plants is equally important. Often in our busy lives we spend only short bits of time working in the garden; if the garden is located conveniently, then all is well. If not, the weeds tend to gain the upper hand and the mint begins to ramble beyond its allocated space.

Field growers also will want to give some thought to these issues. If you are growing on a small acreage, then every inch of space counts. Planning well the location and layout of your garden will maximize production, maintenance ease, and, ultimately, financial gain.

Considering the logistics of access before the garden is planted will make your life much easier. Discovering *after* the garden is planted that a key factor doesn't work very well is one of my most frustrating growing experiences. As an example, imagine that you planted a glorious garden only to discover that there isn't easy access to a hose for watering. Or perhaps you put the garden in your dog's favorite running location and he isn't willing to "give way" to your garden. If you are field growing, make certain that there is appropriate access available for a tiller or tractor, that the irrigation system will cover your growing space adequately, and so on.

 ## Start Small

For new gardeners, it is wise to begin with a small garden space and add to it as you feel comfortable. Start with a space that is 6 to 8 feet (1.8 to 2.4 m) square or round; use the guidelines in this chapter to help you. When you feel ready to expand, enlarge the parameter by 2 to 6 feet (.6 to 1.8 m) and then plant. You may decide to create a different shape for the garden as you're expanding. This is easily done by creating a shape outside of the existing garden and then joining it to the garden as an extension. ✿

If you think about these circumstances after the garden is in place, you will find yourself mumbling as you drag heavy hoses around the yard. And you certainly don't want to be seen driving a tractor up and down the road trying to figure out a point at which you can ride into your field without causing damage to trees, fences, and other items. Just imagine how entertaining that would be for on-lookers, and how disastrous it would be for your field preparation.

Determining Size

Once you know where the garden is going to be located, take a tape measure out to the area and measure the space. I have a few words of advice to you at this point. Be reasonable with yourself in determining how large your garden is going to be. Every one of us has had eyes bigger than our stomachs when it comes to planning a beautiful garden. It's no great pleasure to prepare a huge garden space for planting and discover that it's too much to care for, or that it will be too expensive to plant the entire area.

I suggest starting with a reasonable amount of space that will match your lifestyle in terms of how much of a commitment you can make to gardening. You might even feel conservative, but remember that garden additions are as much fun as the original garden you've planned. Once you have decided on the size, write down those measurements for later reference.

Staking out the dimensions can be a good approach to sizing, especially if you have trouble visualizing the actual size of an area. To do this, measure out the length and width of the garden. Pound a stake into each of the four corners, and then run string between the parallel posts. This will give you a more accurate idea of the garden size you have chosen.

Drafting a Design

I like to work with a piece of graph paper when I am designing a garden space. Pencil out the perimeters of the garden, using whatever scale you prefer. I usually make each square equal to ½ foot (15 cm), so that four graph squares equals 1 square foot (30 cm).

Add the Hard Goods

The next step is to draw in the *hard goods* of the garden. These are the pathways, rocks, benches, focal points, and so on. Be sure to include any existing features of the space, such as patios, fences, and buildings. Make decisions about what types of pathways or stepping-stones you would like to use — flagstones, grass, gravel, and even bark mulch are all very nice choices. Pathways and stepping-stones are one of the most important components of garden design — they give you access to maintain and harvest the garden without stepping on and thus compacting the soil around the plants.

Will you welcome birds into your garden? If so, you should be sure to include a birdbath or bird feeder. Remember that the birds can be beneficial for controlling insect pests. If you want to entice honeybees and bumblebees into the garden to improve pollination, then you should include a water source for them — shallow pottery dishes work well — somewhere in the design.

Will your garden be a place to go and sit for a spell? There are so many wonderful choices for peaceful resting sites. You might decide that you would like an elegant iron bench, or perhaps a willow chair will be more to your taste. Even a glorious old stump or flat boulder makes a lovely sitting place. I often like to combine my bench with an arbor to create a shaded place to sit and read or sketch for a while. Arbors and trellises can also be important in the garden if you plan to grow climbing plants like hops and clematis.

Focal Points

Every garden design benefits from having a focal point from which the rest of the garden flows. Sometimes there might be more than one focal point, especially if the garden is large. You certainly could use one of your hard goods as a focal point, such as a bench, a trellis, a beautiful statue, or a bubbling fountain. The focal point could also be a special plant, like a tree or rosebush. It's also nice to create the focus of the garden around a cluster of plants, such as three or four mullein plants or hollyhocks. Both mullein and hollyhocks are quite tall and their flowers add a splash of color along the spires, making them an eye-catching focal point.

If the garden is also a children's space, it might be fun to create a sunflower and morning glory playhouse as the focal point of the rest of the garden. To do this, train the morning glories to climb up the stalks of the sunflowers, thus filling in the spaces to create "walls." Be sure to make an entry point to the playhouse.

What Plant Where?

As you are drawing all of your ideas on your graph paper, you will want to consider some basic points. Spacing requirements are a common concern. Plant height and flower color are always helpful to know. I really appreciate knowing if a plant will grow in a clump or if it has a spreading nature. In the chart on page 18, you will find specifics for spacing and flower color and other helpful details about the individual plants.

Spacing Requirements

First of all, how much space should you give each plant in your design? Of course, it will vary a bit depending on the individual plant that you

A rock circle enclosing special plants or a water feature creates an appealing focal point in the garden. Pathways are also pleasing to the eye and invite you into the garden.

are working with, but as a general guideline, I recommend that you allow 10 to 12 inches (25 to 30 cm) for most plants. There will be some that can be spaced much more closely than that, and certainly some will need more room to mature.

Do not be deceived in the spring when you are putting out young plants. Most people forget to allow enough room between the plants and they end up with a garden that looks very crowded as the plants come into maturity. The May garden will be much different from the July or August garden, and a second-year perennial garden will look a lot less sparse than it did during its first growing season. If you do plant too closely, most plants can be dug up and moved around a bit to provide more growing space, so crowded conditions are not usually the end of the world. They do, however, create extra work. As you plan which plants you will use, check the spacing requirements and draw them into your design accordingly.

Light Exposure

As you are deciding the plan for your garden, spend some time watching how the sun travels across the space you are considering. Will the garden be located in full sun, partial shade, or full shade? Perhaps the garden will include areas of many types of light exposure. This is important when you begin to select the plants you will grow.

Soil Type

What type of soil will you have available? Is it sandy, rich loam, clay, or gravel? You may have areas that are a combination of soil types. There are very few instances in which the soil would be so poor that a good variety of medicinal herbs could not be grown in that place. However, defining the soil type before you plant will help you choose the most appropriate plants to grow.

Growing black cohosh in a gravelly soil is not the best idea. Penstemons, however, will thrive in such an area. Planning ahead can make your garden a great success.

Plant Height

The next important detail to know is approximately how tall a plant will be when fully grown. You don't want to place short plants behind tall ones. If you plant an herb as a border and later discover that it grows to 3 feet (.9 m) tall while everything planted behind it is only 1 to 2 feet (30 to 60 cm) tall, your border then becomes a living wall that will screen out of vision all that is behind it.

The Color Palette

Designing a garden is like painting a picture. Colors and hues are what make the difference between a complex-looking garden and one that is simply planted with no attention to details.

White flowers and silvery or gray foliage will play a critical role in how lively your garden looks throughout the growing season. I like to make sure that I have 30 to 40 percent of my flower and foliage color in the white/gray/silver range. This allows the garden to look spunky during the late part of the season, when even the best of gardens begin to look weary and faded.

Purples and blues in foliage and flower color are beautiful, but planting from only that palette will produce a bluish hue in the garden when viewed even from a short distance. Those colors are lovely, but they lose their definition from afar. Try planting bright yellow, orange, red, or pink flowers throughout a blue or purple color scheme. This will separate, to the eye, the individual blue and purple flowers in the gardenscape, so that you will see them all specifically, even from a distance.

Red and orange flowers and foliage look great together, but take care when planting a lot

When designing your garden, take advantage of the plants' natural characteristics, such as height and color. You can create a stunning garden from even the most common plants.

of these colors. This is a fiery and spicy combination; it can be a lot of fun, but it can just as easily look very harsh.

Pinks are always pretty, but they sometimes clash with other colors. When using a lot of pinks in the color scheme, I like to utilize white and silver along with blue and purple foliage and flowers to create a watercolor effect.

As you are considering the flower color, don't forget to use foliage textures and colors to make your garden design more interesting. Foliage is always there, even after blooming has finished. In some cases, the foliage distinctions may be what really liven up your garden all year long, as many plants will remain green even through the winter months.

Plant Characteristics and Requirements

This chart gives you the basic information you need to know about each herb in order to be able to incorporate it into a garden plan. Unlike the habitat chart (page 30), which gives a plant's first choices, the growing guidelines I've given here are based on my experience; although some information may not seem typical for a specific plant, I have learned that plants are often more flexible than we assume. Over time you will learn each plant's limits so that you're not asking it to grow in a situation that is too far beyond its natural choices.

HERB	CYCLE	GROWING NATURE	LIGHT REQUIREMENTS	HEIGHT
Alfalfa (*Medicago sativa*)	perennial	clumps	full sun	15–18 inches (38–45 cm)
Angelica (*Angelica archangelica*)	biennial	clumps	full sun, partial shade, shade	4–6 feet (1.2–1.8 m)
Anise hyssop (*Agastache foeniculum*)	perennial	clumps	full sun, partial shade	2–3 feet (.6–.9 m)
Astragalus (*Astragalus membranaceus*)	perennial	clumps	full sun, partial shade	3–4 feet (.9–1.2 m)
Balloon flower (*Platycodon grandiflorus*)	perennial	spreads	full sun, partial shade	12–15 inches (30–38 cm)
Basil (*Ocimum* species)	annual	clumps	full sun	15 inches (38 cm)
Betony (*Betonica officinalis*)	perennial	clumps	full sun, shade, partial shade	12 inches (30 cm)
Black-eyed Susan (*Rudbeckia hirta*)	perennial	clumps	full sun	2–3 feet (.6–.9 m)
Blue vervain (*Verbena hastata*)	perennial	clumps	full sun, partial shade	3–5 feet (.9–1.5 m)
Borage (*Borago officinalis*)	annual	clumps	full sun, partial shade	3 feet (.9 m)
Brickellia (*Brickellia grandiflora*)	perennial	clumps	full sun	2–3 feet (.6–.9 m)
Burdock (*Arctium lappa*)	biennial	clumps	full sun, shade, partial shade	3–4 feet (.9–1.2 m)
Calendula (*Calendula officinalis*)	annual	clumps	full sun	12–15 inches (30–38 cm)
California poppy (*Eschscholzia californica*)	annual	clumps	full sun, partial shade	12 inches (30 cm)
Callirhoe (*Callirhoe involucrata*)	perennial	spreads	full sun, partial shade	8–10 inches (20–25 cm)
Cardinal flower (*Lobelia cardinalis*)	perennial	clumps	shade, partial shade	15–30 inches (38–76 cm)
Catnip (*Nepeta cataria*)	perennial	clumps	full sun, partial shade, shade	15–24 inches (38–60 cm)
Cayenne (*Capsicum* species)	annual	clumps	full sun	to 24 inches (60 cm)
Chamomile (*Matricaria recutita*)	annual	clumps	full sun, partial shade	24 inches (60 cm)
Chamomile (*Chamaemelum nobile*)	perennial	spreads	full sun, partial shade	8–10 inches (20–25 cm)
Chaste berry (*Vitex agnus-castus*)	perennial	clumps	full sun, partial shade	2–10 feet (.6–3.0 m)
Chicory (*Cichorium intybus*)	perennial	clumps	full sun	15–24 inches (38–60 cm)
Cilantro, Coriander (*Coriandrum sativum*)	annual	clumps	full sun, shade, partial shade	10–12 inches (25–30 cm)
Clary sage (*Salvia sclarea*)	biennial	clumps	full sun	3 feet (.9 m)
Comfrey (*Symphytum × uplandicum*)	perennial	clumps	full sun, partial shade	3–4 feet (.9–1.2 m)

Betony

California poppy

Balloon flower

Black-eyed Susan

SPACING	BLOOM COLOR	WATER REQUIREMENTS	SOIL PREFERENCES
12 inches (30 cm)	purple	moderate	high in organic matter
15 inches (38 cm)	yellowish green	moderate to high	rich loam
15 inches (38 cm)	purple	low to moderate	dry, gravelly, or sandy
15 inches (38 cm)	yellow	moderate	dry, sandy, well drained, slightly alkaline
10–12 inches (25–30 cm)	blue, white, pink	moderate	gravelly, well drained
12 inches (30 cm)	white, purple, pink	low to moderate	well drained
10–12 inches (25–30 cm)	purple, pink, white	moderate to high	rich loam
12 inches (30 cm)	yellow	low to moderate	no special needs
12 inches (30 cm)	purple	moderate	well drained and high in organic matter
15 inches (38 cm)	blue	moderate	no special needs
15–20 inches (38–50 cm)	cream	low	sandy
18 inches (45 cm)	green and pink	moderate	rich loam
10 inches (25 cm)	yellow, orange	low to moderate	no special needs
10–12 inches (25–30 cm)	orange	low to moderate	no special needs
12–15 inches (30–38 cm)	pink	low	nutrient-poor
12 inches (30 cm)	scarlet	high	loam or sandy
12 inches (30 cm)	white	low to moderate	no special needs
12 inches (30 cm)	white, red fruit	low	fertile, slightly acid
10 inches (25 cm)	white	low	no special needs
8 inches (20 cm)	white	moderate	well drained
12–24 inches (30–60 cm)	lavender	moderate	well drained
10 inches (25 cm)	blue	low to moderate	no special needs
8–10 inches (20–25 cm)	white	moderate to high	no special needs
24 inches (60 cm)	lavender, pink, white	moderate	well drained
24 inches (60 cm)	purple	moderate	loam or sandy

Plant Characteristics and Requirements—*Continued*

HERB	CYCLE	GROWING NATURE	LIGHT REQUIREMENTS	HEIGHT
Cow parsnip (*Heracleum sphondylium*)	perennial	clumps	shade, partial shade	3–4 feet (.9–1.2 m)
Coyote mint (*Monardella odoratissima*)	perennial	spreads	full sun	10–12 inches (25–30 cm)
Dandelion (*Taraxacum officinale*)	perennial	clumps	full sun, partial shade	8–10 inches (20–25 cm)
Dill (*Anethum graveolens*)	annual	clumps	full sun	3–5 feet (.9–1.5 m)
Echinacea (*Echinacea* species)	perennial	clumps	full sun	2–4 feet (.6–1.2 m)
Elecampane (*Inula helenium*)	perennial	clumps	full sun, partial shade	4–6 feet (1.2–1.8 m)
Epazote (*Chenopodium ambrosioides*)	annual	clumps	full sun	12–15 inches (30–38 cm)
Evening primrose (*Oenothera biennis*)	biennial	clumps	full sun, partial shade	3–4 feet (.9–1.2 m)
Fennel (*Foeniculum vulgare*)	perennial	clumps	full sun	4–5 feet (1.2–1.5 m)
Feverfew (*Tanacetum parthenium*)	perennial	clumps	full sun, partial shade	24 inches (60 cm)
Gayfeather (*Liatris* species)	perennial	clumps	full sun	10–12 inches (25–30 cm)
Ginger (*Zingiber officinale*)	perennial	clumps	shade, partial shade	3–4 feet (.9–1.2 m)
Goldenrod (*Solidago* species)	perennial	clumps	full sun	2–4 feet (.6–1.2 m)
Goldenseal (*Hydrastis canadensis*)	perennial	clumps	shade, partial shade	10–15 inches (25–38 cm)
Gotu kola (*Centella asiatica*)	tender perennial	spreads	shade, partial shade	6–8 inches (15–20 cm)
Grindelia (*Grindelia* species)	perennial	clumps	full sun	24 inches (60 cm)
Hollyhock (*Alcea rosea*)	perennial	clumps	full sun, partial shade	6–8 feet (1.8–2.4 m)
Hops (*Humulus lupulus*)	perennial	spreads	full sun, partial shade	8 feet (2.4 m) and taller
Horehound (*Marrubium vulgare*)	perennial	clumps	full sun	12–24 inches (30–60 cm)
Hyssop (*Hyssopus officinalis*)	perennial	clumps	full sun, partial shade	12–24 inches (30–60 cm)
Inmortal (*Asclepias asperula*)	perennial	spreads	full sun	12–15 inches (30–38 cm)
Lavender (*Lavandula angustifolia*)	perennial	clumps	full sun	24 inches (60 cm)
Lemon balm (*Melissa officinalis*)	perennial	clumps	full sun, partial shade	24 inches (60 cm)
Lemongrass (*Cymbopogon citratus*)	tender perennial	clumps	full sun, partial shade, shade	3–4 feet (.9–1.2 m)
Lemon thyme (*Thymus × citriodorus*)	perennial	spreads	full sun, partial shade	12–15 inches (30–38 cm)
Lemon verbena (*Aloysia triphylla*)	tender perennial	clumps	full sun, partial shade	3–4 feet (.9–1.2 m)

Feverfew

 Goldenseal

 Hollyhock

 Lemon verbena

SPACING	BLOOM COLOR	WATER REQUIREMENTS	SOIL PREFERENCES
24 inches (60 cm)	white	moderate to high	loam or sandy
12–15 inches (30–38 cm)	lavender	low	nutrient-poor
10–12 inches (25–30 cm)	yellow	low to moderate	no special needs
10–12 inches (25–30 cm)	yellow	moderate	well drained, slightly acid
12 inches (30 cm)	pink	low	nutrient-poor to high in organic matter, depending on species
12 inches (30 cm)	yellow	low to moderate	no special needs
10–12 inches (25–30 cm)	green	low	no special needs
10–12 inches (25–30 cm)	yellow	moderate	no special needs
12–15 inches (30–38 cm)	yellow	low to moderate	well worked and well drained
12 inches (30 cm)	white	moderate	rich loam
8–10 inches (20–25 cm)	purple	low to moderate	no special needs
15 inches (38 cm)	yellowish green	high	rich loam
12 inches (30 cm)	yellow	low to moderate	no special needs
8–10 inches (20–25 cm)	greenish white	moderate	humus
10 inches (25 cm)	greenish	high	rich loam
12 inches (30 cm)	yellow	low to moderate	nutrient-poor
15 inches (38 cm)	varies	moderate	no special needs
6–8 feet (1.8–2.4 m)	green	moderate to high	rich loam
12 inches (30 cm)	white	low	nutrient-poor
12 inches (30 cm)	purple	low to moderate	well drained, sandy
24 inches (60 cm)	mauve, cream	low	nutrient-poor, gravelly
12–15 inches (30–38 cm)	purple	low	well drained, sandy
12 inches (30 cm)	white	moderate	well drained
12–15 inches (30–38 cm)	none	moderate to high	rich loam or sandy
12 inches (30 cm)	lavender	low to moderate	well drained
12–15 inches (30–38 cm)	white	moderate to high	rich loam

Plant Characteristics and Requirements— *Continued*

HERB	CYCLE	GROWING NATURE	LIGHT REQUIREMENTS	HEIGHT
Licorice (*Glycyrrhiza glabra*)	perennial	clumps	full sun, partial shade	4–5 feet (1.2–1.5 m)
Lovage (*Levisticum officinale*)	perennial	clumps	full sun, partial shade, shade	2–3 feet (.6–.9 m)
Marsh mallow (*Althaea officinalis*)	perennial	clumps	full sun, partial shade, shade	3–4 feet (.9–1.2 m)
Milk thistle (*Silybum marianum*)	annual	clumps	full sun	2–3 feet (.6–.9 m)
Monarda (*Monarda* species)	perennial	clumps	full sun, partial shade	2–3 feet (.6–.9 m)
Mormon tea (*Ephedra* species)	perennial	clumps	full sun	12–24 inches (30–60 cm)
Motherwort (*Leonurus cardiaca*)	perennial	clumps	full sun, partial shade, shade	2–4 feet (.6–1.2 m)
Mugwort (*Artemisia vulgaris*)	perennial	clumps	full sun, partial shade	4–5 feet (1.2–1.5 m)
Mullein (*Verbascum thapsus*)	biennial	clumps	full sun	5–6 feet (1.5–1.8 m)
Nettle (*Urtica dioica*)	perennial	spreads	full sun, partial shade, shade	2–4 feet (.6–1.2 m)
Oat (*Avena sativa*)	annual	clumps	full sun	4–5 feet (1.2–1.5 m)
Oregano (*Origanum vulgare*)	perennial	spreads	full sun, partial shade	to 24 inches (60 cm)
Oxeye daisy (*Leucanthemum vulgare*)	perennial	clumps	full sun, partial shade	2–4 feet (.6–1.2 m)
Parsley (*Petroselinum crispum*)	biennial	clumps	sun, partial shade	12–20 inches (30–50 cm)
Passionflower (*Passiflora incarnata*)	tender perennial	spreads	shade, partial shade	8 feet (2.4 m) and much taller
Pennyroyal (*Mentha pulegium*)	perennial	spreads	full sun, partial shade, shade	10–12 inches (25–30 cm)
Penstemon (*Penstemon* species)	perennial	clumps	full sun, partial shade	8–36 inches (20–90 cm)
Peppermint (*Mentha × piperita*)	perennial	spreads	full sun, partial shade, shade	24 inches (60 cm)
Periwinkle (*Vinca major, V. minor*)	perennial	spreads	full sun, partial shade, shade	10–12 inches (25–30 cm)
Plantain (*Plantago* species)	perennial	clumps	full sun, partial shade	8–20 inches (20–50 cm)
Pleurisy root (*Asclepias tuberosa*)	perennial	clumps	full sun	24 inches (60 cm)
Potentilla (*Potentilla* species)	perennial	clumps, spreads	full sun, partial shade, shade	6–20 inches (15–50 cm)
Prickly pear (*Opuntia* species)	perennial	clumps, spreads	full sun	10–15 inches (25–38 cm)
Red clover (*Trifolium pratense*)	perennial	clumps	full sun, partial shade	12–15 inches (30–38 cm)

Oregano

 Pleurisy root

 Monarda

 Milk thistle

SPACING	BLOOM COLOR	WATER REQUIREMENTS	SOIL PREFERENCES
24 inches (60 cm)	lavender	moderate	well drained or sandy
24 inches (60 cm)	white	moderate	well drained
12 inches (30 cm)	pale pink	moderate	loam
12–15 inches (30–38 cm)	purple	low	no special needs
12 inches (30 cm)	red, lavender, pinkish, yellow	moderate	rich loam to well drained and sandy, depending on species
12–15 inches (30–38 cm)	yellow	low	nutrient-poor and well drained
15–20 inches (38–50 cm)	purple	low to moderate	no special needs
15–20 inches (38–50 cm)	white	low to moderate	no special needs
15 inches (38 cm)	yellow	low to moderate	well drained
12 inches (30 cm)	cream	moderate to high	high in organic matter
8 inches (20 cm)	green	moderate	high in organic matter
12 inches (30 cm)	lavender	low to moderate	well drained
12–15 inches (30–38 cm)	white	moderate	no special needs
12 inches (30 cm)	white	moderate	no special needs
24 inches (60 cm)	white, lavender	moderate to high	humus
12 inches (30 cm)	lavender	moderate	well drained
12 inches (30 cm)	varies	low to moderate	nutrient-poor, gravelly to normal
12 inches (30 cm)	purple	moderate to high	no special needs
15–20 inches (38–50 cm)	blue	low to moderate	no special needs
12 inches (30 cm)	white	moderate	no special needs
12 inches (30 cm)	orange	low to moderate	well drained
10–15 inches (25–38 cm)	yellow	moderate to high	well drained, sandy
12–15 inches (30–38 cm)	yellow, pink	low	well drained, sandy
12 inches (30 cm)	pink	moderate	no special needs

Plant Characteristics and Requirements—*Continued*

HERB	CYCLE	GROWING NATURE	LIGHT REQUIREMENTS	HEIGHT
Rosemary (*Rosmarinus* species)	tender perennial	clumps	full sun	12–36 inches (30–90 cm) and taller
Rue (*Ruta graveolens*)	perennial	clumps	full sun	12–15 inches (30–38 cm)
Sage (*Salvia officinalis*)	perennial	clumps	full sun	24 inches (60 cm)
St.-John's-wort (*Hypericum perforatum*)	perennial	spreads	full sun	24–30 inches (60–75 cm)
Santolina (*Santolina* species)	perennial	clumps	full sun	12–24 inches (30–60 cm)
Sedum (*Sedum* species)	perennial	spreads	full sun, partial shade	4–36 inches (10–90 cm)
Self-heal (*Prunella vulgaris*)	perennial	spreads	full sun, partial shade	8–10 inches (20–25 cm)
Sheep sorrel (*Rumex acetosella*)	perennial	spreads	full sun	8–12 inches (20–30 cm)
Shepherd's purse (*Capsella bursa-pastoris*)	annual	clumps	full sun	8–24 inches (20–60 cm)
Skullcap (*Scutellaria* species)	perennial	clumps	full sun, partial shade	8–24 inches (20–60 cm)
Spearmint (*Mentha spicata*)	perennial	spreads	full sun, partial shade, shade	24 inches (60 cm)
Spilanthes (*Spilanthes acmella*)	annual	clumps	full sun, partial shade	12–24 inches (30–60 cm)
Stevia (*Stevia rebaudiana*)	annual	clumps	full sun, partial shade, shade	12–15 inches (30–38 cm)
Summer savory (*Satureja hortensis*)	annual	clumps	full sun, partial shade	12–20 inches (30–50 cm)
Sunflower (*Helianthus annuus*)	annual	clumps	full sun	2–12 feet (.6–3.6 m) and taller
Thyme (*Thymus vulgaris*)	perennial	spreads	full sun, partial shade	12–15 inches (30–38 cm)
Valerian (*Valeriana officinalis*)	perennial	clumps	full sun, partial shade, shade	3–4 feet (.9–1.2 m)
Vervain (*Verbena officinalis*)	perennial	spreads, clumps	full sun, partial shade	12–36 inches (30–90 cm) and taller
Violet (*Viola* species)	perennial	clumps	shade, partial shade	4–8 inches (10–20 cm)
White sage (*Salvia apiana*)	tender perennial	clumps	full sun	12–24 inches (30–60 cm)
Wild geranium (*Geranium* species)	perennial	clumps	shade, partial shade	6–24 inches (15–60 cm)
Wormwood (*Artemisia* species)	perennial	spreads	full sun, partial shade	12 inches (30 cm) and taller
Yarrow (*Achillea millefolium*)	perennial	spreads	full sun, partial shade	2–3 feet (.6–.9 m)
Yerba de la negrita (*Sphaeralcea coccinea*)	perennial	spreads	full sun	10–12 inches (25–30 cm)
Yerba mansa (*Anemopsis californica*)	perennial	spreads	full sun, partial shade	12 inches (30 cm)
Yucca (*Yucca* species)	perennial	clumps	full sun	15 inches (38 cm) and taller

Sunflower

 Yarrow

 Santolina

 St.-John's-wort

SPACING	BLOOM COLOR	WATER REQUIREMENTS	SOIL PREFERENCES
12–15 inches (30–38 cm)	blue	low to moderate	well drained
10–12 inches (25–30 cm)	yellow	low to moderate	no special needs
12 inches (30 cm)	purple	low to moderate	well drained
12 inches (30 cm)	yellow	low to moderate	well drained
15 inches (38 cm)	yellow, green	low	well drained
10–15 inches (25–38 cm)	pink, purple, white	low to moderate	well drained
10–12 inches (25–30 cm)	purple, pink, white	moderate	humus
12 inches (30 cm)	reddish purple	low to moderate	no special needs
10 inches (25 cm)	white	moderate	well drained
12 inches (30 cm)	blue	moderate	well drained
12 inches (30 cm)	purple	moderate to high	no special needs
12 inches (30 cm)	yellow and red	moderate to high	moist and high in organic matter
10–12 inches (25–30 cm)	white	moderate to high	humus
10–12 inches (25–30 cm)	lavender, white	low to moderate	well drained
12–15 inches (30–38 cm)	yellow	low to moderate	well drained
10–12 inches (25–30 cm)	purple, white, pink	low to moderate	well drained
12–15 inches (30–38 cm)	white, pale pink	moderate to high	humus
10–12 inches (25–30 cm)	purple	low to moderate	well drained
6–8 inches (15–20 cm)	varies	moderate to high	high in organic matter
12 inches (30 cm)	pale blue	low	well drained
12 inches (30 cm)	pink, purple	moderate to high	well drained
12–15 inches (30–38 cm)	yellow, white	low	well drained
12 inches (30 cm)	white, pink, yellow	low to moderate	well drained
12 inches (30 cm)	orange	low	well drained
12 inches (30 cm)	white	moderate to high	very moist, high in organic matter
15 inches (38 cm)	cream	low	well drained

What Plant When?

As you prepare to plant your garden, you will want to know if the time is right to put out a specific herb. Has all danger of frost passed yet? Many herbs are very tender, especially when they are babies, so they cannot stand up to freezing temperatures. Make sure that you plant these tender ones in the garden late enough in the spring.

Other herbs are very durable and actually may prefer to be planted out in the earlier parts of spring. It will be helpful to know which ones may be started early from seed indoors and then transplanted out in the later spring. Many plants do well if they are divided or transplanted in the fall.

With the help of your local extension service, determine when your approximate frost dates are and plant accordingly. Chapter 10 will give you more details about the best times and methods of seeding and/or transplanting each herb.

Types of Garden Designs

There are so many different styles of medicinal gardens you can create, whether you are starting fresh or adding medicinal plants to an existing garden space. You may even decide to combine traits of one type of garden with another to make it absolutely and wonderfully personalized to you. Let's consider some different ways that you could design your medicinal garden.

Many plants enjoy growing near water, making them ideal for water garden designs. A water garden is a beautiful way to create a peaceful growing environment.

Formal Knot Gardens

These are the most structured of all the garden designs. Traditional knot gardens are shaped using colored gravel and herbs that can be trimmed or hedged to create a very intricate garden design. Historically, a knot garden would duplicate the pattern of a tapestry or rug that existed in the owner's home. If you choose this style of garden, it's important to be symmetrical throughout. In other words, if you plant santolina or a topiary in one part of the garden, you should incorporate those plants in a symmetrical way in other parts of the garden.

Formal knot gardens are reminiscent of beautiful English or French herb gardens from the Middle Ages and can be quite stunning, but they require much detail work and more maintenance than other types of gardens.

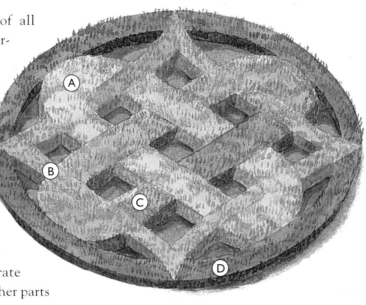

Formal Knot Garden at a Glance
▸ A: Santolina   ▸ C: Lavender
▸ B: Sage   ▸ D: Rosemary

Ecosystem Medicinal Gardens

Perhaps you will choose to simulate a natural environment with your garden. This is an especially nice way to plan your design if the plants you've chosen naturally exist in community with one another in a wild space. For example, you may want to grow medicinals from a prairie region or a woodland environment. Or maybe you live in a tropical climate or a mountain area and you want to grow plants that naturally occur in similar regions. These gardens are very special because they simulate an ecosystem that mimics the environment where the plants might grow if they could choose their own habitat.

There are many different types of ecosystems you may choose to re-create:

Woodland/forest: This habitat is heavily shaded and moist. The tree canopy offers protection for the understory plants and provides decaying leaf matter for soil nutrients.

Prairie/grassland: This is a wide open, sunny area, where plants must compete for water and nutrients. Plants grow intermixed with an abundance of grass species; trees are scarce.

Mountain/meadow: Mountain habitats are at a higher elevation and usually have cooler temperatures and a shorter growing season. Mountains are usually heavily wooded, but contain, open and moist clearings or meadows. Meadows have a richer soil than many of the surrounding areas and plants growing there will have full sun or dappled shade, while mountain plants grow in partial to full shade.

Desert/Mediterranean: A desert habitat is hotter and drier than other habitats. It may offer sun or shade. Water may be abundant for a short time in spring, but usually not the remaining part of the year. Temperatures will be hot as a rule, but winter nights can get extremely cold. The Mediterranean habitat, found in southern Europe and surrounding regions, also offers hot and dry climates, with soil that is not always very nutrient-rich. Night temperatures do not usually go below the mid-30-degree range; these plants will not be hardy in colder climates.

River/stream/lake/pond: This habitat is moisture-rich. Plants growing in any of these areas will require extra moisture and may grow in sun, shade, or partial shade. Often the soil is richer in this type of habitat.

Disturbed area: In this habitat, water, sun, and shade may have altered the soil. Disturbed areas often reflect overuse by humans or animals (i.e., development, recreation, or livestock grazing) and the native habitat is seriously compromised or no longer present at all. Many plants thrive in this type of habitat.

Gardens only: There are some plants that no longer exist outside of a garden environment. They have, for one reason or another, become totally dependent upon humans for their existence.

Temperate: The climatic zones that exist between the tropics and the polar circles are

Ecosystem Garden at a Glance

- A: Cardinal flower
- B: Evening primose
- C: Self-heal
- D: Potentilla
- E: Nettle
- F: Betony
- G: Black-eyed Susan
- H: Violet
- I: Hops
- J: Clematis
- K: Goldenrod
- L: Monarda
- M: Blue vervain
- N: Red clover
- O: Wild geranium
- P: Oxeye daisy
- Q: Pleurisy root
- R: Mint
- S: Anise hyssop
- T: Marsh mallow
- U: St.-John's-wort

duplicated here. In these climates, temperatures never go into the extreme cold or extreme hot range.

Subtropical: This is the climatic region that borders the edges between the tropics and the temperate zones. Temperatures are generally warmer than temperate zones, with more natural moisture, but cold spells and droughts can easily influence these habitats.

Tropical: This climate is very hot and humid. Plants often grow very lush in this habitat. They are not frost- or drought-hardy and care must be taken when growing them to provide adequate moisture and warm temperatures.

The Wild Garden

Some people really enjoy a garden that is designed to look like Mother Nature herself planted it. These types of gardens have many of the basic hard goods in place as well as a main focal point. Imagine how it would feel to walk through a wild meadow; wild gardens feel the same way.

These gardens are not planted with as much organizational detail as other types of gardens — or at least that's how they appear. A little planned chaos works wonders. For instance, it is fine if a taller plant sits slightly in front of a smaller one or if the chamomile seeds itself into the pathways. It's a little bit wild and totally enchanting!

Wild Garden at a Glance

- A: Self-heal
- B: Black-eyed Susan
- C: Oxeye daisy
- D: Echinacea
- E: Clematis
- F: Wormwort
- G: Skullcap
- H: Betony
- I: Yarrow
- J: Violet
- K: Blue vervain
- L: Mullein
- M: California poppy
- N: Chicory
- O: Hops
- P: Penstemon
- Q: Pleurisy root
- R: St.-John's-wort
- S: Nettle
- T: Dandelion
- U: Licorice
- V: Goldenrod
- W: Plantain
- X: White sage
- Y: Chaste berry
- Z: Monarda

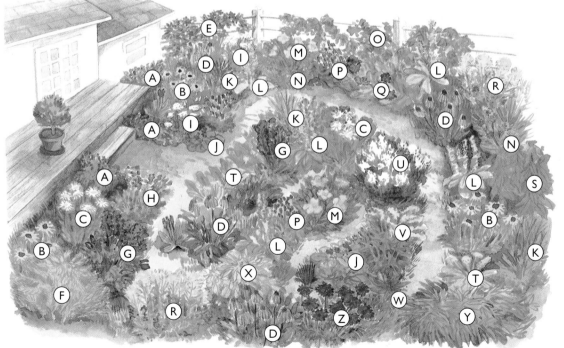

Plant Habitat Preferences

This is a general habitat guide to give you an idea what type of environment these plants may prefer and grow best in. Please remember that these are general guidelines only and every plant will have some degree of tolerance for other circumstances. Look in chapter 10 for more specific growing guidelines.

PLANT	PREFERRED LOCATION	PREFERRED GROWING CLIMATE
Alfalfa (*Medicago sativa*)	prairie/grassland, disturbed area	temperate
Angelica (*Angelica archangelica*)	river/stream/lake/pond	temperate
Anise hyssop (*Agastache foeniculum*)	mountain/meadow	temperate
Astragalus (*Astragalus membranaceus*)	prairie/grassland	temperate, subtropical
Balloon flower (*Platycodon grandiflorus*)	mountain/meadow	temperate
Basil (*Ocimum* species)	gardens only	temperate, subtropical, tropical
Betony (*Betonica officinalis*)	woodland/forest	temperate
Black-eyed Susan (*Rudbeckia hirta*)	prairie/grassland, river/stream/lake/pond	temperate
Blue vervain (*Verbena hastata*)	prairie/grassland	temperate
Borage (*Borago officinalis*)	desert/Mediterranean	temperate
Brickellia (*Brickellia grandiflora*)	desert/Mediterranean	temperate
Burdock (*Arctium lappa*)	river/stream/lake/pond, disturbed area	temperate
Calendula (*Calendula officinalis*)	gardens only	temperate, subtropical
California poppy (*Eschscholzia californica*)	prairie/grassland, disturbed area	temperate
Callirhoe (*Callirhoe involucrata*)	prairie/grassland, desert/Mediterranean	temperate
Cardinal flower (*Lobelia cardinalis*)	river/stream/lake/pond	temperate, subtropical
Catnip (*Nepeta cataria*)	prairie/grassland, river/stream/lake/pond, disturbed area	temperate, subtropical
Cayenne (*Capsicum* species)	desert/Mediterranean, gardens only	temperate, subtropical, tropical
Chamomile (*Matricaria recutita, Chamaemelum nobile*)	prairie/grassland	temperate
Chaste berry (*Vitex agnus-castus*)	desert/Mediterranean	temperate
Chicory (*Cichorium intybus*)	prairie/grassland, disturbed area	temperate
Cilantro, Coriander (*Coriandrum sativum*)	gardens only	temperate, subtropical, tropical
Clary sage (*Salvia sclarea*)	desert/Mediterranean	temperate
Comfrey (*Symphytum × uplandicum*)	river/stream/lake/pond	temperate

PLANT	PREFERRED LOCATION	PREFERRED GROWING CLIMATE
Cow parsnip (*Heracleum sphondylium*)	river/stream/lake/pond	temperate
Coyote mint (*Monardella odoratissima*)	mountain/meadow, desert/Mediterranean	temperate
Dandelion (*Taraxacum officinale*)	prairie/grassland, mountain/meadow, desert/Mediterranean, river/stream/lake/pond, disturbed area	temperate
Dill (*Anethum graveolens*)	gardens only	temperate
Echinacea (*Echinacea* species)	prairie/grassland	temperate
Elecampane (*Inula helenium*)	woodland/forest, river/stream/lake/pond	temperate
Epazote (*Chenopodium ambrosioides*)	desert/Mediterranean	temperate
Evening primrose (*Oenothera biennis*)	prairie/grassland, river/stream/lake/pond, disturbed area	temperate
Fennel (*Foeniculum vulgare*)	desert/Mediterranean, disturbed area	temperate
Feverfew (*Tanacetum parthenium*)	gardens only	temperate
Gayfeather (*Liatris* species)	prairie/grassland, disturbed area	temperate
Ginger (*Zingiber officinale*)	gardens only	tropical
Goldenrod (*Solidago* species)	prairie/grassland, mountain/meadow, river/stream/lake/pond	temperate
Goldenseal (*Hydrastis canadensis*)	woodland/forest	temperate
Gotu kola (*Centella asiatica*)	river/stream/lake/pond, disturbed area	tropical
Grindelia (*Grindelia* species)	prairie/grassland, mountain/meadow, disturbed area	temperate
Hollyhock (*Alcea rosea*)	gardens only	temperate
Hops (*Humulus lupulus*)	woodland/forest, prairie/grassland, mountain/meadow, river/stream/lake/pond	temperate
Horehound (*Marrubium vulgare*)	prairie/grassland, desert/Mediterranean, disturbed area	temperate
Hyssop (*Hyssopus officinalis*)	desert/Mediterranean	temperate
Inmortal (*Asclepias asperula*)	mountain/meadow, desert/Mediterranean	temperate
Lavender (*Lavandula angustifolia*)	desert/Mediterranean	temperate
Lemon balm (*Melissa officinalis*)	desert/Mediterranean	temperate
Lemongrass (*Cymbopogon citratus*)	gardens only	tropical
Lemon thyme (*Thymus × citriodorus*)	gardens only	temperate

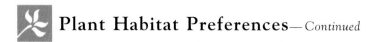
PLANT	PREFERRED LOCATION	PREFERRED GROWING CLIMATE
Lemon verbena (*Aloysia triphylla*)	gardens only	tropical
Licorice (*Glycyrrhiza glabra*)	desert/Mediterranean	temperate
Lovage (*Levisticum officinale*)	desert/Mediterranean	temperate
Marsh mallow (*Althaea officinalis*)	mountain/meadow, river/stream/lake/pond	temperate
Milk thistle (*Silybum marianum*)	desert/Mediterranean	temperate
Monarda (*Monarda* species)	mountain/meadow, river/stream/lake/pond	temperate
Mormon tea (*Ephedra* species)	desert/Mediterranean	temperate
Motherwort (*Leonurus cardiaca*)	disturbed area	temperate
Mugwort (*Artemisia vulgaris*)	mountain/meadow, desert/Mediterranean, disturbed area	temperate
Mullein (*Verbascum thapsus*)	prairie/grassland, mountain/meadow, desert/Mediterranean, river/stream/lake/pond, disturbed area	temperate
Nettle (*Urtica dioica*)	mountain/meadow, river/stream/lake/pond, disturbed area	temperate, subtropical
Oat (*Avena sativa*)	prairie/grassland, mountain/meadow	temperate
Oregano (*Origanum vulgare*)	desert/Mediterranean	temperate
Oxeye daisy (*Leucanthemum vulgare*)	prairie/grassland, mountain/meadow, desert/Mediterranean, disturbed area	temperate
Parsley (*Petroselinum crispum*)	desert/Mediterranean	temperate
Passionflower (*Passiflora incarnata*)	woodland/forest, mountain/meadow	subtropical, tropical
Pennyroyal (*Mentha × pulegium*)	mountain/meadow, desert/Mediterranean	temperate
Penstemon (*Penstemon* species)	prairie/grassland, mountain/meadow, desert/Mediterranean	temperate
Peppermint (*Mentha × piperita*)	river/stream/lake/pond, disturbed area	temperate
Periwinkle (*Vinca major, V. minor*)	woodland/forest	temperate
Plantain (*Plantago* species)	mountain/meadow, river/stream/lake/pond, disturbed area	temperate
Pleurisy root (*Asclepias tuberosa*)	prairie/grassland, mountain/meadow	temperate
Potentilla (*Potentilla* species)	mountain/meadow, river/stream/lake/pond	temperate
Prickly pear (*Opuntia* species)	desert/Mediterranean	subtropical, temperate
Red clover (*Trifolium pratense*)	mountain/meadow, disturbed area	temperate

PLANT	PREFERRED LOCATION	PREFERRED GROWING CLIMATE
Rosemary (*Rosmarinus* species)	desert/Mediterranean	temperate
Rue (*Ruta graveolens*)	desert/Mediterranean, disturbed area	temperate, tropical
Sage (*Salvia officinalis*)	desert/Mediterranean	temperate
St.-John's-wort (*Hypericum perforatum*)	mountain/meadow, disturbed area	temperate
Santolina (*Santolina* species)	desert/Mediterranean	temperate
Sedum (*Sedum* species)	mountain/meadow, desert/Mediterranean	temperate
Self-heal (*Prunella vulgaris*)	woodland/forest, mountain/meadow, river/stream/lake/pond	temperate
Sheep sorrel (*Rumex acetosella*)	disturbed area	temperate
Shepherd's purse (*Capsella bursa-pastoris*)	prairie/grassland, mountain/meadow, disturbed area	temperate
Skullcap (*Scutellaria* species)	mountain/meadow, river/stream/lake/pond	temperate
Spearmint (*Mentha spicata*)	river/stream/lake/pond, disturbed area	temperate
Spilanthes (*Spilanthes acmella*)	prairie/grassland, river/stream/lake/pond	tropical
Stevia (*Stevia rebaudiana*)	river/stream/lake/pond	tropical
Summer savory (*Satureja hortensis*)	desert/Mediterranean	temperate
Sunflower (*Helianthus annuus*)	prairie/grassland, mountain/meadow, desert/Mediterranean, disturbed area	temperate, subtropical, tropical
Thyme (*Thymus vulgaris*)	desert/Mediterranean	temperate
Valerian (*Valeriana officinalis*)	woodland/forest, river/stream/lake/pond	temperate
Vervain (*Verbena officinalis*)	mountain/meadow, desert/Mediterranean, disturbed area	temperate
Violet (*Viola* species)	woodland/forest, mountain/meadow, river/stream/lake/pond	temperate
White sage (*Salvia apiana*)	prairie/grassland, desert/Mediterranean	temperate
Wild geranium (*Geranium* species)	mountain/meadow, river/stream/lake/pond	temperate
Wormwood (*Artemisia* species)	prairie/grassland, mountain/meadow, desert/Mediterranean, disturbed area	temperate
Yarrow (*Achillea millefolium*)	prairie/grassland, mountain/meadow, desert/Mediterranean, disturbed area	temperate
Yerba de la negrita (*Sphaeralcea coccinea*)	desert/Mediterranean	temperate
Yerba mansa (*Anemopsis californica*)	desert/Mediterranean, river/stream/lake/pond	temperate
Yucca (*Yucca* species)	mountain/meadow, desert/Mediterranean	temperate

Space-Saving Gardens

If you have a limited space available or you would like to grow just a small garden near a door or patio, consider creating a wagon wheel or ladder garden. Simply lay a straight wooden ladder or old wagon wheel on the soil where you want the garden to be. Fill the space between the ladder rungs or wheel spokes with good soil, mix this soil with the top 3 to 4 inches (7.5 to 10 cm) of existing soil, and you're ready to plant. Do not place this type of garden over a patch of grass, or the grass will just grow right up through the soil and into the garden.

Another space-saving garden is the checkerboard. First create a checkerboard pattern using 12-inch-square (30 cm) garden stones or patio blocks. Once the pattern is in place, fill the areas between the stones with soil and plant one type of medicinal herb in each soil space. This is a fantastic way to get children involved in gardening, because they can plant something different in each block. Seniors who would like to decrease the size of a garden area for ease of maintenance may find this approach appealing. The benefit of this type of garden is the easy access to every part of it via the stones. The extra heat given off by the stones may also enable you to grow plants that would not normally be hardy in your climate.

🌿 Checkerboard Garden at a Glance

- A: Hops
- B: Mullein
- C: Valerian
- D: Catnip
- E: Lemon balm
- F: Dandelion
- G: Calendula
- H: Skullcap
- I: Echinacea
- J: Oats
- K: Gotu kola
- L: Yerba mansa
- M: Lavender
- N: Self-heal
- O: California poppy

🌿 Ladder Garden at a Glance

- A: Oregano
- B: Thyme
- C: Rosemary
- D: Sage
- E: Parsley

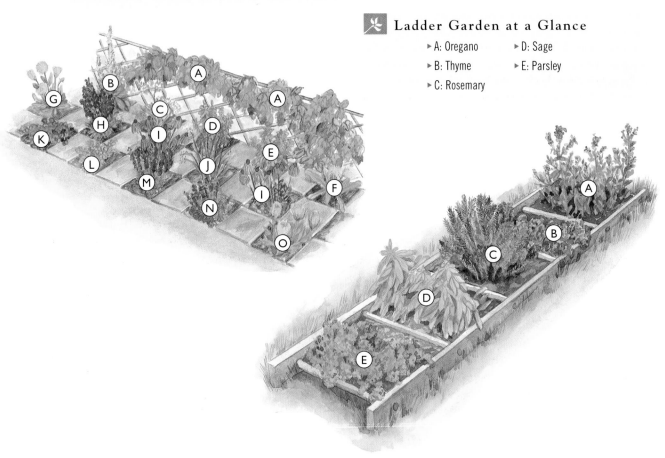

🌿 Raised-Bed Garden at a Glance

- A: Lemon balm
- B: Alfalfa
- C: Catnip
- D: Chamomile
- E: Lavender
- F: Pennyroyal
- G: Evening primrose
- H: Vitex
- I: Skullcap
- J: Dandelion
- K: California poppy
- L: Nettle
- M: Oats
- N: Chicory
- O: Rosemary
- P: Basil
- Q: Dill
- R: Fennel
- S: Peppermint
- T: St.-John's-wort
- U: Valerian
- V: Spearmint
- W: Violet
- X: Cayenne
- Y: Inmortal
- Z: Red clover
- AA: Echinacea
- BB: Astragalus
- CC: Feverfew

Raised-Bed Gardens

Raised beds have become very popular in the last couple of decades, although it was the monks of the European monasteries who originally put this method into place. They created garden beds that were approximately 4 feet (1.2 m) wide and whatever length was desired. Raised beds are easy to reach into for maintenance or harvesting without stepping on the soil and compacting it.

Raised beds can be made by simply raking the soil into bed formations, leaving pathway access on all sides. You can also create the beds using stones or landscaping timbers if you would like to make a more permanent or formalized look. Anything will work! I've used scrap lumber and old bricks that were at my disposal. Note that it is extremely difficult to find untreated landscaping timbers; if you prefer not to use chemically treated lumber, you will most likely have to use woods like redwood and cedar. If you're very ambitious, you could install metal landscaping edging, which will help keep aggressive plants under control.

Container Gardens

Many times the situation will call for planting medicinals in containers or pots. This may be the type of garden that you prefer. There are many fabulous pots, in every size, shape, material, and color imaginable. Planting a container medicine garden can be pure joy. For some individuals, such as apartment-dwellers, this may be the only gardening option they have — but this doesn't mean their gardens can't be interesting.

For others, like me, this method provides a mobile garden that can be rearranged at will. I *love* to incorporate planted containers into my other gardens, because I can give the garden another look or feel just by moving the pots to different locations. It also allows me to provide a much-needed splash of color to any area that

🌿 Container Garden at a Glance

▸ A: Passionflower   ▸ F: Sage   ▸ K: Cayenne

▸ B: Stevia   ▸ G: California poppy   ▸ L: Basil

▸ C: Spilanthes   ▸ H: Calendula   ▸ M: Chaste berry

▸ D: Rosemary   ▸ I: Parsley

▸ E: Lemongrass   ▸ J: Thyme

may be in a blooming lull at a particular time of the season.

I've found that most medicinal herbs grow very well when planted in containers. Clay, pottery, and ceramic pots are easier to care for and the plants seem to thrive in them more than they do in plastic pots. Have fun with containers and don't limit yourself in what you try with them.

Theme Gardens

Planting a theme garden is great fun. The motifs that you might consider are quite varied, and the design possibilities are nearly endless.

You could design beds devoted to herbs used to treat particular body systems. For example, you would plant herbs used for the cardiovascular system in one area, while herbs for the skin may be planted in another area, and so on.

The theme might also be gender or age specific, focusing on the plants for men's or women's health. The garden might be planted with herbs for children's or seniors' unique health concerns.

You could plant medicinals that are very fragrant or generally used as tea herbs. Wouldn't it be great to design a garden that emphasizes medicinal plants that are prepared as foods and can ultimately become a delicious part of every day's menu?

Medicinal wildlife gardens are also very nice, with plants that not only are for medicinal use, but would also attract specific types of wildlife into the space. A hummingbird garden would include a lot of bright orange, red, and pink flowers. Other birds are drawn into gardens that have plants with abundant seeds for food. Birds are so wonderful to watch, and they help immensely with insect problems because the insects are part of the birds' diet. Butterflies are magical in the garden, and bees of all types should be welcomed; these creatures are fantastic pollinators. Bats and moths are also good pollinators and often will pollinate flowers that butterflies and bees do not.

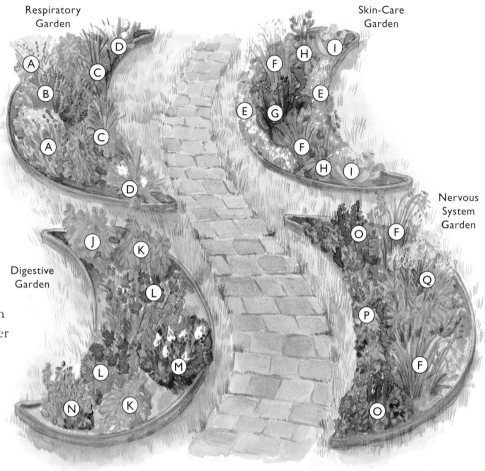

Respiratory Garden

Skin-Care Garden

Nervous System Garden

Digestive Garden

Theme Garden at a Glance

- A: Goldenrod
- B: Rosemary
- C: Blue vervain
- D: Pleurisy root
- E: Chamomile
- F: Oats
- G: Burdock
- H: Borage
- I: Calendula
- J: Spearmint
- K: Sage
- L: Monarda
- M: Licorice
- N: Peppermint
- O: Skullcap
- P: Thyme
- Q: St.-John's-wort

Planning a Theme Garden

Theme gardens can be a great way to organize your planting. Medicinal theme gardens focus on the therapeutic effect of a group of herbs in order to treat or prevent a particular condition. For instance, marsh mallow and parsley might be planted in a urinary-care garden since these plants are used to address conditions of the kidney and bladder. Herbs that are used in the making of soaps, candles, cloth, or dye can be used to create a textile theme garden. What better way to enrich your well-being?

HERB	BEST THEME GARDENS
Alfalfa (*Medicago sativa*)	medicinal food, women's health, men's health, children's health, cold and flu, tonic
Angelica (*Angelica archangelica*)	medicinal food, women's health, cold and flu, heart/circulatory, lungs
Anise hyssop (*Agastache foeniculum*)	tea, fragrance, cold and flu, digestive/liver/intestinal
Astragalus (*Astragalus membranaceus*)	medicinal food, cold and flu, immune/lymph, tonic
Balloon flower (*Platycodon grandiflorus*)	digestive/liver/intestinal, lungs, skin/hair/nails
Basil (*Ocimum* species)	medicinal food, digestive/liver/intestinal, headaches
Betony (*Betonica officinalis*)	tea, stress relief, pain relief, nervous system
Black-eyed Susan (*Rudbeckia hirta*)	women's health, heart/circulatory, urinary
Blue vervain (*Verbena hastata*)	tea, stress relief, cold and flu
Borage (*Borago officinalis*)	tea, medicinal foods, women's health, skin/hair/nails
Brickellia (*Brickellia grandiflora*)	digestive/liver/intestinal
Burdock (*Arctium lappa*)	medicinal foods, digestive/liver/intestinal, skin/hair/nails, urinary
Calendula (*Calendula officinalis*)	digestive/liver/intestinal, skin/hair/nails
California poppy (*Eschscholzia californica*)	stress relief, pain relief, nervous system
Callirhoe (*Callirhoe involucrata*)	digestive/liver/intestinal, skin/hair/nails
Cardinal flower (*Lobelia cardinalis*)	allergy relief, muscles/bones, lungs
Catnip (*Nepeta cataria*)	medicinal food, children's health, stress relief, cold and flu, pain relief, digestive/liver/intestinal, nervous system
Cayenne (*Capsicum* species)	medicinal food, cold and flu, pain relief, heart/circulatory, muscles/bones, digestive/liver/intestinal, lungs, eyes/ears/nose/throat
Chamomile (*Matricaria recutita, Chamaemelum nobile*)	tea, fragrance, women's health, children's health, stress relief, pain relief, muscles/bones, digestive/liver/intestinal, nervous system, skin/hair/nails
Chaste berry (*Vitex agnus-castus*)	women's health, men's health, tonic
Chicory (*Cichorium intybus*)	tea, digestive/liver/intestinal, urinary, tonic
Cilantro, Coriander (*Coriandrum sativum*)	medicinal food
Clary sage (*Salvia sclarea*)	fragrance, women's health

HERB	BEST THEME GARDENS
Comfrey (*Symphytum × uplandicum*)	muscles/bones, digestive/liver/intestinal, skin/hair/nails
Cow parsnip (*Heracleum sphondylium*)	digestive/liver/intestinal, nervous system
Coyote mint (*Monardella odoratissima*)	tea, cold and flu, digestive/liver/intestinal, lungs, eyes/ears/nose/throat
Dandelion (*Taraxacum officinale*)	tea, medicinal foods, women's health, digestive/liver/intestinal, skin/hair/nails, urinary, tonic
Dill (*Anethum graveolens*)	tea, medicinal foods, children's health, digestive/liver/intestinal
Echinacea (*Echinacea* species)	cold and flu, immune/lymph, lungs, eyes/ears/nose/throat, skin/hair/nails
Elecampane (*Inula helenium*)	cold and flu, lungs, eyes/ears/nose/throat, digestive/liver
Epazote (*Chenopodium ambrosioides*)	medicinal foods, digestive/liver/intestinal
Evening primrose (*Oenothera biennis*)	women's health, skin/hair/nails
Fennel (*Foeniculum vulgare*)	tea, medicinal foods, women's health, children's health, digestive/liver/intestinal, lungs, eyes/ears/nose/throat
Feverfew (*Tanacetum parthenium*)	medicinal foods, pain relief, brain/memory
Gayfeather (*Liatris* species)	women's health, men's health, lungs, eyes/ears/nose/throat, urinary
Ginger (*Zingiber officinale*)	tea, fragrance, medicinal foods, women's health, children's health, cold and flu, heart/circulatory, immune/lymph, digestive/liver/intestinal, lungs, eyes/ears/nose/throat, tonic
Goldenrod (*Solidago* species)	allergy relief, lungs, eyes/ears/nose/throat, urinary
Goldenseal (*Hydrastis canadensis*)	allergy relief, cold and flu, lungs, eyes/ears/nose/throat, skin/hair/nails
Gotu kola (*Centella asiatica*)	tea, medicinal foods, nervous system, brain/memory, skin/hair/nails
Grindelia (*Grindelia* species)	allergy relief, heart/circulatory, lungs, eyes/ears/nose/throat
Hollyhock (*Alcea rosea*)	medicinal foods, digestive/liver/intestinal, eyes/ears/nose/throat
Hops (*Humulus lupulus*)	stress relief, pain relief, nervous system
Horehound (*Marrubium vulgare*)	cold and flu, lungs, eyes/ears/nose/throat
Hyssop (*Hyssopus officinalis*)	tea, cold and flu, lungs, eyes/ears/nose/throat
Inmortal (*Asclepias asperula*)	heart/circulatory, lungs
Lavender (*Lavandula angustifolia*)	fragrance, textile, women's health, children's health, stress relief, pain relief, muscles/bones, nervous system, brain/memory, skin/hair/nails
Lemon balm (*Melissa officinalis*)	tea, fragrance, medicinal foods, children's health, stress relief, cold and flu, pain relief, immune/lymph, digestive/liver/intestinal, nervous system
Lemongrass (*Cymbopogon citratus*)	tea, fragrance, medicinal foods
Lemon thyme (*Thymus × citriodorus*)	tea, fragrance, medicinal foods, children's health, digestive/liver/intestinal
Lemon verbena (*Aloysia triphylla*)	tea, fragrance, medicinal foods
Licorice (*Glycyrrhiza glabra*)	tea, medicinal foods, children's health, stress relief, cold and flu, immune/lymph, digestive/liver/intestinal, lungs, eyes/ears/nose/throat

Planning a Theme Garden—*Continued*

HERB	BEST THEME GARDENS
Lovage (*Levisticum officinale*)	medicinal foods, cold and flu, lungs
Marsh mallow (*Althaea officinalis*)	cold and flu, digestive/liver/intestinal, eyes/ears/nose/throat, skin/hair/nails, urinary
Milk thistle (*Silybum marianum*)	women's health, stress relief, allergy relief, digestive/liver/intestinal, skin/hair/nails, tonic
Monarda (*Monarda* species)	tea, cold and flu, digestive/liver/intestinal, lungs
Mormon tea (*Ephedra* species)	allergy relief, lungs, urinary
Motherwort (*Leonurus cardiaca*)	women's health, stress relief, heart/circulatory, digestive/liver/intestinal, nervous system
Mugwort (*Artemisia vulgaris*)	women's health, digestive/liver/intestinal
Mullein (*Verbascum thapsus*)	allergy relief, pain relief, lungs, eyes/ears/nose/throat, skin/hair/nails, urinary
Nettle (*Urtica dioica*)	tea, medicinal foods, textile, women's health, men's health, children's health, allergy relief, immune/lymph, lungs, eyes/ears/nose/throat, skin/hair/nails, urinary, tonic
Oat (*Avena sativa*)	medicinal foods, women's health, men's health, children's health, stress relief, pain relief, heart/circulatory, immune/lymph, muscles/bones, digestive/liver/intestinal, nervous system, eyes/ears/nose/throat, tonic
Oregano (*Origanum vulgare*)	medicinal foods, cold and flu, digestive/liver/intestinal
Oxeye daisy (*Leucanthemum vulgare*)	women's health, heart/circulatory, digestive/liver/intestinal, eyes/ears/nose/throat, skin/hair/nails, urinary
Parsley (*Petroselinum crispum*)	medicinal foods, digestive/liver/intestinal, urinary
Passionflower (*Passiflora incarnata*)	stress relief, pain relief, nervous system, brain/memory
Pennyroyal (*Mentha pulegium*)	tea, women's health, cold and flu, digestive/liver/intestinal
Penstemon (*Penstemon* species)	skin/hair/nails
Peppermint (*Mentha × piperita*)	tea, fragrance, medicinal food, women's health, children's health, stress relief, cold and flu, pain relief, muscles/bones, digestive/liver/intestinal, lungs, skin/hair/nails
Periwinkle (*Vinca major, V. minor*)	skin/hair/nails
Plantain (*Plantago* species)	children's health, digestive/liver/intestinal, skin/hair/nails, urinary
Pleurisy root (*Asclepias tuberosa*)	cold and flu, lungs
Potentilla (*Potentilla* species)	digestive/liver/intestinal, eyes/ears/nose/throat, skin/hair/nails
Prickly pear (*Opuntia* species)	medicinal foods, digestive/liver/intestinal, skin/hair/nails
Red clover (*Trifolium pratense*)	tea, medicinal foods, women's health, children's health, stress relief, cold and flu, immune/lymph, tonic
Rosemary (*Rosmarinus* species)	fragrance, medicinal foods, cold and flu, heart/circulatory, immune/lymph, muscles/bones, digestive/liver/intestinal, brain/memory, lungs, skin/hair/nails
Rue (*Ruta graveolens*)	women's health, eyes/ears/nose/throat

HERB	BEST THEME GARDENS
Sage (*Salvia officinalis*)	medicinal foods, women's health, cold and flu, digestive/liver/intestinal, lungs, eyes/ears/nose/throat, skin/hair/nails
St.-John's-wort (*Hypericum perforatum*)	stress relief, cold and flu, pain relief, immune/lymph, muscles/bones, nervous system, eyes/ears/nose/throat, skin/hair/nails
Santolina (*Santolina* species)	fragrance, textile
Sedum (*Sedum* species)	medicinal foods, digestive/liver/intestinal, urinary
Self-heal (*Prunella vulgaris*)	tea, women's health, digestive/liver/intestinal, eyes/ears/nose/throat, skin/hair/nails
Sheep sorrel (*Rumex acetosella*)	immune/lymph
Shepherd's purse (*Capsella bursa-pastoris*)	medicinal foods, women's health, heart/circulatory, digestive/liver/intestinal, urinary
Skullcap (*Scutellaria* species)	stress relief, pain relief, nervous system, brain/memory
Spearmint (*Mentha spicata*)	tea, fragrance, medicinal foods, women's health, children's health, stress relief, cold and flu, pain relief, muscles/bones, digestive/liver/intestinal, nervous system, brain/memory, lungs, eyes/ears/nose/throat, skin/hair/nails, tonic
Spilanthes (*Spilanthes acmella*)	cold and flu, immune/lymph, digestive/liver/intestinal, lungs, eyes/ears/nose/throat
Stevia (*Stevia rebaudiana*)	tea, medicinal foods, digestive/liver/intestinal
Summer savory (*Satureja hortensis*)	digestive/liver/intestinal, lungs, eyes/ears/nose/throat, skin/hair/nails, urinary
Sunflower (*Helianthus annuus*)	cold and flu, digestive/liver/intestinal, lungs, urinary
Thyme (*Thymus vulgaris*)	fragrance, medicinal foods, cold and flu, immune/lymph, muscles/bones, digestive/liver/intestinal, nervous system, lungs, eyes/ears/nose/throat, skin/hair/nails
Valerian (*Valeriana officinalis*)	stress relief, pain relief, nervous system
Vervain (*Verbena officinalis*)	children's health, stress relief, cold and flu, muscles/bones, digestive/liver/intestinal, nervous system, lungs
Violet (*Viola* species)	tea, medicinal food, women's health, children's health, stress relief, heart/circulatory, digestive/liver/intestinal, nervous system, lungs, eyes/ears/nose/throat, skin/hair/nails
White sage (*Salvia apiana*)	women's health, cold and flu, digestive/liver/intestinal, lungs, eyes/ears/nose/throat, skin/hair/nails
Wild geranium (*Geranium* species)	digestive/liver/intestinal, eyes/ears/nose/throat, skin/hair/nails
Wormwood (*Artemisia* species)	women's health, digestive/liver/intestinal
Yarrow (*Achillea millefolium*)	women's health children's health, cold and flu, heart/circulatory, muscles/bones, digestive/liver/intestinal, lungs, eyes/ears/nose/throat, skin/hair/nails
Yerba de la negrita (*Sphaeralcea coccinea*)	digestive/liver/intestinal, skin/hair/nails, urinary
Yerba mansa (*Anemopsis californica*)	allergy relief, cold and flu, immune/lymph, lungs, eyes/ears/nose/throat
Yucca (*Yucca* species)	men's health, muscles/bones

Three

secrets to great soil

 The health of your plants begins with the soil. Most new gardeners think that taking care of plants is all that's involved in growing medicinal herbs, but as an organic grower you will need to cultivate healthy soil, just as you cultivate healthy plants. Evaluate the nature of your soil to determine how you can best improve and maintain it. Nourishing the soil on a continuous basis is critical for growing the best-quality herbs. Plants utilize nutrients available in the soil to become vibrantly healthy, and producing viable soil is the first important step toward a gorgeous and useful medicinal garden. ❦

How Will Your Garden Grow?

Once the location has been determined and you know what size your garden space will be, you should make a decision as to whether you will be growing in beds, rows, containers, or raised beds. This will help you decide how to treat the soil for maximum effect.

Bed Cropping

I prefer to grow in garden beds. It is a way for me to maximize the space by using less area to accommodate pathways. It also means that the growing areas are not walked in, thus preventing the soil from becoming compacted and depleted. It allows less soil to be exposed to the elements, reducing soil loss due to wind and erosion.

I live in the high mountain desert of southern Colorado, where water conservation is critical. Bed cropping allows for drip-style or careful sprinkler irrigation, using less precious water while still meeting the growing needs of the plants. Even if you live in a region where water is more abundant, you should be acting with a global consciousness to use as little of our water resources as possible.

Prepare the soil by digging up the beds and mixing in organic matter (see page 46 for more information on organic matter). Ideally, this is done in the fall or spring. Just before planting, till the soil again and then rake it smooth. Incorporate walking space into the area to allow for easy access to the beds. Proceed with planting in mid- to late spring.

Row Cropping

If sprinkler or drip irrigation is not a possibility, then planting in rows may be your best choice. Some gardeners prefer row planting simply because it allows easier access for a tractor.

These beautiful basil plants are an excellent example of row cropping. Mulching is critical for this type of herb growing.

For small-scale farming or gardening, I suggest you use a tiller or hand tools whenever possible. Using a tractor on more than a very occasional basis will compact the soil and make it harder for your plants to develop an extensive root structure. It will also make it a lot more work for you when root harvesttime comes and you're trying to dig them out of compacted soil.

Row cropping is often flood irrigated. This allows more water to run off, contributing to potential soil erosion, more leaching of soil nutrients, and often using water in a less prudent manner. If you have decided to row crop in your garden or field plot, it will be important to incorporate mulching practices to help nourish the soil and hold in moisture. Mulching also helps prevent soil erosion and cuts down on the amount of weeds.

Container and Raised-Bed Gardening

Preparing planter boxes in the form of raised beds or growing in containers is also an excellent way to garden with medicinal plants. If you have very limited space — a patio or balcony, for example — this may be your best option. In addition, containers allow for a better growing medium (soil) if the soil where you live is exceptionally poor or polluted, making for poor-quality medicinals.

For physically challenged individuals, containers or planter boxes may make gardening a much simpler task. This type of growing can allow for easier, safer access for those who use wheelchairs, canes, and other aids. It is also a style of gardening that may increase the comfort level of gardeners who aren't able to bend and stoop as much as a traditional garden requires.

Containers or planter boxes should be filled with a good-quality soil. The soil should be light enough that it doesn't compact over time, yet heavy enough to hold moisture. Good container and planter box soil mixes are available at garden centers and nurseries as "planter's mix" and "perennial soil mix." These mixes can be purchased by the bag or in bulk (cubic yard); the garden center or nursery staff will help you calculate how much you need.

Growing herbs in containers is a great way to maximize limited space and provide easy access to the medicinal garden.

Preparing the Soil

Now that the location of the garden has been determined, it's time to nourish the soil. If the soil is very rich and good, then you are a lucky gardener. Most of us will discover that our soil needs some type of nourishment. All soil must have caretaking to maintain its ability to grow healthy plants.

Adding Organic Matter

By far the most critical component to your soil is organic matter. Organic matter is materials like leaves, manure, and cover crops that decompose in the soil and provide it with the nutrients

 garden profile

Gram-D Farm

Gram-D Farm was begun as a source of medicinal herbs for the products that Denise Blume and Belinda Pardue manufacture. When they started a botanical extracts company in 1990, they knew that their success would depend upon a ready supply of raw materials. The first home of their company, Natural Products, Inc., was in Boone, North Carolina. It was perfectly located in the Appalachian Mountains, surrounded by a rich natural flora and a deep tradition of trappers and wildcrafters. Even today, much of the wild-harvested herbs come from eastern mountain ranges.

In their first year of operation, Denise obtained a grant from the North Carolina Rural Center to study the feasibility of growing botanicals in their state. The grant provided funds for contracting with gardeners and farmers to grow a number of different botanicals in the mountain, piedmont, and coastal areas of North Carolina. The results of the two-year study were significant: The botanicals were not easy to grow (with a few exceptions), and most people lost interest when the weeds grew too fast.

Ready to take on a challenge, Belinda and Denise decided to move their business down from the mountains to the foothills and purchased 31 acres in tobacco-growing country. The site they selected had three different soil types, several natural springs, and a large wooded tract. Fortunately, two of the fields had been fallow for 10 years, so they were able to immediately start the organic certification process.

Denise bought an old Super A tractor and started planting months before ground was broken for the new manufacturing facility. The first year she planted calendula, echinacea, rue, comfrey, and a few species for their homeopathic customers. The next summer, Natural Products, Inc. dedicated its new facility and farm, now called Gram-D Farm, in honor of Denise's grandmother.

The crops at Gram-D Farm have expanded to include both annuals and perennials and 15 species of medicinal shrubs. Soil rebuilding became a major issue in the spring of 1998, following two devastating El Niño floods that stripped away topsoil and brought in tons of sand. Composted chicken litter from local poultry farmers and buckwheat cover crops were used for soil management.

Farm records for the past four years show that the most labor is required for weed control, followed by transplanting and watering. Manual labor costs exceed other production costs by a ratio of 4 to 1! Farm products are sold directly to Natural Products, Inc.; prices are determined by total production costs divided by total farm poundage.

needed to grow healthy plants. Organic matter also offers soil "roughage," which helps maintain good soil consistency, making it possible for plants to develop a healthy root structure. Adding organic matter can improve and maintain soil health. It is an ongoing process that must be repeated every year.

To determine if your soil is of good quality, put a bit of the moist earth in your hand. Squeeze your hand into a fist. When you open the hand, the soil should crumble through your fingers, rather than forming a tight ball. If you have sandy soil, you'll need to examine it visually. Bits of soil, composted matter, and sand should all be present in your sample, and it, too, should crumble even after being squeezed.

For most plants, the ideal level of organic matter is between 4 and 5 percent. You can send a soil sample off to your local County Extension Service to be tested so that you know if you need to add organic matter before planting your garden. Pick up a kit from the extension service — it will tell you how to prepare your soil sample for testing. Be sure to state what type of testing you would like to have done. In most cases, the soil can be tested for organic matter levels, nutrient levels, salt levels, and soil pH.

Start with the Basics

Each year you will want to add organic matter to your garden or field soil. This is an ongoing process that provides the soil with the nutrients it needs to remain healthy.

Organic matter, such as leaves, compost, or manure, is best added to the soil in the late fall. If you can't add any in late fall, make it a point to add the organic matter in early spring. Use a wheelbarrow to transport the organic matter to the garden, and spread the material evenly on top of the soil. You can also use a manure spreader if you're tending a larger area.

The next step is tilling: Till as soon as possible once the organic matter has been spread over the soil. Delaying this step will result in nitrogen loss through breakdown from exposure to the air.

Use Cover Crops

Cover crops, like organic matter, also help build good-quality soil. They are living "manures" that will add vital nutrients to the earth. Typically, these crops are grown in the garden or field during the off-season or whenever a field space is being left fallow to regenerate before being cultivated again. Cover crops grow and thrive throughout the off-season, protecting the soil from wind and water erosion while also providing much-needed food for wildlife.

The seeds of the cover crop are planted in the fall (or at the end of the normal growing season). For us in Colorado, that means late September or mid-October. In very early spring, or at least four weeks before the planting season begins, the growing cover crop should be tilled into the soil. The tilled soil is allowed to sit for a week or two. After that time, the soil is retilled to prepare it for the actual spring planting of the herbs.

Common plants to use as cover crops are grasses and legumes. Winter rye, oats, buckwheat, clovers, and alfalfa are all good choices. Short-term cover crops — such as buckwheat, winter rye, and oats — are left in place for only a season or two. If the land is being left fallow for several seasons to a few years, legumes, red clover, and alfalfa are good choices for long-term cover crops. All of these plants are deep-rooted and nitrogen-rich, excellent for replenishing the nutrients in tired soil.

Clover makes a wonderful and attractive cover crop that can be used to nourish your soil between planting seasons. Use clover as either a long- or a short-term crop.

Evaluating pH

A soil's pH level will indicate its degree of acidity or alkalinity. Plants are directly affected by pH, as this influences what nutrients are available to the plants' roots. It will also determine how deep a plant can root, since subsoils may have a different pH level.

Most plants will grow best in a pH level between 6.0 and 6.5, providing there is adequate organic matter and nutrients available in the soil. Different soil components like sulfur and lime will raise or lower the pH level by increasing or decreasing acidity and alkalinity. As the soil pH changes, you will be able to detect changes in a plant's growth habits and health. Changing pH levels can also affect the herb's medicinal and nutritional potency.

We humans are not known to be very good soil caretakers. By this I mean that when we try to adjust the pH to a level that *we* feel is ideal, we often can lose sight of what the plants may need for the region that we are growing in. Everything in a growing environment is interwoven: soil, available water, temperature, insect populations, and pollinators. The type of trees that may be growing in your garden space will also influence the soil's pH.

In short, I feel you will have better success growing your medicinals if you first ensure that you have sufficient organic matter in your garden, and then work with the existing pH level of the soil. The soil is integrated with all the other growing factors available to you; if you choose plants that can grow at the existing pH level, they will do very well. If you manipulate the pH of the soil, you will have to be a really good scientist or an excellent wizard to avoid messing up the overall environmental picture. It's a much bigger issue than just adjusting the soil, and I find that we throw things *out of balance* more often than we keep things *in balance*.

For instance, if you adjust the pH for acid-loving plants in a soil that is normally more alkaline, you may create a soil that doesn't sustain any of the plants as well as it needs to for optimum growth. This can be very frustrating, but it could also throw off the medicinal constituents and potency levels in the plants you are growing. That might prevent you from being able to experience the medicinal benefits the plant normally offers. In a worst-case scenario, it might influence toxicity levels of a plant, making it inappropriate or unsafe to use in a medicinal way.

Learn what your soil pH is through a soil test (see page 47) and then work with that rather

Container Growing Is Not a Cure-All

Growing plants in containers can help alleviate problems you might have with your backyard soil, but it isn't a cure-all. Passionflower, for example, is a semi-tropical to tropical plant that requires bat pollinators. I can grow it in containers in my garden, but there are no bats to pollinate the flowers where I live, so the plant will not grow fruits or mature seeds unless I hand-pollinate the flowers.

Similarly, I can container grow American ginseng, an eastern woodlands plant. I can provide the acid soil and the shade this plant needs, but the air in southern Colorado is very dry and the temperatures are extremely hot for the herb. It will grow, but I would be lucky to have it live long enough (six to eight years) to actually harvest this plant. With so many growing variables it would be questionable if the American ginseng I harvested would be medicinally active enough to use for my health and well-being. ❦

than trying to change it. There are so many herbs, and they grow in all different types of soil. You should find no lack of medicinal plants to choose from.

If you would really like to grow an herb that normally grows in a radically different soil pH, and if you feel the plant will not be able to adapt to the soil in your area, then consider growing that plant in a container. You will be able to control the type of soil the herb will grow in, but keep in mind the influence of the elements and the integration of the total environment. You won't be able to control everything — insects, for instance — and you will need to consider if the plant you're growing in the container will be able to complete its life cycles in the environment you have provided it.

Composting

One of the most important parts of organic growing is the use of compost. You will want to incorporate into your compost all sorts of ingredients. Soil, manure, very small twigs and leaves, trimmings from garden maintenance work, and vegetable or fruit scraps from the kitchen (do not use dairy or meat products) are all good things to put into your compost. After these items have decomposed, they will be added back into the soil of the garden or field as a very nutrient-rich organic soil builder. Be sure your composter is in full sun or partial shade; full sun is best, while composting in full shade is rarely successful.

When you first begin your compost pile, it's best to build a surrounding structure for the compost materials. You can create a compost pile without one, but I find that a structure helps to keep the compost ingredients all together so that the decomposition process is more efficient. It also gives a tidier appearance.

There are several ways you can build a structure. It can be made from wire, wooden pallets, cinder blocks, or a 55-gallon metal drum. Some people prefer to dig a pit in the soil and put their compost ingredients into the pit. You could forgo building a structure and instead purchase a ready-made compost bin from a garden supply shop.

Wire, Wood, or Cinderblock Structures

Use wire, wood, or cinder blocks to form a square or circular shape. Pasture wire or chicken wire works well and can be formed into a tube and tied closed with baling wire or twine. Four wooden pallets can be formed into a square, and the corners fastened with wire. When the time comes to turn the compost pile, untie the wire, reverse the structure like an accordion, and retie it into place.

The importance of composting cannot be overlooked. This nutrient-rich soil-booster will help your plants grow strong and healthy.

Cinder blocks will make the most permanent type of structure. Build a three-sided square, leaving the fourth side open for easier access. Turn the compost ingredients with a garden fork to facilitate the decomposition process.

Pit or Pile Composting

For pit composting, a hole is dug in the ground. The hole should be 2 to 3 feet (.6 to .9 m) deep and unlined. Compost ingredients are added until the pit is filled sufficiently. The compost is then covered with soil and allowed to decompose. When the process is completed, the compost is unearthed and added to the garden.

The simplest compost is a pile in a corner of the garden or field. This works fine if you are diligent about turning your pile and keeping it moist. This is not the most attractive type of compost, but it certainly is functional and the least expensive to create.

Many gardeners opt to compost in a pile, since it is the simplest way to create this soil fertilizer and conditioner. Regular turning of the pile is necessary to ensure proper decomposition.

Drum Composters

When choosing a drum for your composter, be aware that you should *never* use one that has been used to store toxic or petroleum-based substances. Clean the drum using a pressure nozzle on the end of a hose. After rinsing well, fill with water and an environmentally friendly cleaner such as a citrus-based detergent. Scrub the drum's interior with an old broom, and then rinse thoroughly.

If you are making your compost bin from a 55-gallon metal drum, you will need to hire a welder to create a door of sorts in the side of the compost barrel. The door will provide access for adding ingredients and removing finished compost to be used in your garden. You will also need to create some holes in the ends of the barrel for air circulation. This type of bin works best if it can be put onto a horseshoe-shaped metal frame. The frame will act as a cradle, allowing you to roll the barrel to mix your compost. If you are using a plastic drum, be sure it is food-safe to prevent chemicals from leaching into the compost.

What *Not* to Use in Compost

Along with dairy products and meats, there are a few types of plant materials to avoid using in your compost. Do not use succulent types of plants like houseleek (also known as hen-and-chickens), because they don't decompose very easily. Annual or perennial weeds that have gone to seed are also best avoided. You should never use plants that are infected with a virus or bacteria (see chapter 6 for more information on plant diseases). Large branches should not be added to the compost unless they have been put through a chipper or shredder first. Last, human waste is not an appropriate ingredient for compost because of the health hazards it could introduce. ❧

Creating the Compost

Once you have made a structure to hold the compost ingredients, you will begin adding the vital components to create compost. This is the best way I have found to layer the ingredients:

1. Place several small twigs in the bottom of the bin. These twigs will take some time to decompose; in the initial stages of your compost's life they will form air pockets at the bottom of your pile, providing ventilation for the other ingredients.

2. Add a layer of soil, about 8 to 10 inches (20 to 25 cm) deep.

3. Cover the soil with a 4- to 6-inch (10 to 15 cm) layer of manure (for more information, see below).

4. Steps 1 through 3 contain the early building blocks of your compost pile. Now you can begin layering additional ingredients. There are many choices for appropriate compost ingredients (see below). I feel that utilizing a variety of components facilitates faster decomposition of the compost.

5. As you layer ingredients into your compost, add a 6-inch (10 cm) layer of soil and a 2- to 4-inch (5 to 10 cm) layer of manure about every 24 inches (60 cm) to ensure that you have incorporated all of the healthy elements of compost into your pile.

Manure

Use whatever type of livestock manure is available to you, as long as it is from a good organic source. (Feedlot livestock and poultry farm animals are often fed growth hormones and antibiotics, making their manure unsafe for your garden use.) Do *not* use dog or cat manure at all in your compost.

The more aged the manure is, the faster it will compost. Fresh manure takes a bit longer to break down. Never put fresh manure directly on your garden; it can burn the plants and increase the amount of *E. coli* bacteria in your harvested herbs.

Additional Ingredients

In step 4, I instruct you to add additional ingredients to your compost. What exactly comprises this category?

Kitchen scraps like vegetable and fruit trimmings, grains, eggshells, tea, and tea leaves are all good to use in compost. You should not put meat or a lot of dairy products into your compost pile. A little bit of cheese, milk, or eggs won't hurt, but large amounts of these items should be avoided. A constant, very high temperature is required to break down meat and dairy products so that they can safely be used in the garden. It is extremely difficult to keep the compost temperature hot enough on an ongoing basis, and if that high temperature is not maintained, those types of food can become a health hazard. They also attract undesirable animal and insect visitors to the compost. Also avoid adding food materials that are highly processed and those that contain animal fats.

Leaves, garden trimmings, and grass clippings are very good ingredients in your compost. Whenever you weed, deadhead flowers, trim the skullcap, or do other housekeeping garden tasks, add those trimmings to your compost. It's important to mix grass clippings with other ingredients when adding them to the compost; large layers of grass clippings will mat together, dry out, get very hot, and prevent water from moving through the compost efficiently.

Activating Compost

Garden shops offer compost activator products. These can be used to really get your compost working, but it isn't necessary to purchase a compost activator. Consider making your own.

Nettle leaves, comfrey leaves, seaweed, and fish emulsion are all excellent compost activators. Make a compost tea of any or all of these ingredients (see recipe next page) and add it to your compost once every three months. This supplies the components that your compost will need to begin working and breaking down the other ingredients to make a supreme composted matter.

I don't feel it is necessary to buy worms to add to your compost. You could do this if you choose to, but if you are working your compost on a regular basis and you are adding healthy ingredients to it, the worms will find their way to your compost bin.

Working the Compost

It is important to turn your compost once a month during warm and hot weather. During the cold winter months, the compost pile is not hot enough to decompose much, so turning it is less crucial.

Turning the compost can be done using a shovel or garden fork. I find it easier to work with a garden fork, but give both a try and see what you prefer. The goal is to flip the pile. Ideally you want all of the material on the top of the pile to become the bottom of the new pile and the material that is nearer the bottom will become the top. Everything in the middle usually stays in the middle, but it gets all mixed up in the process, which is perfect.

As you turn the pile you may find that at the very bottom is a small amount of composted material. This material will look like a rich, dark brown soil. That's the compost that is ready to use. You may choose either to use it immediately or to mix it back into the pile for later use. If you have a very large compost pile, such as might be the case on a small farm, you will need to use a tractor to turn it.

Watering the compost is a key component to its quality. Your compost should stay evenly moist. It should not be soaking wet, nor should it be completely dried out. I live in a very dry, hot, and sometimes windy region, and I need to water my compost about once a month during hot weather. In climates where there is more

precipitation, you would need to water your compost less often. Simply water it with a hose, making sure that every part of the pile has been watered evenly.

Incorporating Compost into Your Garden

Once the composted material is ready for use, it can be worked into the garden soil. If the garden will be freshly tilled, apply a 1- to 3-inch (2.5 to 7.5 cm) layer of compost to the top of the soil. Till or work the compost into the soil until it is well mixed. If you are adding compost to an existing perennial garden, apply a top dressing of compost ½ to 1 inch (1.25 to 2.5 cm) thick. Rake the compost into the soil all around the existing plants.

The ideal time to add compost is spring, but it can really be added at any time of the year. Once the compost has been incorporated into the soil, water the garden thoroughly. This will encourage the plants' roots to begin drawing up the nutrients the compost provides.

▶ compost activator tea

Be sure to wear gloves whenever working with fresh nettles to avoid skin irritation. Don't allow the mixture to sit in your house while it's steeping — it doesn't smell very good! This makes enough activator for up to a 64-cubic-foot (1.8 m³) compost pile.

- 6 cups dried or 12 cups fresh nettles
- 6 cups dried or 12 cups fresh comfrey leaves
- 2 cups flaked or powdered kelp
- 1 cup liquid fish emulsion

Put all ingredients into a 5-gallon bucket and fill the bucket with water. Allow this mixture to sit in a warm place for 4 to 8 hours. Pour all the contents of the bucket into your compost pile.

Four

propagation
methods

When you begin to work with medicinal plants, you will need to leave behind most of your preconceptions about how propagation is supposed to be done. Many of the medicinal plants will be successful if you grow them in the same way that you handle vegetables or annual flowers, but far more of them will have at least one special requirement in order to sprout or root and begin a thriving life. Get acquainted with your chosen plants by browsing through chapter 10. You can also consult nurseries or other growers in your area for advice. 🌾

Do Your Homework

If you are a horticulturist or Master Gardener, I challenge you to use your training as tools or guidelines, rather than as rules. If you are new to growing medicinal plants, then remember that the *only* rule is that there are no rules. Open yourself to experimentation and flexibility. Many of the medicinal plants — especially those closest to their wild roots — seem to hate rules, and they are very good at breaking them. Set aside technology for a moment and begin to think like the plant you want to grow.

Each Plant Is an Individual

I don't mean to scare you from trying to propagate these plants yourself. Quite the contrary: My hope is simply to save you a bit of frustration. If you approach this task from a less restricted perspective, you *will* have excellent success.

The first step is to learn a bit about the individual plant. Ask yourself:

▸ What part of the world is it native to?

▸ Where would this plant grow if it could choose its ideal place?

▸ What type of climate exists in the place the plant is indigenous to?

▸ What other plants grow in community with this plant?

▸ What types of animals and insects have a relationship with this plant?

Learn as much as you can about where the plant might grow naturally — chapter 10 will provide more insight into each herb's personality traits. Also check wild-plant identification books; they are a good source of information about a plant's natural habitat. In addition, I utilize geography books and naturalist guidebooks. Knowing about an herb's natural preferences is the key that will make you successful in growing the plants of your choice.

Create a "Native" Environment

Once I have an idea about a plant's natural growing environment, I try to offer the seeds, root divisions, or cuttings support by duplicating that environment as closely as possible. In the past I have had all the latest technology available to me, and while that can be a lot of fun and looks quite impressive, without remembering details about the plant's native environment, all other tools would have been useless.

I am now fortunate to have a growing facility that is simple and practical. I don't miss all the bells and whistles, because they didn't offer me greater success over the methods I currently use. Success is not realized by equipment or fancy supplies; it is due to plant knowledge and hard work.

As much as possible, match the plant's desired temperature range. Provide some shade, if needed, and keep the herbs appropriately moist. See chapter 3 for tips on getting your soil into the best possible shape. Careful monitoring of changes in the plant's environment will yield consistent, positive results.

Growing from Seed

There are a number of propagation methods; the one you choose will be determined by the needs of each specific plant (see chapter 10 for individual plant requirements).

Whenever possible, I prefer to start my plants from seed. I feel this gives me the strongest plant. Some plants do not produce viable seed, however, or they may have a very poor seed germination percentage. For those plants, propagation by cuttings, runners, or root and crown divisions may be a better choice.

Some plants have desirable qualities that will not be manifested when they are produced from seed. For instance, peppermint that is very strong in taste and fragrance has high levels of volatile oils; because of this, it will normally have much stronger medicinal properties. This plant would need to be propagated from a cutting or root division; mints grown from seed don't normally carry that quality of high volatile oil content.

Keep in mind that while this principle applies to many types of mints, it does not necessarily hold true for all mints or other types of plants. *Every plant is an individual with its own specific requirements*. Don't fall into the trap of lumping all plants into the same growing categories. Chapter 10 and the propagation chart on page 68 will give you more information, so that you can start your garden off right.

I am often told that starting plants from seed is just too difficult and intimidating. That does not need to be the case. Remembering that every plant is an individual and learning about its growing preferences is the first place to begin when propagating from seed. Many seeds require special treatments prior to being sown, while others have no special needs. Nearly all seeds will follow some basic guidelines.

Echinacea, like many other medicinal plants, is generally easy to propagate and maintain. But some species of the herb are more difficult to propagate. The key is becoming familiar with each plant's individual preferences and requirements.

Saving Seeds

When growing plants from seed you'll have two choices for what seeds you use: buying seed from a seed house that provides good-quality stock or saving and cleaning your own seed. Both are good options, but in truth I think it is important to know how to save your own seed and do the cleaning process even if you opt never to do the task again.

Saving your own seed is a part of our ancestral traditions just like growing your own food or preparing your own medicines. It is a skill that should be honored as a sacred part of our ability to care for ourselves. We should all endeavor to pass on this traditional skill to our children, grandchildren, and beyond.

Another good reason to know how to save your own seed is the rising popularity of genetic engineering. Genetic engineering limits plant and animal diversity, gives inappropriate control or power to corporate entities and governmental agencies, and can have negative repercussions on health, nutrition, and healing. If you save your own seed from non-genetically engineered plants, you will be exercising your right to eat what you feel is best and make plant-based medicines and textiles from crops you feel are most appropriate for your own needs.

The process of saving seed is not a difficult one, but in order to keep the seed viable you must harvest, clean, and store it properly.

Harvesting. Harvesting should be done when the seed is ripe; look for seeds that are fully formed, showing evidence of a seed embryo inside (the seed should look plump). Ripe seeds usually have turned from green to a more unique color — anything from brown, tans, black, and white to exotic colors like maroon and speckled hues. The mature seeds will also often have a somewhat dried appearance. If the seeds are fully ripe, pick them by hand or by using a pair of snips or scis-

sors. I like to gather my seeds in paper bags or tightly woven baskets. Do not use containers that are airtight, as these can encourage the growth of mold if the seed contains any moisture in or on it.

Cleaning. To begin the cleaning process, spread out newspaper on a table. A shallow cardboard box will also work nicely for this purpose. Seeds are normally contained within some type of shell, cone, or husk, to protect them from wind and harsh weather or browsing animals/insects. You will have to dislodge the seed from that protective "house" and then attempt to remove as much of the chaff (the clinging bits of the seed's house) as possible. I use various-sized screens and baskets to accomplish this. As the seeds are sifted through a screen, they are separated from the chaff. It will be nearly impossible to remove 100 percent of the chaff, but don't worry; a bit of chaff

Harvest sunflower seeds by gently rubbing them from the head of the plant.

doesn't hinder the sowing process much when you actually plant the seeds.

Storing. Once you have cleaned the seeds to your satisfaction, put them in a plain paper envelope. Remember to label the envelope with the plant name, when and where the seed was harvested, and any other information you would like to include. I sometimes note the elevation of the harvest location and weather conditions at the time of harvest. If the seed is nontropical, it will stay viable longer if it is stored in the freezer. Put your envelopes in a plastic zipper-lock bag and put the whole package in the freezer. Stored in this fashion, seeds will often stay viable for several years. If the seeds are from a tropical plant, store them at room temperature in a dry place, protected from bright light. These seeds will also hold their viability for up to several years. For any type of seed, be sure to avoid excessive heat (over 100°F (38°C) for extended periods of time), bright light, and direct contact with moisture. Do

 What to Use as a Seed-Cleaning Screen

Be creative! Use sprouting screens, different-sized tea strainers and colanders, and old window screens for your seed-cleaning. I create screens by using different sizes of fabric netting (available at fabric or craft stores) or different-sized nylon or metal window screening (available at hardware stores). I stretch the netting/screening material between embroidery hoops (also available at fabric or craft stores) until they are taut. This gives me many different-sized, inexpensive cleaning screens to work with. If making screens does not suit your fancy, you can easily purchase a set of seed-cleaning screens at an upscale garden center or a mail-order gardening supply house. 🌸

whatever is possible to prevent pests like insects and mice from getting into the seed, too.

Selecting and Purchasing Seeds

If you find that saving your own seed is not possible, buy your seed from a reputable seed house. Large seed companies are not automatically quality seed companies. Seed companies, large and small, should sell you seed that is labeled correctly with common and Latin names. You should also source seed that has not been treated chemically in any way (no fungicides or sprouting or pelletizing agents). In addition, I look for seeds that are not heavily contaminated by weed seeds, and I want to make sure they have not been stored for years and years before being sold to me. Ask your supplier these questions *before* you buy.

There are a number of excellent seed companies, and I have listed many of my favorites in Resources. I find that each year I come across a seed house I wasn't aware of before. I always give new companies a try (I wouldn't want to be known as a seed snob) to see if the seeds perform well. If so, I become a loyal customer. I boycott seed houses that handle genetically modified/engineered seeds. I feel that propagating these seeds is unethical and dangerous both to the environment and to our bodies. As a medical herbalist, I believe that it's impossible to know how plants grown from such seeds will behave physiologically when they are ingested as foods or medicines.

Apply Seed Treatments

Some seeds will need extra treatment before being sown. This is where your previous research on the individual plant is most critical. What happens to that seed when it matures on a plant out in nature? Does it drop immediately to the ground or does the wind carry it off? Is it likely to be eaten by an animal or a bird? Will it spend several months exposed to the winter snow or a rainy season? Factors such as these will affect the germination of the seed. Put your mind in the place of the plant, and when you have thought about what the seed would experience out in nature, ponder how you can duplicate those factors in your growing situation.

Stratification. If the seed would normally experience a period of winter with cold temperatures, ice, and freezing and thawing conditions, that seed will most likely benefit — indeed require — stratification. Stratification is the process of chilling or freezing moistened seeds to simulate winter. If the plant would normally experience an icy winter, then the seeds should be stratified in the freezer. Place seeds in a reclosable freezer bag with a few drops of water. Shake the bag to coat the seeds with moisture and then put the bag into the freezer for 2 to 3 months. Remove the bag from the freezer once a month and allow the seeds to thaw for a few hours. Then return the bag of seeds to the freezer. This method, which is also called wet stratification, creates the freezing/thawing effect that many plants experience in their natural habitat.

If the seeds would normally experience a cold winter but not necessarily a frozen one, then do the stratification in the refrigerator. In this case, put the seeds into moistened peat moss or sand in a reclosable plastic bag and place the bag in the refrigerator until the seeds start to sprout. Then plant the seeds as usual. This technique is often referred to as cold stratification.

Scarification. Perhaps the seeds you want to germinate would experience some type of situation that would cause the seed coat to get slightly damaged or nicked. This process allows moisture to more easily penetrate the seed and cause germination. Maybe the wind would carry that seed across a gravelly or sandy surface, for example. Artificially inducing this is called scarification. There are several ways to scarify a seed. I prefer to lay a piece of coarse sandpaper in the bottom of a shoe box. I place the seeds on top of the sandpaper and ever so gently rub the seeds back and forth a few times. This will scar the seed coat surface. Another method is to place the seeds in a small coffee can with some coarse sand. Cover and gently shake the can a few times; the friction of the seeds against the sand will cause scarification. For very large seeds or those that have an especially hard coat, you may have to nick each seed with a small sharp knife. Use extreme care in this process; you don't want to injure yourself or damage the fragile embryo of the seed just inside the coat. The goal is to nick the seed coat without going any deeper.

After harvesting, place the seeds on some newspaper or a screen and sift through them. Discard any chaff, insects, or pieces of plant matter.

Soaking. Some seeds need to experience extended periods of wetness. In nature, this could be accomplished by snow cover or a native habitat along a stream bank. This soaking time allows the seed coat to soften so that the seed may sprout more easily. If I think a seed will germinate more easily if soaked, I place the seeds in a small bowl, pour hot water over them, and let them soak. Hot water is used because it softens the seed coat more quickly; this is important since simulated soaking will be for a shorter duration than the natural soaking process. The soaking time varies depending on the seed; refer to chapter 10 for more information. After the appropriate soaking time, the seeds are sown immediately.

Hydrogen peroxide soaking. If you know that the plant you're propagating has seeds that usually get eaten and exposed to the digestive juices of an animal before germinating, then consider doing a hydrogen peroxide soak. I use regular 3 percent hydrogen peroxide — the kind you might have in your bathroom cabinet for first-aid purposes. Many native dryland or desert plants seem to respond well to this type of treatment. The peroxide, like digestive juices, breaks down the seed coat more quickly so that germination is easier. This type of soak should not be done for a long period of time. Small or fragile seeds should be soaked only for 15 to 20 minutes; larger or more durable seeds can be soaked for up to 45 minutes. Sow the seeds immediately after soaking.

Choose a Soil Medium and Prepare the Seed Flats

Choose a soil medium that is not too heavy for planting seeds. You can purchase premade seed mixes or you can prepare your own (see the box below). Fill seed flats or boxes with your soil medium and water the flats well. I prefer a watering wand with a rosette sprinkler head for a soft, even water flow. (This waters thoroughly and evenly without washing the soil medium out of the flats.) Press the soil medium gently to eliminate any air pockets and to give an even sowing surface.

 Make Your Own Soil Medium

For years, I've used an excellent, easy-to-make soil medium that works equally well for seed sowing and for cuttings. To make it, mix 1 part soil, 2 parts peat moss, and ¼ part perlite. Blend well. Use this medium to fill your flats, and proceed as directed. ❀

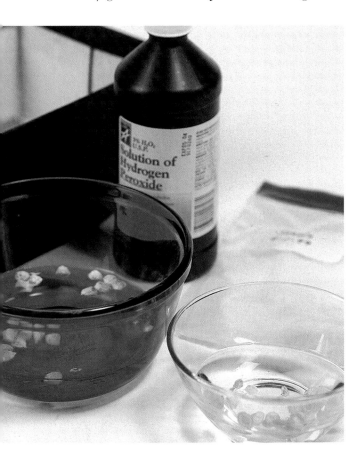

In order to grow, some seeds require a pretreatment, such as a water soak, a hydrogen peroxide soak, scarification, or stratification.

STEP-BY-STEP SEED SOWING

As you are sowing the seeds, you should attempt to keep the spacing as even as possible. Seeds that all fall in a clump will make transplanting more difficult, and the seedlings undergo more stress and shock when roots must be pulled apart during transplanting. Large seeds like sage and burdock are pretty easy to keep evenly spaced, whereas really tiny seeds like mullein and chamomile can be very difficult to space. If seeds are extremely tiny, mix 1 part seed with 2 parts cornmeal and then sow as usual, cornmeal and all. The cornmeal acts as an automatic spacing agent.

One of the most important steps in sowing seed is to sow it at the proper depth. It is a common practice for people to plant their seeds too deep. Once again, it is important to know about the individual plant you are sowing. Seeds that have been planted too deep will not sprout. Look closely at the seeds you are sowing. How big around are they? Double the diameter of the seed, and then plant it in the soil medium at that depth.

After the seeds are sown, you will need to cover them. Some seeds will require complete darkness, but most will need some light. I prefer to cover my seeds with vermiculite. Vermiculite allows light to penetrate, while at the same time offering the seeds some protection and helping to maintain moisture in the flat.

Keep the Seeds Moist

Another critical step in germinating seeds is keeping the seeds evenly moist (not soggy). They must never dry out! If the seeds dry out, they won't sprout; if they have already sprouted and then dry out, the tiny seedlings will die. Take great care to keep your seed flats moist.

Remember that your seed flat was watered in when you prepared it for sowing, so it is usually only the surface soil that needs to have moisture

1 **Once you've prepared a flat or pots, poke small holes in the soil with your fingertips.**

2 **Sow the seeds evenly in the pots or across the flat, then cover with a bit of the soil medium.**

renewed regularly. On a small scale, I find a spray bottle filled with water works great for this task; a gentle spray will give the seeds moisture without washing them out of the flat. On a larger, greenhouse scale, a rosette watering wand can be used if it is held at shoulder height and moved evenly and slowly above the flats, gently watering the seed surface.

In addition, I cover my seed flats with pieces of shade cloth. This can be purchased at garden shops or nursery supply companies. The shade cloth helps to hold in moisture longer and also offers a bit of extra protection to the germinating seeds. Once germination occurs and the seedlings begin to come up, remove the shade cloth from the flats so the seedlings have greater access to sunlight. If you have sown your seeds directly into the garden or field, it is just as important to keep them moist. Use a soft spray sprinkler to keep the seeds moist in a large area.

 Protect Small Seeds from the Elements

If you have sown tiny seeds directly into the garden, the challenge to keep them moist and prevent them from blowing away in the breeze will be even greater than with those sown in flats. I sometimes cover tiny or delicate seeds with lengths of burlap. Sow your seeds as usual and then lay the burlap cloth over the top of the seedbed. Burlap is great because it does not prevent light from filtering through to the seeds, and it holds moisture fairly well. Secure the burlap with stones or metal stakes to keep the wind from displacing it. Once the seeds have germinated, remove the burlap so the seedlings have greater access to sunlight. ❀

Other Propagation Methods

Some plants cannot be propagated from seed because they don't produce seed or the seed isn't viable. Comfrey, for example, doesn't produce seed, and wild geranium produces seeds that won't sprout. Other herbs have a unique characteristic like color variegation (such as lemon thyme) or extra-high amounts of volatile oil (such as peppermint and spearmint) that will not grow "true" when propagation is done by seed.

Tip cuttings, layering root divides, and crown propagation are other ways to start a new generation of young plants.

STEP-BY-STEP CUTTINGS

Cuttings are my second choice for propagating a plant. Some herbs will be very difficult to root from cuttings, but many plants will develop roots easily. Propagation by cuttings is easier to do in quantity than other non-seed propagation methods.

Preparation. Fill a plug flat (a flat divided into many small cells) or small pots with the same soil medium you use for seeding. Water in the flats.

After the flats are prepared, you will need a rooting hormone to get your cuttings off to a good start. Rooting hormone contains Indole-3-butyric acid and 1-Naphthaleneacetic acid, two naturally occurring plant growth hormones that stimulate sprouting along the stem nodes. There are three types of rooting hormone you can use.

Powdered rooting hormone is available at garden shops. The cutting tips are rolled in the powder and then stuck into the soil. This type of rooting hormone, while convenient, is actually my least favorite choice because there is no way to adjust the level of hormone used. Some plants require little rooting hormone in order to produce good roots; other types of plants, especially those with woody stems, require a higher level of hormone.

Liquid concentrate rooting hormone is the one that I prefer. Label directions will give the appropriate dilution for the kind of plant you are trying to root. With this type of hormone, I can prepare the mixture as strong or as weak as necessary for the plant I am working with.

Homemade rooting hormone can be prepared from liquid kelp concentrate. Use 1 teaspoon of concentrate per ounce of water. I find that kelp rooting hormone works pretty well for most cuttings, but some dryland native and desert plants don't seem to like this substitute.

Tips on Cuttings

• Take only one-third to one-half of the tender growth available. If you take more than that, you will increase the stress on the mother plant.

• A quick rooting-hormone dip is fine for most plants.

• Use a small, thin stick to poke a hole into the soil, and then place the stem in the hole. Be sure that all peeled nodes are beneath the soil level.

• Place the flat of cuttings in a place out of direct sunlight. The area should be warm (68–70°F; 20–21°C), with good air circulation. Cover the cuttings lightly with a piece of shade cloth. Keep the soil moist in the plug flat. Cuttings will root in 1 to 4 weeks, depending on the plant. 🌿

1 **To take cuttings from the mother plant, snip off 1 to 3 inches (2.5 to 7.5 cm) of the tender tip growth.**

2 **Gently peel the leaves off the bottom two nodes, or joints, where they attach to the stem.**

3 **Dip the end of the stem into rooting hormone, then stick the cutting into the soil medium.**

4 **With your thumb and finger, gently pinch the soil up around the stem of the cutting.**

STEP-BY-STEP LAYERING

If the plant you are working with has runners or offshoots, layering is best. Runners or off-shoots are stems that grow laterally along the soil surface. They root readily whenever a node has direct contact with the soil, resulting in plantlets all along the stems. Layering simply takes advantage of what nature already does.

Preparation. Fill an open flat with the soil medium and water it in well. Unfold several paper clips and bend them into a simple horse-shoe shape. Spacing them evenly, use the horse-shoe clips to hold the runners onto the soil. Place the clips carefully so that every node or offshoot is firmly in contact with the soil.

 Tips on Layering in Pots

Place the plug flat of layerings where it will be out of direct sunlight. The area should be warm (68–70°F; 20–21°C), with good air circulation. The layerings do not need to be covered, and they will root in 1 to 2 weeks. Test for rooting by very gently tugging on the plantlet. If it has started to root, it will not lift from the gentle pressure. At this stage, clip the stem connection between the rooted plantlets with a pair of sharp scissors. When the herbs are ready to transplant, simply break apart the soil to create little plants with their own bit of soil around the roots. ❧

1 **To layer in a pot, snip the runners near the point where they grow out of the mother plant.**

2 **To layer in the garden, dig a shallow trench where you will place the runner.**

3 **Set the runner on top of the soil and secure with a forked piece of twig or a bent, U-shaped paper clip.**

4 **If planted in the garden, fill in the trench lightly with soil.**

STEP-BY-STEP ROOT DIVISION

Whenever a plant has a branching root system, root divisions are a possible propagation method. Plants with a taproot — a single, long root rather than branching multiple roots — do not usually divide well by root divisions. This method will usually work for rhizomatous plants, which have roots that grow laterally just under the soil surface, but again, you should research the individual plant before beginning to propagate in this way. It is always best to do root divisions in early spring or early fall, when it is the least stressful for the mature plant.

Keep Detailed Records

As you begin trying various ways of propagating herbs, do keep a plant journal. Take detailed notes about what you have done and what results you get. Every detail you note may be useful at another time, so don't be stingy.

I have plant journals going back 16 years, and many times I have been grateful to look through them to see what technique I used to grow a specific plant. Reviewing my notes helps me recall if it was better to plant a seed in August or April, what suppliers I liked best for a particular plant, what strength rooting hormone worked best, and more. ✿

1 **Carefully dig up the mature plant you wish to divide, gently removing soil from around the roots.**

2 **Turn the plant on its side, and, using a very sharp knife, slice through the root clump.**

3 **Make sure that each division has a sufficient amount of roots attached to the crown.**

4 **Replant each division piece in the garden or field or in pots. Keep the soil moist.**

STEP-BY-STEP CROWN PROPAGATION

When a perennial plant is dug up from the garden or field and the roots are harvested, the crowns (which normally sit just at the soil surface) may sometimes be replanted. I have found this to be one of the least effective propagation methods, but it does work sometimes. Use this system as a last resort, if no other method is available.

Once planted, keep the soil moist until crowns have developed a new root structure. If new stem growth begins to sprout from the top of the crown, or if gentle tugging on the crown is met with resistance, you will know that new roots are developing.

These crown cuttings from elecampane were all propagated from one plant.

1 Dig full plant out of ground. Cut excess stem and leaf growth to about 1 inch (2.5 cm) above the crown.

2 Divide the crown into several pieces using a spade.

3 Separate the crown pieces and prepare a spot in the garden or field to replant them.

4 Plant the crowns, being careful not to put them too deep; they should be just at the soil surface.

Propagation at a Glance

You'll find general propagation information in this chart. Keep in mind, however, that many plants will have unique requirements. See chapter 10 for more detailed information.

HERB	PROPAGATION METHOD	WHERE TO START	SPECIAL TREATMENT
Alfalfa (*Medicago sativa*)	seeds	outdoors	none
Angelica (*Angelica archangelica*)	seeds	indoors	cold stratification
Anise hyssop (*Agastache foeniculum*)	seeds	indoors	cold stratification
Astragalus (*Astragalus membranaceus*)	seeds	indoors, outdoors	cold stratification, water soak, scarification
Balloon flower (*Platycodon grandiflorus*)	seeds	indoors	cold stratification, water soak
Basil (*Ocimum* species)	seeds	indoors	none
Betony (*Betonica officinalis*)	seeds	indoors	cold stratification
Black-eyed Susan (*Rudbeckia hirta*)	seeds	indoors, outdoors	cold stratification
Blue vervain (*Verbena hastata*)	seeds	indoors	cold stratification
Borage (*Borago officinalis*)	seeds	indoors, outdoors	none
Brickellia (*Brickellia grandiflora*)	cuttings, layering	indoors	rooting hormone; needs extra heat
Burdock (*Arctium lappa*)	seeds	indoors, outdoors	cold stratification
Calendula (*Calendula officinalis*)	seeds	indoors, outdoors	none
California poppy (*Eschscholzia californica*)	seeds	indoors, outdoors	cold stratification
Callirhoe (*Callirhoe involucrata*)	seeds	indoors	cold stratification, peroxide soak, scarification
Cardinal flower (*Lobelia cardinalis*)	seeds	indoors	cold stratification
Catnip (*Nepeta cataria*)	seeds	indoors, outdoors	cold stratification
Cayenne (*Capsicum* species)	seeds	indoors	needs extra heat to germinate
Chamomile (*Matricaria recutita*, *Chamaemelum nobile*)	seeds	indoors, outdoors	none
Chaste berry (*Vitex agnus-castus*)	seeds	indoors	cold stratification, water soak, scarification
Chicory (*Cichorium intybus*)	seeds	indoors, outdoors	cold stratification
Cilantro, Coriander (*Coriandrum sativum*)	seeds	indoors, outdoors	none
Clary sage (*Salvia sclarea*)	seeds	indoors, outdoors	none
Comfrey (*Symphytum × uplandicum*)	root division	outdoors	none
Cow parsnip (*Heracleum sphondylium*)	seeds	indoors, outdoors	cold stratification
Coyote mint (*Monardella odoratissima*)	cuttings, layering, seeds	indoors	rooting hormone, cold stratification

HERB	PROPAGATION METHOD	WHERE TO START	SPECIAL TREATMENT
Dandelion (*Taraxacum officinale*)	seeds	indoors, outdoors	cold stratification
Dill (*Anethum graveolens*)	seeds	indoors, outdoors	none
Echinacea (*Echinacea* species)	seeds	indoors, outdoors	cold stratification
Elecampane (*Inula helenium*)	seeds	indoors, outdoors	cold stratification
Epazote (*Chenopodium ambrosioides*)	seeds	indoors, outdoors	none
Evening primrose (*Oenothera biennis*)	seeds	indoors, outdoors	cold stratification
Fennel (*Foeniculum vulgare*)	seeds	indoors, outdoors	cold stratification
Feverfew (*Tanacetum parthenium*)	seeds	indoors, outdoors	cold stratification
Gayfeather (*Liatris* species)	seeds	indoors, outdoors	cold stratification, peroxide soak
Ginger (*Zingiber officinale*)	root divisions	indoors	none
Goldenrod (*Solidago* species)	seeds	indoors	wet stratification
Goldenseal (*Hydrastis canadensis*)	root divisions, seeds	indoors, outdoors	wet stratification
Gotu kola (*Centella asiatica*)	cuttings, layering	indoors	none
Grindelia (*Grindelia* species)	seeds	indoors, outdoors	cold stratification
Hollyhock (*Alcea rosea*)	seeds	indoors, outdoors	cold stratification
Hops (*Humulus lupulus*)	root divisions, cuttings, layering	indoors, outdoors	rooting hormone
Horehound (*Marrubium vulgare*)	seeds	indoors, outdoors	cold stratification
Hyssop (*Hyssopus officinalis*)	seeds	indoors, outdoors	cold stratification
Inmortal (*Asclepias asperula*)	root divisions, seeds	indoors, outdoors	cold stratification, water soak, scarification
Lavender (*Lavandula angustifolia*)	cuttings, layering, seeds	indoors	rooting hormone, cold stratification
Lemon balm (*Melissa officinalis*)	cuttings, layering, seeds	indoors	rooting hormone, cold stratification
Lemongrass (*Cymbopogon citratus*)	root divisions, seeds	indoors	needs extra heat to germinate
Lemon thyme (*Thymus × citriodorus*)	cuttings, layering	indoors	rooting hormone
Lemon verbena (*Aloysia triphylla*)	cuttings, layering	indoors	rooting hormone; needs extra heat to germinate
Licorice (*Glycyrrhiza glabra*)	seeds	indoors, outdoors	cold stratification, water soak, scarification
Lovage (*Levisticum officinale*)	seeds	indoors	cold stratification
Marsh mallow (*Althaea officinalis*)	seeds	indoors, outdoors	cold stratification
Milk thistle (*Silybum marianum*)	seeds	outdoors	none

Propagation at a Glance — *Continued*

HERB	PROPAGATION METHOD	WHERE TO START	SPECIAL TREATMENT
Monarda (*Monarda* species)	root divisions, cuttings, layering, seeds	indoors, outdoors	rooting hormone, cold stratification
Mormon tea (*Ephedra* species)	seeds	indoors	cold stratification, peroxide soak; needs extra heat
Motherwort (*Leonurus cardiaca*)	seeds	indoors, outdoors	cold stratification
Mugwort (*Artemisia vulgaris*)	seeds	indoors	cold stratification
Mullein (*Verbascum thapsus*)	seeds	indoors, outdoors	cold stratification
Nettle (*Urtica dioica*)	root divisions, seeds	indoors, outdoors	cold stratification
Oat (*Avena sativa*)	seeds	outdoors	none
Oregano (*Origanum vulgare*)	cuttings, layering, seeds	indoors	rooting hormone, cold stratification
Oxeye daisy (*Leucanthemum vulgare*)	root divisions, seeds	indoors	cold stratification
Parsley (*Petroselinum crispum*)	seeds	indoors, outdoors	cold stratification, water soak
Passionflower (*Passiflora incarnata*)	cuttings, layering, seeds	indoors	rooting hormone, wet stratification; needs extra heat
Pennyroyal (*Mentha pulegium*)	root divisions, cuttings, layering, seeds	indoors	none
Penstemon (*Penstemon* species)	cuttings, layering, seeds	indoors, outdoors	rooting hormone, cold stratification, peroxide soak, other soak, scarification
Peppermint (*Mentha × piperita*)	root divisions, cuttings, layering	indoors, outdoors	none
Periwinkle (*Vinca* species)	root divisions, cuttings, layering	indoors, outdoors	none
Plantain (*Plantago* species)	seeds	indoors, outdoors	cold stratification
Pleurisy root (*Asclepias tuberosa*)	seeds	indoors, outdoors	cold stratification, water soak
Potentilla (*Potentilla* species)	root divisions, cuttings, layering	indoors, outdoors	rooting hormone
Prickly pear (*Opuntia* species)	cuttings, layering, seeds	indoors, outdoors	cold stratification, peroxide soak; needs extra heat
Red clover (*Trifolium pratense*)	seeds	outdoors	cold stratification
Rosemary (*Rosmarinus* species)	cuttings, layering	indoors	rooting hormone; needs extra heat to germinate
Rue (*Ruta graveolens*)	seeds	indoors	cold stratification

HERB	PROPAGATION METHOD	WHERE TO START	SPECIAL TREATMENT
Sage (*Salvia officinalis*)	seeds	indoors	cold stratification
St.-John's-wort (*Hypericum perforatum*)	root divisions, seeds	indoors, outdoors	cold stratification
Santolina (*Santolina* species)	cuttings, layering	indoors	rooting hormone
Sedum (*Sedum* species)	root divisions, cuttings, layering	indoors, outdoors	none
Self-heal (*Prunella vulgaris*)	seeds	indoors	cold stratification
Sheep sorrel (*Rumex acetosella*)	seeds	indoors, outdoors	none
Shepherd's purse (*Capsella bursa-pastoris*)	seeds	outdoors	cold stratification
Skullcap (*Scutellaria* species)	seeds	indoors	cold stratification
Spearmint (*Mentha spicata*)	root divisions, cuttings, layering	indoors, outdoors	none
Spilanthes (*Spilanthes acmella*)	seeds	indoors	none
Stevia (*Stevia rebaudiana*)	cuttings, layering, seeds	indoors	rooting hormone; needs extra heat to germinate
Summer savory (*Satureja hortensis*)	seeds	indoors	none
Sunflower (*Helianthus annuus*)	seeds	indoors, outdoors	none
Thyme (*Thymus vulgaris*)	root divisions, cuttings, ayering, seeds	indoors	rooting hormone, cold stratification
Valerian (*Valeriana officinalis*)	seeds	indoors	none
Vervain (*Verbena officinalis*)	seeds	indoors	cold stratification
Violet (*Viola* species)	seeds	indoors	cold stratification
White sage (*Salvia apiana*)	seeds	indoors	cold stratification; needs extra heat to germinate
Wild geranium (*Geranium* species)	cuttings, layering	indoors	rooting hormone
Wormwood (*Artemisia* species)	root divisions, cuttings, layering, seeds	indoor, outdoors	rooting hormone, cold stratification
Yarrow (*Achillea millefolium*)	root divisions, seeds	indoors, outdoors	cold stratification
Yerba de la negrita (*Sphaeralcea coccinea*)	seeds	indoors	cold stratification, water soak, scarification; needs extra heat
Yerba mansa (*Anemopsis californica*)	seeds	indoors	other soak; needs extra heat to germinate
Yucca (*Yucca* species)	seeds	indoors	cold stratification, wet stratification; needs extra heat to germinate

Five

garden maintenance

Garden maintenance is often viewed as an unpleasant chore or a necessary evil, but I think that approach should be rethought. I like to call this part of garden work caretaking. It's a great way to feel refreshed and alive, exercising your body and your spirit and giving your mind time to rest from daily work and hassles. It is continuation, as you shape the garden into a reflection of your relationship with the plants that are growing there. Even if you are growing on a small scale, you will find that so much of your time is required to do field maintenance that taking a positive approach gets the work done while keeping your attitude cheerful. ❦

Spring Cleanup

Around the end of January, I begin to feel garden fever coming on. I always envy those of you with year-round growing seasons as you garden through every month. But I also think it's a positive thing for the garden to rest through winter. Indeed, I'm usually badly in need of some quiet and rest myself after a busy growing season. My own restlessness probably has to do with all of those glorious seed catalogs that arrive in the mail. By February I've ordered all my seeds, and as these things go, I have usually ordered far more than is really reasonable.

There are also those nice days popping up by February when I stroll through my gardens and can hardly restrain myself from putting on my work gloves and beginning the task of garden cleanup. As hard as it is to be patient, I would encourage you to sip a cup of hot tea in your February garden and wait until a bit more time has passed before you begin snipping, digging, and planting. There are still several weeks of winter to come, and the perennial plants in the garden appreciate the extra protection last year's growth provides for them. The birds and other wildlife also need the protection, as well as the food from all those seed heads that are still standing on the plants from last fall.

As soon as I see the beginning signs of new green growth coming around the base of the perennial plants, I get more serious about cleaning up the garden space. Here in southern Colorado that is around the last week of March or the first week of April. Even waiting an additional week or two would be best, but I usually can't stand it any longer and out I go — snips and gloves in hand.

Removing Old Annuals

I begin cleaning up the garden by pulling out all of last year's annuals. I always leave them in the garden through the winter to give the garden more texture and interest. I am also a firm believer in being generous to wild animal and bird friends. They have worked hard all during the growing season to help with pest control, so it seems only right to leave them plenty of food sources and winter protection in exchange.

Leave annuals, like basil, in the ground until spring. These plants should be removed from the garden each year before planting begins.

Managing Aggressive Perennials

Once the annuals are pulled out and added to the compost pile, I begin working on managing the mints, artemisias, St.-John's-wort, and other perennial plants that have spread beyond their designated spaces during the past year. Plants that spread aggressively always seem to get a raised eyebrow from gardeners. Ask all the gardeners you know how they feel about mints; they will tell you that they love them or hate them and there is usually not much in between. But I really enjoy having these plants in the garden, and I like a lot of varieties of spreading plants.

There are many methods of keeping these plants under tight control; I'll share some of them with you.

Container growing. Aggressive spreaders like yarrow and sweetgrass can be grown in containers if you absolutely do not want them wandering about your garden of their own free will. Containers work fine for these types of plants, but be prepared to empty the containers every year or so and start fresh. Spreading plants quickly become root bound and use up all the available soil and nutrients, leaving you with no alternative except to take everything out of the container, put in fresh soil, and start with a new plant. But this is the preferred method of growing these types of plants if you want to be absolutely sure you can control them.

Garden barriers. Some gardeners find that placing a physical barrier in the ground prevents the plants from spreading too much. I've tried this method and it works reasonably well. Cut the bottom out of a 5-gallon bucket, sink the bucket into the garden space, and then plant your mint or wormwood in it. Leave about 2 inches (5 cm) of bucket rim above the ground to slow plant runners from rooting in the soil around the bucket. You can also install metal landscaping edging in the ground around the plants. The edging must be at least 18 inches (45 cm) deep, or it won't do any good; the roots will travel underneath the edging if it is too shallow.

Both of these methods will give you greater control over spreading plants, but if a plant uses runners as part of its propagation arsenal (mints, gotu kola), the runners will often travel right over the edge of the barrier and continue business as usual.

Growing in containers is a good way to control aggressive herbs and to extend the garden to small places around the yard.

Pulling. I believe that the best method for managing aggressive perennials is pulling. By using the pulling method I don't have unmanageable problems with any of these plants. They are happy and so am I.

Early in the spring, when a fresh snow has melted or a soaking rain has just passed, put on a pair of rubber gloves and head to the garden (I prefer rubber gloves because my hands stay drier and do not become so cold). Scrutinize the plant and determine what is a reasonable amount of garden space for it to claim. Then start at the outside edge of the patch and begin pulling from the roots. Work from the outside edge toward the center. When you have pulled out enough of the plant to keep it in its designated space, pull out yet another 4 to 6 inches (10 to 15 cm). This will leave that patch starting out smaller than you might like, but during the growing season the plant will easily fill in the area.

Water your herbs during the garden season, but don't lavish water on them; you will find that your mints, yarrows, and other aggressive growers will behave themselves reasonably well.

Cutting Back Perennials

Next I work at trimming off all of the dead growth on perennial plants. With few exceptions, you can trim off all of the previous year's growth down to 1 to 2 inches (2.5 to 5 cm) above the ground. Do not trim back any tender new growth that you see.

There are a couple of perennials I don't trim back until their new growth has fully come out in the later parts of spring. In Colorado, that means not before the last weekend in May. Lavender and

Mint plants can be highly invasive in the garden, sending out runners as seen here.

Leave echinacea to mature in the fall garden and cut it back in early spring.

vitex (chaste berry tree) will leaf out all along the existing stems; if you trim them back early, you will have trimmed off parts that were alive. I like these plants to become very large and bushy, so I am careful not to trim off any living growth.

Relocating Perennials

Early spring (as early as the ground thaws) is the best time to relocate any plants that you have decided aren't in the best location. After watching the plants and seeing how they thrive in a given area, you may find that some of them would grow better in a different location. Perhaps the plants received too much sun, or not enough. Maybe the existing location did not have the proper water conditions. It may be that you simply did not enjoy the way the plant looked in that spot. All of these are good reasons to relocate a plant or to remove it completely and give it to a friend who would enjoy it in her garden.

To relocate a plant, dig it up carefully — disturb the roots as little as possible. Then dig a hole slightly larger than the root clump in the new location. Gently replant the herb. Finish by giving it a generous watering. Water the plant daily or every other day, depending on the weather, for a week or so. This will help the plant establish itself in its new home.

 ### Dividing Perennials

Spring is a perfect time to divide perennials that have gotten too large. Perhaps you are hoping to cover a larger area of the garden with some existing plants. Be sure to keep divided plants well watered for a week or so to encourage them to root in well in their new location.

See chapter 4 for details on the best ways to divide plants.

Keeping Weeds Under Control

Spring moisture is followed by warmer temperatures. This means weeds begin to grow. When my daughter was very little she used to believe that the weed fairy came every night and danced over the garden, planting seeds to grow weeds. She very likely may have been right. Weeds never seem to have any difficulty growing, and pop up almost overnight.

Weeds can be a problem if you let them get out of control. The good news is that if you choose to stay on top of the situation, the task of weeding is not a big deal and actually becomes a part of the many therapeutic benefits the garden offers us.

The bad news is that there are no natural herbicides that meet certified organic standards and are safe to use in your garden. Do not be deceived by companies that promote their weed-killing products as Earth-friendly and with no residual effects. These claims are absolutely false; upon closer look you will discover that these products are indeed not harmless, as we are led to believe.

As we enter the new millennium, there is not a single safe chemical product to use to get rid of weeds. But there are a number of ways in which you can keep weeds under control and still rest assured that the plants you harvest have not been subjected to dangerous chemicals, and are safe to use for foods, medicines, body-care products, and other health-care items. By utilizing nonchemical weeding methods, you will also have the peace of mind that comes from knowing you are taking care of your piece of the Earth in a responsible and ethical fashion. What better reason can there be for doing the job by hand?

What Is a Weed?

When discussing weed management, I should first clarify what I consider a weed. In my opinion, a weed is simply a plant that is growing in an inappropriate place. This could be a plant like purslane, which always comes into my garden of its own accord and in great abundance each summer. California poppy could also be considered a weed if it has self-sown in places I prefer that it not grow.

Many important medicinal plants are considered weeds in the minds of some gardeners. Dandelion, burdock, and St.-John's-wort might be classified as weeds, but if they are planted and grown appropriately, they become very beautiful and useful garden additions. I once had a fence line planted with burdock. It was beautiful, large, and added privacy between my and the neighbor's yards. But my neighbor would have been very distressed to think it was burdock, which he considered a "weed." One night he came for dinner and I served a roast cooked with burdock, dandelion, and carrots. He was admittedly enlightened, and thought of burdock and dandelion in a much more positive manner from that night onward.

Pulling Weeds

There are no two ways about it: Organic growers must pull weeds. The trick is to be efficient at the pulling so that you don't have to pull any more often than necessary.

Pull on a day when the ground is moist. Weeding is a much easier and faster task when the ground is damp. Grasp the weed as close to the ground as possible. Tug firmly on the weed to pull up as much of the root as possible. Some weeds have a very complex root system and it is impossible to pull up 100 percent of the roots. Thistle and bindweed, for example, have root systems that are very difficult to pull up in one

weeding. My husband, Chris, manages our farm, and it is his expert opinion that bindweed is really a great sleeping giant under the Earth and pulling it amounts only to clipping the giant's fingernails, which will grow yet again.

Do not get discouraged by persistent weeds; if you stay in charge of them, at some point they will begin to weaken and will eventually give you less of a problem. I find that if I spend 10 to 15 minutes a day, even with my extensive gardens, I can keep weeds under control and never have a weed disaster to deal with. Unfortunately, I *have* let my weeds get the upper hand on occasion. When this happens I make a large pitcher of herbal iced tea for myself, and I have a day of weeding frenzy to get things back on track.

A "winged weeder" or "Cape Cod weeder" is useful for removing weeds around an established lavender.

Which Tools Should I Use?

There are several tools that I feel are invaluable to the task of weeding:

▸ **Old-fashioned dandelion digger.** These hand tools are great for getting out most of the root system, especially taproots. Dandelion diggers have an 8-inch (20 cm) rounded blade with a blunt-forked end. The tool is stuck into the ground near the base of the plant and pushed down to pry the plant loose.

▸ **Hori hori.** Sometimes called a Japanese weeder, this is a 6- to 8-inch (15 to 20 cm) narrowly tapered hand spade that has toothed edges. It easily digs, pries, and saws weeds out of existence.

▸ **Winged weeder.** I have a hand-size winged weeder and one on a long handle to use as I would a hoe. This tool has a triangular blade that looks like a kite at the end of a curved neck. The long sides of the triangle are sharp. You work this tool just on the soil surface, going into the soil ½ to 1 inch (1.25 to 2.5 cm). The shape allows you to get very close to the base of garden plants, and the sharp edges cut off weeds as you go. This is a fast-weeding tool that also cultivates the soil a bit to keep it nice and loose.

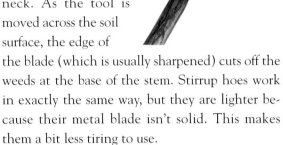

▸ **Traditional hoes and stirrup hoes** are also useful for weeding. A traditional hoe has a long handle and a flat metal blade on a curved neck. As the tool is moved across the soil surface, the edge of the blade (which is usually sharpened) cuts off the weeds at the base of the stem. Stirrup hoes work in exactly the same way, but they are lighter because their metal blade isn't solid. This makes them a bit less tiring to use.

▸ **Hands.** By far the best tools for weeding are your hands. Nothing is more efficient, because they can perform a great variety of functions.

Special Weeding Tips

It will make a big difference in your weed population if you can pull out weeds before they go to seed. Weeds have incredible survival instincts and they produce seed like crazy. Try to pull them out before the seed matures and you will be far ahead of the game.

Do not leave weeds that are in flower lying in the garden for later removal. Remember those survival instincts: Some weeds, like thistles, will still go to seed even after they have been pulled out! To prevent those unexpected weed seeds, remove the pulled weeds from the garden immediately.

Purslane is another great survivor, but in a different way. Also called portulaca, purslane is a succulent plant that will reroot where it is lying on the ground after being pulled out. Again, the key is to remove these weeds immediately from your garden area. ❧

Protect Your Plants with Mulch

Mulch serves many purposes in the garden. It can be used to keep weeds from becoming problematic. It retains moisture and warmth so that plants grow more vigorously and with greater water conservation. Mulch can also be used to create walking areas within the garden. The best part is that often mulch is either free or very inexpensive.

To apply a mulch, simply spread the mulching material in a layer a few inches deep around the plants or in the walkways of your garden. Most mulching materials will last at least one growing season and many of them will give you years of service.

Wood and Cloth Mulch

Many materials can be used to create a mulch. Recycled materials like cardboard and newspapers and even shredded trees can make a great mulch. Wood-based mulch is readily avail-

Fabulous Fish Emulsion

Fish emulsion is one the best organic fertilizers available. Made up of ground fish and fish excrement, this fertilizer gives much-needed nutrition to the plants without burning tender roots or leaves. It is a very good source of nitrogen that becomes available to the plants immediately after application. I apply extra fish emulsion only in the early summer as a way to give the plants an extra boost. Container plants benefit from a monthly dose of this fertilizer, while greenhouse plants need no more than a weekly application.

Purchase fish emulsion in either powdered or liquid form at garden centers and nurseries. Follow the instructions on the label for mixing and diluting. ❀

Straw is a great all-natural mulch. Spread it around the base of your plants to protect them and help keep weeds to a minimum.

able, slow to break down, and retains moisture quite well.

There are weed-barrier cloths that you can buy by the roll. These not only prevent weeds from growing through, but they also allow water to seep down to the plant roots. Because these barriers are made from black cloth, they absorb a lot of heat, helping to provide extra warmth for your plants. Although it is possible for the black cloth to absorb excess heat in summer, this is much more common with black plastic.

Rock Mulch

Gravel and pebbles make good mulch in some areas. They too collect solar heat, especially dark-colored rock. A word of caution about black lava rock: It often collects too much heat and makes a space so hot that plants cannot survive, so use this type of rock mulch with care.

Grass Mulch

Many people like to recycle their grass clippings into garden mulch. This works great for pathway mulching, but I don't really care for its use around the plants themselves, for a variety of reasons. If you apply a layer of clippings that is too thick, it will become compacted; water will not be able to pass through to the plants, but will just roll off the top. Thick, compacted grass clippings also get very hot as they begin to decompose. This can raise the soil temperature around the base of your plants too much and may even kill them.

Never use clippings from lawns that have been treated with synthetic chemical fertilizers, pesticides, and herbicides, as this will contaminate the soil in your garden.

Synthetic Mulches

Plastic and other synthetic materials, such as indoor/outdoor carpeting, tar paper, and so on, make terrible mulches and are extremely unfriendly to the earth. These materials prevent water and oxygen from penetrating the soil.

In addition, synthetic mulches often contain substances that are toxic to the plants and to animal/insect life that thrives in the garden, and these creatures help maintain the health of the garden. For example, using plastics or an old carpet will help to keep the weeds from growing, but it also kills earthworms, which are terrific healthy-soil builders.

The Importance of Deadheading and Pinching

This is the section on "plant torture." I am just kidding, of course, but many times that is what I get accused of when I talk to people about deadheading their flowers and pinching back foliage to encourage good growth patterns. For some reason, it's difficult to convince people to adopt these practices.

How to Deadhead

Deadheading is simply the removal of spent flower blooms by pinching or snipping them off. Many plants will bloom continuously through the growing season as long as the old blooms are removed. Otherwise, that plant begins to put its energy into seed formation, and the blooming process either slows greatly or stops altogether.

Deadhead lavender regularly to remove old growth and promote continuous blooming throughout the growing season.

For plants that bloom only during a certain period, you can often stretch that time out a bit by deadheading. In any case, deadheading helps to keep the garden looking spunky and vibrant, rather than frazzled and tired. It also helps to limit disease, insect, and pest problems. Note, however, that if you want to save seed from a specific plant, do not deadhead it. If you do, the plant will have no way to develop seed, which is formed from the spent flowers.

To deadhead, you need to pinch off the flowers right where they join the stems. If the plant has thorns or a tough stem that can't be easily pinched, use a small pair of scissors to snip off the

bloom. Deadheading will prompt new flower buds to form, and blooming will continue for a much longer period of time.

How to Pinch

It is also wise to keep bushy plants pinched. In this case, you'll pinch off the young tender tips of the foliage. This *might* include flowers, but it isn't necessary to wait for blooming before pinching your plants.

Neglecting to keep them pinched appropriately will result in leggy, weaker plants, which will become more likely to experience disease or insect problems. It also ultimately makes the

To keep plants from growing leggy, pinch back the tender tips of the foliage. It may or may not be necessary to pinch off flowers as well.

garden look untidy. Plants like hyssop and lemon verbena will grow sturdier and more abundantly if you pinch them back. I usually do this every 1½ to 2 weeks, and the parts that I pinch off are used to prepare medicines, teas, food, and other health-care items.

You can pinch the upper 2 to 4 inches (5 to 10 cm) off the plants with your fingernails or you can use a small pair of scissors. I keep a very small pair of embroidery scissors in my pocket at all times when I'm gardening. They are just the right size to do many types of garden maintenance and harvesting tasks (except for working on thick-stemmed plants or trees; you'll need larger snips for that). Because they are small and light, my hand does not get sore from using them a lot. Give it a try and see if they work well for you.

 ## garden profile

The Irrepressible Garden

Fifteen years ago I moved into a house in May (planting time!) and the only place to create a garden was in the back corner where a rock garden already existed. This was the literal definition of a rock garden, because it contained only rocks and *no* plants at all.

I thought it would be easy to remove the rock and use it to create garden pathways. So I began the process and was horrified to find a layer of indoor/outdoor carpeting beneath the rock. Below that was a layer of tar paper, and below *that* was a layer of black plastic! Needless to say, I was pretty convinced that absolutely nothing would grow in that depleted soil. My worst fears were confirmed by neighbors who told me the previous owners had sterilized the soil and put in all those layers at least 20 years prior. It never fails to amaze me to what lengths people will go for their own convenience, failing to consider how that might affect the well-being of the Earth and the creatures that live there.

Well, I borrowed a neighbor's rototiller and spent my $25 gardening budget buying plants instead of building the soil. Surprisingly, nearly everything grew well, and beginning that fall I started a strong soil health regeneration plan. I began incorporating organic matter into the garden, including mulched autumn leaves. Every spring I added compost and cottonseed meal as a top dressing. That garden got better each year and was beautiful eight years later when I moved out of that home.

Six

pest and disease control

Plant diseases and insect problems, fortunately, aren't usually as much of a concern for herb gardeners as they can be for vegetable and flower gardeners. My theory about this is that there is so much diversity among these plants that they become less attractive to insects. Diseases often are focused on more specific groups of plants; diversity would seem to be a great ally. Nonetheless, every grower must deal with pests and diseases at one time or another.

Invest in one or two good books on organic insect and disease management (see Recommended Reading). I also like being able to prepare my own natural pesticides or disease treatments at home, so I've included many recipes here for your use. 🕸

Identifying Plant Diseases

Plant diseases can be very intimidating. It's often frustrating to identify the problem and determine how to control it. There are numerous types of plant diseases; I will be offering only a basic look at some disease categories in this chapter. Use a good resource book or the local extension service for additional information.

Disease prevention will always be your best tool, and I encourage you to practice it seriously and become an expert at warding off the problems rather than fixing them. The following is a general overview of fungi, bacteria, and viruses, the three main disease categories.

Fungi

Fungal diseases are the most common plant diseases that confront growers. There are many different fungal diseases, but they all fall into two groups: soilborne and airborne. Both types are reproduced by spores, which can be spread by air, water, contaminated soil, tools and pots, even animals or humans.

Most fungi prefer warm temperatures to thrive, but a few actually favor cool temperatures. All are influenced by moisture. Keep plants well drained, provide good air circulation by weeding and ensuring that the herbs are appropriately spaced, and practice crop rotation for your best prevention.

Soilborne fungi live in the soil and will often attack roots and crowns of plants. This type of fungus should be destroyed by removing the plants and the affected surrounding soil, if possible. Plastic laid over the soil for several weeks during the hot part of the growing season will help "bake" the spores and kill the fungus remaining in the soil. The plants can be discarded into a *hot* compost pile, or disposed of with your rubbish.

This sage plant has been damaged by root rot, a common soilborne fungus. Plants infected with this disease should be removed from the garden.

You can also try sealing the diseased plants in a plastic bag and leaving it out in the sun, or even burning the plants — if your town permits.

There is a type of beneficial soil fungus that is called mycorrhizal fungus. This specific fungus affects plant roots, but in a beneficial way: It helps to improve the plant's nutrient absorption and it assists the plant in dealing with drought conditions.

Airborne fungi attack the aboveground parts of the plant. To help control this type of fungus, prune off the affected plant parts carefully and spray the plant with a fungicide treatment. If it is badly affected, you may need to sacrifice the entire plant to a hot compost pile or discard it with your rubbish.

Use superior oils, very light and purified horticultural oils that suffocate fungal spores and even soft-bodied insects without being absorbed by the plant, to help prevent spores of airborne fungi from reproducing and penetrating the plant parts. Baking soda sprays and garlic sprays are sometimes effective for airborne fungi if the problem has not become too widespread.

Bacteria

Fortunately, most bacteria found with plants are of a beneficial nature and actually help to increase soil fertility. Damaging bacteria that cause plant diseases are promoted by very warm and moist environments. That is why tropical and greenhouse gardeners have more difficulty with them than do gardeners in moderate climates.

Bacteria have cells that are large enough to see under a basic light microscope and are mainly rod-shaped. These cells are capable of reproducing themselves every 30 minutes under ideal circumstances, so bacterial diseases can spread rapidly. The spread of bacterial infection is facilitated by water, insects, contaminated tools, animals, and by touching other infected plants. The bacteria infect the plant through wounds (such as pruning cuts) or natural openings.

Once again, prevention is your best defense. Keep tools clean and control insect populations, especially those of pest insects. Water can be a

Powdery mildew, a common airborne fungal disease, has attacked this sage plant. The infection will stunt the growth of, but not kill, the plant.

▸ baking soda spray

This treatment can be helpful in controlling powdery mildew. Castile soap and the Ivory brand are good choices for the dishwashing liquid, but almost any kind will work providing it is unscented and doesn't contain degreasing agents. You'll get 2 or 3 treatments from this recipe.

- 1 teaspoon baking soda
- 1 quart warm water
- 1 teaspoon dishwashing liquid

Dissolve baking soda in warm water. Add dishwashing liquid. Mix well and pour into a spray bottle. To use, spray plant thoroughly, especially the undersides of the leaves. Space treatments 3 to 5 days apart.

▶ horsetail spray

This is a natural fungicide that is effective on powdery mildew, botrytis, leaf spot, and other fungal diseases. Success with this spray varies, so you'll need to experiment a bit to see which plants and diseases it will be most effective on in your area.

¼ cup dried horsetail
1 gallon water

In a large pot, combine the horsetail and water. Bring to a boil, reduce heat, and simmer gently for 20–30 minutes. Remove from heat; strain. To use, combine ¼ cup horsetail brew and 1½ cups water in a spray bottle. Spray on affected plants. Repeat application every 1–2 weeks if symptoms persist.

Common Fungal Diseases

• **Botrytis**, an airborne and waterborne disease, is a gray fuzzy mold on the stems and leaves that causes the plant stems to cave in on themselves.

• **Damping off** kills young seedlings by rotting them at the soil line. This fungus is transmitted through air and soil.

• **Downy mildew** is an airborne disease, and shows up as white to purple fuzz, turning black, on the undersides of the leaves and stems. It usually kills the plant quickly.

• **Powdery mildew** is a white to grayish fuzz on the leaves, shoots, and other aerial parts of the plant. It is airborne and causes poor growth and lower yields, but does not kill the plant.

• **Rust** is both airborne and waterborne, and shows up as orange and white spots on the leaves and stems. The plants become weak and yield is reduced, but they won't necessarily die. ❧

carrier of these diseases, so make sure that water draining out of infected plants will not be wicked up by a healthy plant in a nearby area. Just touching an infected plant and then handling a healthy one can spread the problem, so use care to wash your hands and gloves after working with bacteria-infected plants. Finally, practice crop rotation. This lessens the possibility that further plantings of the same crop will become infected.

Suspect bacterial infection if the plant wilts dramatically despite being in moist soil. Sometimes plant tissue will have mushy or slimy areas, especially within the stem wall. Some plants may even develop cankers or galls (oozing growths on leaves, stems, or roots). Once plants have become infected with a bacterial disease, you can try pruning off the affected parts of the plants (remember to disinfect your snips or scissors between each cut). This may help, but if it does not solve the problem, your only alternative is to destroy the plants by discarding them with your rubbish or burning them.

Viruses

Virus diseases are certainly the most difficult to identify, and there are no successful treatments once plants have become infected. Prevention is an absolute must, especially if you have an environment that is likely to foster viruses. Poor ventilation, standing water, extreme hot or cold temperatures, overabundance of pest populations, and contaminants such as chewing tobacco can all encourage the spread of viral infections.

Viral symptoms are tricky to discern because they can vary from plant to plant, depending on a plant's age and the growing conditions. It's even possible for plants to be carriers and show no symptoms. Occasionally, a plant can be harboring a virus but the only signs of it are slow growth and eventual death — hardly the foolproof symptom

A Simple Disinfectant

Clean and disinfect tools and pots by washing them in a solution of 9 parts water to 1 part bleach. Rinse with a solution of 1 part vinegar and 9 parts water to remove any bleach residue from the tools and pots. ❧

picture I appreciate having. It should be noted that viruses rarely live in seeds or plant pollens, so the virus won't be spread by bees, bats, or other pollinators. Leaf-chewing and sap-sucking insects, however, can help spread viral diseases.

Viruses can be spread in a number of ways, but water and wind are the primary culprits. Insects that bite into plant tissues are another common way that viruses spread. As an insect bites an infected plant, it picks up the virus. When the insect bites into the next plant, it injects the virus (often in a concentrated form) into it. Common virus-spreading insects include aphids, leafhoppers, mites, nematodes, and whiteflies.

Fungus spores are great ways for viruses to hitch a ride to an unsuspecting plant. Propagating plants by cuttings or grafting with contaminated tools can cause the infection to spread, and tobacco users often carry the tobacco mosaic virus on their hands (from handling cigarettes, pipe tobacco, or chewing tobacco), unintentionally contaminating soil, seeds, or plants as they work.

I cannot stress enough how important the proverbial ounce of prevention is when dealing with plant diseases and insect problems. Keep those hands washed really well, and tools too. Ruthlessly eradicate all infected plants by pulling them out of the greenhouse, garden, or field. *Do not* compost them! Viruses can live for years in a dormant state in the soil or decaying plant material. Weeds often are prime candi-

Leaf spot is the viral culprit affecting this otherwise healthy-looking catnip plant. The herb must be destroyed to prevent spreading.

Common Viruses and Their Symptoms

• **Mosaic.** The leaves and fruits will show patches of mottling light green, yellow, and sometimes white. Flowers often become disfigured with unusual color variations.

• **Ring spot.** Leaves may show rounded spots that are light yellow.

• **Leaf curl.** Leaves will begin to grow in a distorted fashion and curl for no apparent reason. ❧

dates for viruses, so keep up on your weeding tasks to decrease the possibility that they will become infected with a virus and spread it to your plants. Last, manage insect populations carefully to lessen the possibility that they will spread a virus infection.

Insect Management

The topic of insect management is very broad. The first and foremost step is proper identification of any insects you see on your plants. Some of them will likely be problematic and require a control of some sort, but you will also learn that many of the insects are beneficial and great helpers in caring for your garden. It's wise to learn the difference and take advantage of those insect helpers.

As with plant diseases, I suggest investing in one or two good reference books (see Recommended Reading) to make the tasks of identification and treatment much simpler.

The list of pest insects seems very long, so for the sake of space and what is most relevant to medicinal herbs, I have included only the most common problem bugs. There are beneficial insects that can help you manage some pest situations. Natural preparations are a possibility as well. I also make suggestions for both control methods under each pest name. For more in-depth information about treating difficult pests, please refer to a good resource book. The art of plant pest control is indeed a whole book's topic.

Aphids

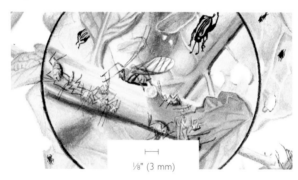

⅛" (3 mm)

What they look like: There are many different types of aphids — black, red, white, green, even golden in color — and many different ways to deal with them. This insect is oval or tear-shaped with two "tubes" protruding from the back end (this is how they give birth to live young). Aphids have several tiny legs and a pair of antennae. Some have wings.

What they do: Aphids suck the juice out of the stems, leaves, and flowers of plants. They excrete a sticky substance that may foster mold growth, and can even spread disease as they travel from plant to plant. Plants become deformed as the aphids feed on them.

How to treat them: I find it best to have a few different tricks in my bag when dealing with aphids, as they tend to develop resistance to control methods. Many beneficial insects help control aphids. These include aphid midges, braconid wasps, damsel bugs, parasitic wasps, beneficial nematodes, ladybugs, and lacewings. Check with your local garden center for more information, or contact one of the companies listed in Resources.

Soap sprays and quassia sprays coat the aphids' bodies, effectively suffocating them. Quassia sprays seem to have a less negative impact on beneficial insects than soap sprays do. Neem tree extract is yet another approach. We use a brand called Azitin XL, which qualifies for organic certification regulations (not every brand of natural insecticide meets organic standards, as they often contain inert ingredients that are not Earth-friendly). A last recommendation for aphids is a garlic oil spray. You can also plant garlic near the plants that seem especially susceptible to aphids. This preventive measure can offer the plants additional protection.

Beetles

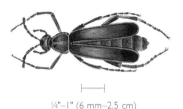

1/4"–1" (6 mm–2.5 cm)

What they look like: As with aphids, there are many types of pest beetles. These insects have hard-shelled, oval-shaped bodies between 1/4 and 1 inch (6 mm and 2.5 cm) long. Color also varies, but most beetles are some shade of black, blue, or brown. They have tiny heads in comparison to their bodies. Beetles that tend to create problems with herbs include blister beetles, flea beetles, and Japanese beetles.

What they do: Beetles are chewing insects that eat stems, leaves, and flowers. They prefer tender new growth, but will also eat older growth.

How to treat them: Beneficial insects that offer some protection from various types of beetles are parasitic wasps and beneficial nematodes. Natural pesticide preparations for beetles include soap sprays, bug juice (see recipe, page 99) made with beetles, and neem tree extract.

Cabbage Loopers

1" (2.5 cm)

What they look like: This pest looks like a green, 1-inch-long (2.5 cm) caterpillar. Cabbage loopers have white lines on their bodies and become a distinctive loop shape as they move.

What they do: A very destructive pest, cabbage loopers eat primarily leaves but will often attack the whole plant, chewing large holes as they go.

How to treat them: If you are experiencing a large population of cabbage loopers, control them with beneficial parasitic wasps. Smaller populations can be nicely managed with a garlic oil spray.

Corn Earworms, Tomato Fruitworms

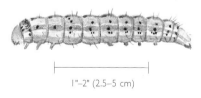

1"–2" (2.5–5 cm)

What they look like: This pest goes by different names, but it is the same distressing creature. These 1- to 2-inch-long (2.5 to 5 cm), caterpillar-like worms are green to brown in color with dark stripes and black legs.

What they do: Corn earworms/tomato fruitworms create a lot of damage to fruiting plants like passionflower. The larvae burrow into fruits and flower buds, eating as they go. They also chew on leaves.

How to treat them: Lacewings are helpful in controlling corn earworms and tomato fruitworms. Parasitic wasps are also quite good, and predatory insects like assassin bugs and spined soldier bugs will all do their part to eradicate these pests from your garden.

Cutworms

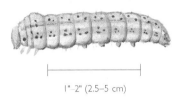

I"-2" (2.5–5 cm)

What they look like: These 1- to 2-inch (2.5 to 5 cm) caterpillars are gray or brown in color. They have many legs and often look slimy.

What they do: A nocturnal insect, the cutworm does its damage at night. It will chew through an entire plant stem just above the soil surface and then eat off all of the tender new growth of the cut plant.

How to treat them: Try beneficial nematodes for cutworms. Once nematodes have been introduced into the garden, you should see positive results throughout the growing season — without repeat applications.

Earwigs

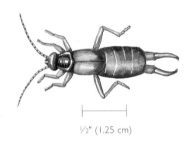

½" (1.25 cm)

What they look like: Long, narrow, semi-hard-shelled bodies characterize the hungry earwig. This insect is brown, with a set of pincers on its rear end.

What they do: Earwigs eat nearly everything in their path. All types of plants and plant parts satisfy their diet.

How to treat them: I have just one method to control earwigs and it works incredibly well. Roll up damp newspaper into moderately tight logs and lay them around the base of the plants you are having trouble protecting. Do this in the early morning and then collect the logs in the early evening. Throw the paper logs into the trash, for they will be loaded with earwigs that have crawled into them throughout the hot part of the day. Repeat as necessary.

Fungus Gnats and Shore Flies

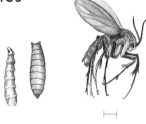

⅛" (3.2 mm)

What they look like: These tiny, flying, gnat-like creatures are often a problem for indoor gardeners. They are black, and some have dots on their wings. They actually resemble very small houseflies.

What they do: Fungus gnats and shore flies signal that sanitation and/or watering practices need to be improved. They lay their eggs in the soil and the larvae find a perfect home under fallen leaves and other decaying plant debris.

How to treat them: Make sure that all fallen or yellowing leaves are removed. Next, make sure you are not overwatering or leaving water to stand in pot trays.

If you do have a problem, treat the plants with neem tree extract, garlic spray, or beneficial nematodes. These nematodes are watered into the soil, where they will eat the larvae of many pest insects.

Grasshoppers and Crickets

length varies

length varies

What they look like: Grasshoppers can grow very large — some are several inches long. They all have long back legs and big eyes. Colors range from greens and yellows to browns and blacks. Some even have wings and can fly.

Crickets are black with long legs and antennae. These fast-moving insects make a distinguishing hopping movement. They are generally 1 to 2 inches (2.5 to 5 cm) in length.

What they do: Grasshoppers and crickets eat a wide variety of plants, and are especially fond of alfalfa, comfrey, and lemon balm. They are chewing insects that feed on leaves, buds, and flowers.

How to treat them: I find grasshoppers and crickets difficult to control. They are ferocious eaters and aren't easily affected by natural control methods. Chris and I have found that beneficial nematodes help in initially controlling the grasshopper population. Birds are also a fantastic ally because they adore a grasshopper meal and can eat a lot of those little critters. If you keep livestock, young turkeys are the best method of making a serious dent in your grasshopper and cricket populations.

Nolo Bait, an insect-specific bacterium injected into bran, is a long-term commitment to keeping the grasshoppers and crickets under control. It takes awhile to have an effect, but if you stick with it, you will not only help your current problem but you will also be making an impact on next year's "crop" by influencing the reproductive cycle of the pests. Nolo Bait works by making grasshoppers and crickets lethargic, thus leaving them prey to others of their kind. It also prevents them from reproducing.

Neem tree extract is very helpful on these pests in two ways. First, the pests don't like the taste of it, so they are deterred from eating your plants. Second, if they do indulge in a meal, the neem begins making them lethargic and they soon stop eating. As grasshoppers become sick, other grasshoppers will cannibalize them and in turn become infected. Neem tree extract has definitely saved some of our young, early-spring crops when the grasshoppers were feasting faster than the plants could get established. Without this control, we would have lost some important crops.

Leafhoppers

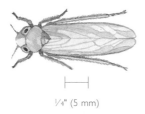

¼" (5 mm)

What they look like: Another hopping and flying creature, a leafhopper has a soft body and wings. The insects are usually green, brown, or yellowish, and have very large eyes.

What they do: This insect sucks the juices from the stems and leaves of plants, spreading disease as it travels. Its saliva stunts and deforms plants.

How to treat them: Predatory bugs and parasitic wasps may be introduced to control leafhoppers. Leafhoppers are great carriers of plant diseases, so it's always best to check them before they become a large problem.

Soap sprays and neem tree extract sprays will both be helpful in controlling leafhoppers before they get out of hand.

Leaf Miners

⅛" (3.2 mm)

What they look like: You would need a magnifying lens to see these tiny black-and-yellow flying bugs.

What they do: Leaf miners can cause a lot of damage to the foliage of your plants as they tunnel through the leaves. The damage appears as white winding marks on the leaves that resemble a worm pattern.

How to treat them: Control leaf miners by using parasitic wasps. Once you have introduced parasitic wasps into your garden or greenhouse space, they should always be there, working hard to control pest insects.

Neem tree extract is also beneficial in managing leaf miners. We find that spraying the neem tree extract in the early evening seems to give us the best results.

Scale

⅛" (3.2 mm)

What they look like: Scale are hard or soft round bumps that cluster on stems. They have no legs, wings, or other visible body parts. Their color can be white, yellow, red, brown, or black.

What they do: This pest sucks the juice from stems, fruit, and leaves. Scale may also inject toxins into the plant via their saliva. Rosemary is susceptible to scale.

How to treat them: There are many different types of scale and some can be difficult to check. Use parasitic wasps, soldier beetles, and ladybugs to help control this pest. Remember that scale spreads easily, so act quickly, as soon as you notice you have a problem.

Dormant oil and superior oil are also helpful with scale. Use these solutions carefully and according to label directions. They are best applied during times of the day when the sun is not at its most intense, to lessen the possibility of burning your plants.

Slugs and Snails

length varies   length varies

What they look like: Soft-bodied and slimy, slugs and snails are usually shades of gray, brown, or black. They have two antennae on their head, and some carry a shell on their back.

What they do: Slugs are very hungry creatures and if left unchecked, they will quickly eat massive quantities of your plants. Slugs and snails both are especially fond of basil.

How to treat them: You can control slugs and snails with a slug bait sold through organic growing supply sources (see Resources). It's toxic to them and a bit gory, but works really well.

You can also use a homemade remedy. Raw potato slices should work well; put them out in the evening and collect them very early the next morning. Slugs will cluster on the potato for a feast and you will be able to eliminate a good number of them by discarding the slices.

Try lightly sprinkling wood ashes around the area where slugs are a problem. As slugs pass through the ashes, they are literally dried up.

Spider Mites

less than 1/50" (.5 mm)

What they look like: Another very tiny insect that requires a magnifying glass to see, a spider mite looks like a miniature spider. They are red, green, or yellow.

What they do: Spider mites suck the juice from the undersides of leaves, thus weakening the plants. This pest causes yellow speckling of the leaves as it covers the plant with its tiny webs. The plant's leaves will eventually turn yellow and fall off.

How to treat them: I find spider mites one of the more difficult pests to deal with, partly because they are so difficult to see and also because they are so persistent. A goldenseal grower once shared the following control method with me (goldenseal is especially susceptible to spider mite problems). When you see evidence of spider mites, sprinkle a light dusting of white sugar (yes, there is something good to do with white sugar after all!) on the soil and on the plants themselves. Ants will move in and eat the sugar *and* the spider mites. Once the sugar and mites are gone, the ants usually disappear again and all is well.

You can also use predatory mites to control the spider mites. The difference between these two mites is that the beneficial mites don't feed on plants, as the spider mites do.

Neem tree extract, soap sprays, and dormant oil sprays can all help you get rid of your spider mite problem. Spray all the plant surfaces very well with these solutions. Sprays aren't as effective as beneficial insects, however, because spider mites are tiny and they hide in the foliage of the plants easily.

Stinkbugs

1/2" (1.25 cm)

What they look like: This distinctive insect has a hard shell in the shape of a shield. It can be shades of green, brown, or black.

What they do: Stinkbugs also suck the sap from the plant, although they prefer the herb's aerial parts. Their feeding leaves behind scarring. Too much stinkbug damage will weaken the plant and make it susceptible to other pests and diseases.

How to treat them: One of the best ways to prevent stinkbugs from becoming a big problem is by weeding. Common weeds seem to attract these pests, so controlling weeds becomes your first line of defense. Parasitic wasps are also very good allies in managing stinkbug populations.

Thrips

less than 1/25" (1 mm)

What they look like: Yellow, brown, or black in color, thrips are minute, bullet-shaped insects that are best seen with a magnifying lens.

What they do: Thrips suck juices from plant leaves and flowers. Their feeding leaves behind tiny white speckles that end up creating an ugly, unhealthy appearance on the plant.

Thrips can spread viruses as they travel from plant to plant.

How to treat them: Controlling thrips is every gardener's and greenhouse grower's difficulty. They are so tiny and they get down into the crevices of the plants, making them nearly impossible to control with natural pesticides. Beneficial insects will be your best approach. Use pirate bugs, lacewings, ladybugs, and predatory mites. You can also make a dent in the thrips population by using sticky monitoring cards as insect traps. Thousands of thrips can be trapped using one sticky card alone.

If you do decide to work with natural pesticides, try dormant oil sprays, neem tree extract, or soap sprays. Garlic oil spray is also helpful.

Whiteflies

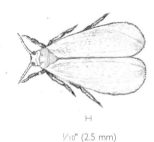

H

1/10" (2.5 mm)

What they look like: Whiteflies are very small, triangular insects with wings. As their name suggests, they are totally white.

What they do: Plants are weakened by whiteflies, which suck the juices out of the leaves and stems. In turn, the plant becomes more susceptible to other pests and diseases. After biting into an infected plant, a whitefly can then spread viruses to healthy plants.

How to treat them: If you see whiteflies, address the situation immediately. The success in controlling whiteflies is to do something about the problem before it gets too far out of hand. Use either beneficial insects or natural pesticides, but do it immediately.

A small parasitic wasp, *Encarsia formosa*, is especially good at handling whiteflies. This wasp is so small you can barely see it without a magnifying glass, and it will not cause any harm to humans. Predatory beetles work well too. Sticky monitoring cards can act as whitefly traps, catching thousands of the pests on a single card.

Soap or garlic sprays can work pretty well for whiteflies. If the problem is still small enough, either of these will often do the trick. Neem tree extract is also a possibility. If you have a severe whitefly infestation, however, the best thing to do is to get rid of the host plant, especially if the problem is indoors. Once these creatures get a foothold, they are extremely difficult to control with organic measures.

All-Natural Pest Treatments

There are numerous methods for controlling insect pests in the garden, field, or greenhouse. Prevention will always be your best approach, but if that fails, consider beneficial insects or non-chemical pest controls. Do your best to address problems when they begin; controlling pests at this point will be much easier, less expensive, and will require less time and energy.

Monitor your garden or greenhouse regularly to stay in touch with pest populations. If you're careful, you should be able to keep small problems from getting out of hand. It's a simple step toward keeping the garden healthy.

Monitoring Sticky Cards

You can purchase monitoring cards, sometimes called yellow sticky cards, to use as both a tracking tool and a trapping control method for insect pests. The cards are a bright, sunny yellow and are covered with a sticky substance that attacks and traps insects. The insects can be counted once a week and appropriate control methods determined based on which pests you are seeing a problem with. Because cards actually trap insects, this in and of itself becomes a control method.

When you use sticky cards, there are a few things to keep in mind. First, always place your cards in the foliage area of the plants (don't place them high above the plants, because not all pests are flying insects). Second, put them in the same place in the garden from one week to the next. This will help you have an accurate picture of how well you are maintaining insect populations. Third, use a magnifying glass when looking at the cards, so that you can properly identify the insects. Keep a log of how many of each insect you see on the cards from week to week: This gives

Hang sticky cards at the level of the foliage for most efficient monitoring of pest populations.

you a tracking record and establishes whether any patterns exist.

Sticky cards can be purchased at garden centers or you can make your own. To prepare your own sticky cards, buy a package of bright yellow (color is important, as insects are attracted to this sunny hue) plastic picnic plates. Make a mixture of equal parts vegetable oil and honey. Smear a thin layer over the plates, front and back. Hang from a string, or clip to a wooden stake with a clothespin in the garden, to catch pests. Once a week, these plates can be looked at and insects counted. Then wash the plates, allow them to dry, and reapply the sticky goo, and you're set to begin a new week of bug catching.

Beneficial Insects

Working with beneficial insects can be the most effective way to control pest insects if you educate yourself as to which beneficial insects stalk which pest insects. When you get a balance of beneficials in your space, the pests nearly disappear. There are a number of excellent beneficial insectary houses that raise and sell these creatures. They really know what they are doing with these bugs! Chris and I have found them wonderfully helpful in identifying what pest problems we have in the greenhouse, cold frames, and gardens and determining which beneficial insects we need to introduce.

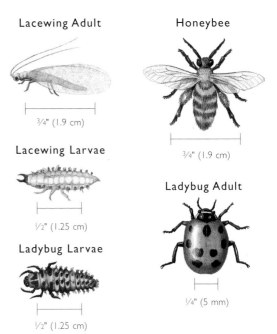

Lacewing Adult
¾" (1.9 cm)

Lacewing Larvae
½" (1.25 cm)

Ladybug Larvae
½" (1.25 cm)

Honeybee
¾" (1.9 cm)

Ladybug Adult
¼" (5 mm)

A Guide to Beneficial Insects

BENEFICIAL INSECT	PEST INSECT	OTHER BENEFICIAL EFFECTS
Aphid midges	aphids	
Assassin bugs	flies, caterpillars	
Braconid wasps	elm beetles, cabbageworms, hornworms, aphids, houseflies, horseflies	
Bumblebees, honeybees		great pollinators
Centipedes, millipedes	soil-dwelling mites, soil-dwelling larvae	help decompose dead plant material into compost
Damsel bugs	aphids, leafhoppers, thrips, small caterpillars	
Lacewings	aphids, corn earworms, tomato fruitworms	great general predator
Ladybugs	aphids, soft-bodied pests, spider mites, soft scale, mealybugs	
Parasitic wasps	aphids, whiteflies	
Predatory mites	spider mites, thrips	
Beneficial nematodes	root weevils, crown and stem borers, fungus gnats, shore flies	great compost workers
Praying mantis	all the insects it can catch, both pests and beneficials	
Soldier beetles	grasshopper eggs, caterpillars, beetle larvae	
Spiders (all types)	many different insects	
Spined soldier bugs	caterpillars, grubs, Mexican bean beetle larvae	

I much prefer to control bug problems this way rather than spraying pesticides — even approved certified organic pesticides. Spraying tampers with the ideal environmental balance, even when done properly, using safe preparations. I'll concur that it is more desirable to spray than to have an insect problem, but I feel it's always better to let nature handle her own difficulties, with my support, whenever possible. Besides, spraying takes a lot of time that I would rather spend doing something else in the garden.

Natural and Homemade Organic Pest-Control Preparations

There are several all-natural pest-control preparations on the market, and you can certainly make some of your own. Remember that these are still pesticides, even though they aren't made from synthetic chemicals; they can be very toxic and should be used and stored appropriately.

Wear the proper protective clothing (long sleeves and pants), waterproof boots and gloves, and proper eye protection when applying any type of pesticide. If you are using a sprayer, learn ahead of time how it works so that you can apply these preparations safely and effectively. Take care not to apply them in places that are close to children's or pets' play spaces or water areas, such as ponds and streams.

Read label instructions carefully before you begin to apply the substance, and never store any of these or other preparations where children or pets can reach them, in open containers, or in containers that are not

Spray bottle for bug juice.

fully labeled. If you make the preparation yourself, you *must* label it completely with the preparation name and every single ingredient used. Also clearly mark containers with cautionary information if appropriate. Wait at least 24 hours before using a sprayed plant for medicinal purposes.

Neem Tree Extract

Neem tree extract works by killing the insects, acting as a growth regulator in some insects, and simply repelling insects from the plants (they seem to dislike the taste). We use the brand Azitin XL, as it qualifies for certified

▶ bug juice

Many pests, especially beetles, will not feed on plants if they smell the dead of their own species. This preparation works especially well for Colorado potato beetles, Mexican bean beetles, and cabbage loopers. If there are virus-infected plants in the area, this method should not be used; there is the potential of spreading viruses to healthy plants from the bodies of insects that might have fed on the affected plants.

1 cup pest bugs
3–4 cups water

1. *Grind the pest bugs in an old blender. Please don't use the kitchen blender — go to a secondhand shop and purchase a blender that can be used just for preparing garden remedies.*
2. *Add enough water to get the ground insects to the consistency of milk. Strain the bug juice before putting it in the sprayer.*
3. *To use, spray the plants, covering all the surfaces. This should help repel similar pests from those plants for 3–4 weeks. You can reapply at this time if necessary.*

▸ garlic oil

Nearly all pests hate garlic, so this is an excellent control method. It's especially effective against aphids, whiteflies, spider mites, leafhoppers, squash bugs, and young grasshoppers. It's important to use mineral oil in this recipe, as this will not be absorbed by the plant.

Note: Some plants are sensitive or allergic to this spray, so do a test patch first. Spray one or two plants with the garlic oil. If the leaves turn yellow or brown within 24 hours, do not use the spray on that particular type of plant. If no burning occurs, go ahead and use the spray on the remaining plants. This spray is best used around dusk; the oil content can provoke a "sunburn" reaction during the hot periods of the day.

6–8 cloves garlic, peeled and finely chopped

1 tablespoon mineral oil

1 pint water

1 teaspoon dishwashing liquid

1. *Place the garlic in a clean glass jar and pour the mineral oil over it. Cap the jar tightly and store at room temperature for 24 hours.*
2. *Line a strainer with a piece of cloth and then pour the oil mixture through it. Gather up the cloth and squeeze the remaining oil from the garlic. Discard the pieces of garlic and reserve the garlic-infused oil.*
3. *Combine the water and dishwashing liquid.*
4. *To use, mix 1–2 tablespoons of the infused oil into a pint of water in a spray bottle. Spray plant thoroughly.*

▸ ant bait

This bait will attract ants of all kinds. Use it with caution around small children or animals, and do not inhale the dust when mixing. Mark your Ant Bait label with a skull and crossbones; it is poisonous.

3 teaspoons boric acid

1 cup sugar

3 cups water

Cotton balls

1. *Combine boric acid, sugar, and water and blend well.*
2. *Fill each of several glass jars halfway with cotton balls. Pour 1 cup of the mixture into the jars and cover tightly. Punch small holes in the lids and label the jars clearly.*
3. *Lay out the jars in the garden in places where ants are a problem. The ants will carry the mixture back to the anthill and it will destroy the colony. Replace the bait every 1 to 2 weeks, as needed, until ants are no longer a problem.*

organic standards, and have found it to be very effective against beetles of many types, whiteflies, aphids, spider mites, thrips, leaf miners, mealybugs, and grasshoppers.

Use neem tree extract according to the manufacturer's directions. Generally, you spray it onto plants that are being eaten or damaged by the pests. It acts in some capacity as a repellent, but when bugs ingest it, it will poison young, weak, or sick insects. If healthy insects ingest the extract, it disrupts their reproductive system, making them unable reproduce.

When plants have neem applied as a soil drench (a heavy soaking of the soil with the preparation), it has a systemic effect on the plants: The plant draws up the neem into its leaves and

Butterflies, like the one pictured here on an echinacea plant, are colorful and welcome visitors to any garden. Keep in mind that commercial pest preparations can also affect beneficial insects, so choose your preparations wisely.

stems, thus affecting the pest when it eats the plant. Neem may be toxic to some beneficial insects as well, but it does not seem to bother honeybees or spiders very much. Neem is not toxic to people or animals, and it is biodegradable.

Nolo Bait

This is a biological suppression bait for use on grasshoppers, locusts, and some species of crickets. Unlike chemical-based insecticides, Nolo Bait contains a naturally occurring spore called *Nosema locustae* that infects these insects. It is not toxic to humans, livestock, wild animals, birds, fish, or life-forms other than grasshoppers and closely related insects.

The spore is injected into wheat bran, which grasshoppers like to eat. Most pest species of grasshoppers, particularly younger instars, will eat the bran; the resulting infection helps to con-trol grasshopper populations without adverse effects on the environment. Depending upon age and species, a grasshopper that eats even one flake of Nolo Bait may become infected. When infected and sick, the insect eats less and less. Other grasshoppers often cannibalize the sick ones and then become infected, spreading the disease among the healthy population. In addition, infected females can pass the disease through their eggs, helping to control future generations of offspring.

Nolo Bait does not work rapidly, however. According to the Fremont County CSU Extension Service, the age and amounts of the insects influence how quickly results are seen. Follow-up applications each year that grasshopper populations are on the rise will help manage the problem. Grasshoppers migrate over great distances; it is best to spread Nolo Bait over your area

▸ quassia tea spray

Quassia (*Quassia amara*) is a tree that grows in Latin America. The wood from it is used to prepare a spray. Aphids, beetles, flies, and caterpillars can all be controlled with this spray.

> ¼ cup chopped quassia wood
> (available at natural products stores)
> 1 quart water

1. *In a saucepan, combine the quassia wood and the water. Bring to a boil, reduce heat, and simmer gently for 20–30 minutes. Strain and cool; pour into a spray bottle.*
2. *To use, spray the quassia tea onto the plant; be sure to coat all the plant's surfaces. The treatment can be repeated one or two times weekly until pests are controlled.*

▸ soap spray

This is a broad-spectrum control method used to treat spider mites, aphids, earwigs, whiteflies, mealybugs, thrips, and scale. It may also be helpful against ticks, beetles, and caterpillars. The spray works by both repelling insects and suffocating any that are already on the plants. This is just as effective as commercial insecticidal soap products that are available from your garden store. If you choose to purchase a soap spray, follow the label directions to prepare and apply.

> 1–2 teaspoons dishwashing liquid
> 1 quart water

1. *Combine dishwashing liquid and water in a spray bottle; shake to mix.*
2. *To use, spray over the entire plant, coating all the surfaces well. Repeat every 5–7 days, as necessary, until pests are controlled.*

frequently during the growing season. Ask the neighbors if they would like to participate; this will also increase your success.

Slug and Snail Bait

Although I have heard about many different methods to control slugs and snails, the one that seems to work really well for us is potatoes. Just before dark, place large slices of raw potatoes on the ground where slugs are a problem. Slugs love these potato feasts and will munch happily all night long.

The worst part of this method is that you must get up very early the next morning, just as there are beginning traces of light. Gather the potato slices into a box or can. They should be loaded with slugs (you may want to wear a pair of gloves if touching slimy slugs bothers you). Discard the "slug hotels" in the trash. Do this every day until you are no longer noticing slug-related damage. If you don't check the potatoes

 ## Managing Pests

Preparation	Pest Insect
Ant bait	ants
Bug juice	beetles, cabbage loopers
Garlic oil	aphids, whiteflies, spider mites, leafhoppers, squash bugs, young grasshoppers
Neem extract	whiteflies, aphids, spider mites, thrips, leaf miners, mealybugs, grasshoppers
Nolo Bait	grasshoppers, locusts, crickets
Quassia tea	aphids, beetles, flies, caterpillars
Slug bait	slugs, snails
Soap sprays	spider mites, earwigs, whiteflies, mealybugs, thrips, soft scale, ticks, beetles, caterpillars

early enough in the morning, the slugs will have retreated back into the soil — and your plant roots — for the day. If you prefer not to kill the slugs, make sure you transport them at least 200 feet (30 m) away from your gardens; slugs can travel quite a distance.

You can also purchase pelletized slug bait and sprinkle it on the greenhouse floor or on the soil in the garden wherever slugs and snails have become a problem (follow the directions on the package). This slug bait works really well, and is just the ticket for people who don't wish to get up at the crack of dawn to gather and discard slug-coated potato slices.

Let Mother Nature and Friends Help You

As a closing thought to this subject, I would like to remind you that there are lots of other valuable allies you may have on hand to control pest problems in your garden. For example, cats help control rodents. Birds are great friends to have in the garden; they eat a variety of insects and are especially fond of caterpillars. Bats should be welcomed too. They control evening flying insects quite nicely. Salamanders have an appetite for insects, while nonpoisonous snakes and lizards are wonderful for eating both insects and rodents. As a bonus, nonpoisonous snakes often keep poisonous snakes away from your garden or field areas. Last, don't forget about toads and frogs. These amphibians have hearty appetites, and they provide an evening concert free of charge.

All of these creatures are assets that I hope you will welcome into your garden space. They provide valuable services to you in your efforts to manage pests, and many of them, like salamanders and frogs, are experiencing environmental hardships of their own. It's only right that we

Frogs and toads make superb all-natural insect controls that are never harmful to plants. These amphibians will dispense with a wide variety of insect pests.

should offer them our support in making a garden home available to them.

Don't forget all the incredible resources you have at your disposal when looking for information or help in managing pest and disease problems. Besides the great books that are available, state extension services are immensely helpful in identifying garden troubles. Local garden centers, nurseries, and botanical gardens usually have staff members who can assist you. Be sure to network with other gardeners, farmers, and landscapers, to benefit from their experience. We can all help one another on occasion when it comes to pest and disease management.

Seven

harvesting from your garden

Harvest is a time of abundance and prosperity. There are so many fantastic plants to utilize from the garden. Picking and preparing medicines and foods, personal-care preparations, even herbal bouquets will bring beauty, good health, and happiness into your home or workspace. Even most of the weeds I pull out of the garden may be used in a positive fashion for medicinal foods and preparations — or even in compost. Enjoy your harvesting experiences. For me, this certainly is one of the most rewarding parts of growing plants and using them. As you harvest each plant, you will begin to think of all the different ways you will prepare it for use. There is no better definition of abundance and prosperity, in my opinion, than this time in the garden. ❧

A Little Knowledge Goes a Long Way

It's important to learn as much as you can as you look forward to harvesting. If you know which types of tools work best for the plant part you are harvesting, your time will be spent very efficiently and enjoyably. Proper methods and good tools will cause the plants less stress as you are harvesting them.

Learn which time of the year is most appropriate to harvest certain parts of the plants. Harvesting at the wrong time can result in compromising the health of the plant. It's also true that harvesting in the wrong season may mean that the plant you picked is not as medicinally potent or nutritious as you may wish it to be.

Once the plants have been picked, it is most helpful to know the best ways to process them. Have you ever thought about the difference between a fresh apple and a dehydrated apple? Certainly they are both good, nutritious foods, but the fresh apple has vitality, whereas some of the nutrients may have been compromised during the process of drying the plant. This is a normal occurrence and shouldn't be viewed as a bad thing; after all, dried plants are perfect for use during the long winter. If you had a choice, however, would you not choose to eat the fresh apple? Knowing which herbs are best used fresh and which are easier to adapt when dried is a great help during harvesttime.

Good storage practices are important for maintaining a plant's potency as long as possible. Proper harvesting and storing of herbs is just as important to learn as proper growing techniques, especially when you plan to use these herbs for health and well-being.

Each part of a plant will have a harvesting method that works best for it. Roots should be dug up with a spade or garden fork. Flowers need to be picked gently to prevent bruising. Fruits and seeds must be picked when they are fully ripe, and some should even be gathered after a frost. Harvesting too soon will not make for a strong plant medicine. There are general guidelines that help the harvesting go more smoothly but, as is always the case with plants, remember that they are individuals, and each one may have its own specific requirements. Refer to each plant's profile in chapter 10 for special harvesting requirements.

Harvesting from your plants is a rewarding task that will allow you to truly enjoy the fruits of your labor.

Knowing When to Harvest

As important as it is to know how to harvest each part of a plant, it will do you little good if you don't harvest it at the right time of the year. Annuals are not harvested at the same time as biennials or perennials. Roots must be harvested at different times than flowers, and so on.

Roots and Rhizomes

Roots, rhizomes, and bulbs are generally harvested during the spring or the fall. Sometimes they will be dug in the winter months, if you live in an area where the ground does not freeze. Remember that whenever you harvest roots, you will be putting an end to the plant's life. Plant perennials and biennials accordingly, so that you will have some roots to harvest and some to leave in the garden for later.

Annual roots can be harvested at any point during their growing cycle, as long as they are harvested before the plant goes into seed. Once it has gone to seed it will die and the root will be wasted.

Biennial roots should be harvested in the fall of the first year's growth or in the spring of the second year's growth. If you harvest in the spring of the first year, the root will not be large enough to be valuable to you. If you wait until the fall of the second year, the plant will have seeded and then died, leaving you with a pithy, woody root that is not going to make a good food or medicine.

Perennial roots are best harvested in the spring, fall, or winter. If the plant is one that has flowers or seeds you would also like to use, it's best to let it go for a full cycle and then harvest the roots after that — in late fall or winter.

 ## At-Risk and Endangered Wild Roots

One of the reasons many plants have become at risk or endangered is because of improper and unethical wildcrafting (harvesting in the wild) that called for the roots and rhizomes to be dug up during the wrong season. Some wildcrafters harvest perennial roots and rhizomes during the early spring to satisfy eager customers. Thus the plant is not allowed to flower and reproduce seed for that year, and this in turn jeopardizes self-propagation. When a plant becomes at risk or endangered, it needs to be given every possible opportunity to survive; at-risk perennials especially should be allowed to produce seed. Gardeners can help by growing these plants in their own gardens, eliminating the need to wildcraft them. Making your own medicinal herb products, or buying those whose labels state the plants have been cultivated or ethically harvested, will also help protect these wildcrafted plants.

Whole Plants and Aerial Parts

Whole plants are harvested either when they are actively growing or when they are in flower or seed/fruit, depending on the requirements for the specific herb. The same is true for the aerial parts.

Obviously, the flowers, buds, seeds, and fruits will be harvested when those parts of the plant are available. As a general rule, berries and other fruits are usually picked in late summer or sometimes in fall, depending on when they ripen. Seeds are often harvested in early and late fall, but some seeds will ripen earlier; you must keep a close eye on them if you want to harvest the seeds before the plant disperses them into the air or onto the ground.

The Tools for the Job

Choose good-quality tools for your plant harvesting. Tools greatly influence how pleasurable your harvest experience is! I consider my equipment an investment and I save money until I can afford a good-quality tool. I'm not suggesting that you need anything fancy, just that what you buy is well made.

What to Use and When to Use It

Although you should experiment to find out which tools work best for you and your plants, here are a few of my favorites:

▸ **Needle-nose spade.** I find this tool, which some garden stores call a nurseryman's spade, indispensable for harvesting whole plants and roots.

▸ **Garden fork.** My absolute favorite root-digging tool is a garden fork. Buy one that has strong prongs that won't bend easily. I have an old one that belonged to my great-grandfather and the prongs on it are long with sharp points. It's fantastic for lifting out even some of the longest taproots.

▸ **Hand snips.** A high-quality pair of harvesting or pruning hand snips is critical for every gardener. Choose a quality pair that will last a lifetime, replacing the springs and blades as needed. I have to replace blades annually and the springs about every five years, but my snips get an excessive amount of use. Buy a pair that is the right size for your hand and be sure to determine whether they are right- or left-handed snips. It is important to get a good pair with a proper fit so that you don't injure your hand while using them. Poor snips are easy to find; good ones are worth the trouble of seeking them out.

▸ **Scissors.** I also carry a small pair of scissors. These easily fit in a harvesting basket or utility belt, making them readily available for all types of plant work throughout the day. I use them for everything, from pruning to harvesting.

▸ **Hands.** Finally, I would like to put in a positive word for handpicking. Sometimes there is not a tool that can work better than the human hand. For instance, flowers, seeds, and fruits need the careful harvesting provided by hands.

Harvesting Roots, Rhizomes, and Bulbs

The underground parts of a plant often require the most energy to harvest, since these parts must be dug up. Use caution, though, or you may end up chopping off a valuable piece of the root or piercing a nice juicy bulb.

I prefer to loosen the soil around the root area and then gently lift the root out of the soil with a garden fork or needle-nose spade. A broad shovel won't work as well as a long spade will.

We grow in strong clay soil in southern Colorado. I find it easier to harvest underground parts on a day when the soil is evenly moist rather than very dry or totally wet. If the soil is too wet, it is nearly impossible to extract the root from that clay soil. If the soil is very dry, trying to get a spade or fork into the soil is like trying to penetrate concrete.

If you look closely at the root, you will notice that there is a definite line where the plant begins to grow out of the soil. This is where the stems and leaves grow out of the roots, and this part of the plant is called the root crown.

 Fresh-Processing Roots

Wash the roots thoroughly. It is important that any manure or compost be cleaned off the roots to prevent *E. coli* or other bacterial contamination. Process roots, rhizomes, or bulbs fresh as soon as possible. If it will be a few hours before you can process it, cool the plant part in a refrigerator or root cellar for no longer than 24 to 48 hours.

Chop the roots into small chunks (1 to 2 inches; 2.5 to 5 cm) or grind them in a blender or food processor. Proceed as usual with your medicine making. 🌿

1 **Once the roots are out of the ground, trim off the tops or aerial parts of the plant to ¼ to 1 inch (5 mm to 2.5 cm) above the root crown.**

2 **Separate the roots from the crown.**

3 **Gently rub the roots free of much soil and stones, then wash well with a hose sprayer or faucet.**

Drying Roots

You can dry roots in their whole form, chopped into small chunks (1 to 2 inches; 2.5 to 5 cm), or sliced. Whenever possible, I prefer to dry all of my plant parts whole. Whole dried plants will store better and maintain potency levels longer than sliced or cut plants. Some roots, such as yucca and burdock, should be sliced before drying; once they have dried, they become extremely hard, and it will take a very strong piece of equipment (like a milling machine) to cut them up.

Lay out the whole, sliced, or chopped roots on a nonmetal screen (old nylon window screens work great for drying plants) in an area that is out of direct sunlight and gets good warm air circulation. Roots will take a week to several weeks to dry fully. They should feel brittle and easily snap in two when they are dry. At that point they can be stored for later use. It is extremely important that the roots are completely dry before being stored; even a small amount of moisture can encourage the growth of mold.

garden profile

Paula's Intuitive Medicinal Garden

"Let the beauty you love be what you do. There are a thousand ways to kiss the earth." — Rumi

Paula Randall gardens in Canon City, in the southern Colorado high mountain desert. She shares this account of her special herb garden:

"The beauty I love is the earth and I most love the earth's children-plants. Some of these children live with my cats and me.

"When I moved into my house two years ago, the earth surrounding it was in a dismal state of neglect. The month was February. Seed catalogs covered the table; odd containers of seeds from previous gardens and wild places were unpacked first so they could be sown direct in winter's ground.

"The warm sun arrived in April, as well as compost, manure, and visions of color. The clay was like concrete and my dreams started to fade. I wondered if any seed could sprout or any root survive ... worms did not live in this soil! But the old lilac bloomed, the black walnut leafed out, and I planted under the watchful eye of my garden cat, Zoe. Friends and family weeded and tilled with great love and were rewarded with unbounded beauty. The earth's children grew and welcomed siblings gifted by people who loved me.

"This garden lives on its own terms. I set new plants and spread seed. The compost grew. It seems it did not get hot enough over the winter and all the old pickling spice seeds sprouted. I found myself wondering, on a daily basis, 'What is this?' There was celery, dill, fennel, and mustard growing among the tomatoes, carrots, echinacea, cronewort, and St.-John's-wort. Dandelions, hyssop, calendula, and sunflowers bloomed. The tall plants protected the more fragile ones from our brutal sun. Some went out of season, as others needed growing room.

"Then the worms returned and the bees arrived. The guardian sunflowers attracted aphids, the tansy discouraged other insects. The cats found hiding places. I turned brown in the sun. My plant friends fed me and anyone else who asked. The kitchen is now full of vinegars and tinctures. There are racks of flowers for tea.

"My eyes are filled with every imaginable color. I have kissed the earth in a thousand ways."

Harvesting Whole Plants

Harvesting whole plants is done in basically the same way as roots, rhizomes, and bulbs. Before harvesting a whole plant, it is wise to double-check whether the plant should be in flower or have seed formed at the time you harvest it (see chapter 10).

1 **To harvest a whole plant, use a spade or garden fork, penetrate the soil deep beneath the roots, and lift.**

2 **Shake the plant to get rid of loose soil, then wash it clean of all soil and debris using a hose sprayer.**

 **Drying**

Whole plants may be dried using the screen method described on page 110, or by tying a rubber band or a slipknot around the roots of the plants and then hanging them upside down to dry. It is important that hanging plants be spaced far enough apart to allow for good warm air circulation. Never hang them in direct sunlight, as this will degrade the plant material quickly. Once dried, store the whole plants in a brown paper sack that has been taped closed at the top. You could also chop the plants into large pieces and store them in glass jars. The less the herb is chopped or ground, however, the more medicinal potency it will retain and the better it will store. ❀

3 **Hang the entire plant upside down to dry in a warm place out of direct sunlight.**

Harvesting Aerial Parts

Often it is desirable to use all of the aerial parts of the plant. Aerial parts can include leaves, stems, flowers, and seeds or fruits. It's unusual to harvest leaves or stems when the plant is in flower, seed, or fruit. Check each individual plant's requirements to learn if the plant should be in flower or seed when this type of harvesting is carried out.

How to Harvest

To harvest aerial parts of an annual plant, I often cut the plant just above the soil surface. When harvesting aerial parts of perennials, I cut the upper half to third of the plant. This allows the plant to recover more easily and begin growing again sooner. I like to use a pair of sharp scissors, but good snips will work also. Use whichever tool you are most comfortable with.

Processing

After I have cut the aerial parts, I remove any dead or dying plant material and make sure that the plant is free of dirt. If the plants have been grown properly and are healthy, I don't find it necessary to wash them, unless they have gotten muddy. But this is a personal judgment call for each of us. If you do wash your plants, be aware that you will be removing some of the water-soluble vitamins from the plant surfaces, as well as some of the volatile oils.

Fresh processing. I like to process many aerial plant parts into fresh preparations. If you are making fresh preparations with any above-ground parts of the plant, try to process them no more than 24 hours after harvesttime. It is best to get them put up within minutes of harvest. The sooner a plant is processed, the better and fresher it is. This makes a difference that you will be able to notice in your final product.

Gently snip aerial parts halfway down the plant and then bunch together small groups for drying.

Drying. Tie the plants into bundles and hang them upside down for drying, or lay them on a nonmetal screen to dry. If you dry aerial parts on a screen, be careful not to layer them too thickly. A layer no more than 4 inches (10 cm) thick will allow the plant material to dry more evenly. Turn the plants frequently to ensure even drying. Store dried plants for later use.

Mullein flowers are fresh picked and then processed immediately into tincture or infused oil.

Harvesting Flowers and Buds

I love to harvest medicinal flowers. They remind me of all the vitality a plant holds in such a delicate but important part. Be gentle with flowers, as they bruise easily and will turn brown quickly if picked improperly.

How to Harvest

Normally I handpick flowers only. Sometimes, as is the case with chamomile, I harvest the flowering tops too, removing the flowers plus 2 to 4 inches (5 to 10 cm) of leafy stems. This type of harvesting is best accomplished with scissors. I use a basket to catch the flowers as I am picking them, but my husband prefers a 5-gallon bucket, which he feels is sturdier and protects the flowers better.

Processing

Gently shaking the flowers will remove any bugs or extra soil. Washing isn't necessary unless the flowers are muddy.

Fresh processing. If you plan to use the flowers fresh, immediately cool them in the refrigerator until you are ready to process them.

Drying

To dry the flowers, lay them out in a shallow layer on a nonmetal screen. Avoid direct sunlight and be sure the air circulation is good and temperatures are warm. I also like drying flowers in large, shallow baskets. The baskets can be gently shaken every day or so to redistribute the flowers, so that they all get exposed to the air and dry properly. I love the way baskets of drying flowers look and smell in my home. It's a beautiful and practical way to dry flowers and buds.

Once the flowers or buds are dried, they are put into storage (see page 117 for information on storage). I often dry extra baskets of flowers and buds, which I simply leave out in the house throughout the year to add beautiful color and fragrance. Since these flowers will gather dust and are exposed to the air constantly, I don't use them for making preparations. They are only to please the eye and nose.

Whole flowers dry quite easily when laid out in a shallow layer across a screen. Stir gently every day or two to facilitate even drying.

Harvesting Seeds and Fruits

Most seeds and fruits should be picked when they are fully ripe. Occasionally a plant will be harvested when the seeds are still green. Check the individual plant's requirements to know when to harvest seeds.

How to Harvest

I usually handpick most seeds, but occasionally I use scissors to harvest entire seed heads. Fruits should be individually picked. It's best to place your harvested seeds in a bucket, close-woven basket, or paper bag.

Processing

Organically grown seeds and fruits rarely require washing. Rinse any muddy fruits, but take care not to wash too much; excessive washing can rinse away valuable water-soluble vitamins.

Fresh processing. Even though seeds and fruits may be fully ripe and appear dry when they are harvested, they are considered for fresh use if they are processed immediately after harvest.

Drying. I find it best to put seeds and fruits into a close-woven basket for a few days to a couple of weeks to let them finish drying. Nothing is more disappointing than storing fruits or seeds before they are fully dried and having them mold.

Once dried, seeds and fruits are best stored in paper bags or glass jars. The freezer presents optimum storage conditions for seeds. I often put my seeds in a paper bag, place that bag into a freezer bag, and then put the whole package in the freezer. Fruits, on the other hand, may be stored at room temperature in a dry place.

Harvesting plants from your garden can be a wonderful sensory experience for both eyes and nose.

Drying for Optimal Quality

There are several different methods you can use to dry plants, from hanging bundles, to screen and basket drying, to drying in paper sacks and cardboard boxes. Regardless of the method you choose, it is important to be sure that the plant is fully dry before storing or it will mold.

Attics usually work very well for drying plants; basements generally aren't good drying places because they often have poor air movement and cooler temperatures. I dry plants on our covered patio in Colorado, but the climate here is dry. People in areas with high humidity will have more difficulty. You may need to assist the process by setting up fans to improve air circulation and remove some of the moisture from the air. If your plants are dried improperly, they may show signs of mold and mildew in the form of a white downy or black slimy coating. The plants will often smell musty or rotten; these plants must be discarded.

Please do not dry your plants in buildings where machine oils or other fumes will be present. Plants can absorb these substances, and that is the last thing you want if you plan to use them for health and well-being.

Hanging Bundles

If you choose to dry your herbs by hanging them upside down in bundles, it's important to pay attention to the size of the batch. As you are putting together a bundle, look at the stems and be sure that the diameter of the bunch where the stems are tied together is no bigger than that of a pencil. This will allow for good airflow through the bundle, preventing the growth of mold and mildew.

Tying herbs with a simple slipknot or a rubber band will allow you to keep the bundle together as it shrinks during the drying process. If you use string tied in a basic knot, stems will fall out as the plant shrinks.

Don't hang bunches of herbs too close together; crowding produces poor air circulation.

What about Ovens and Dehydrators?

I'm often asked if I dry my plants in a food dehydrator or in the oven. Personally, I don't wish to expose my plants to any temperature that would be above that of normal warm air; heat can change or degrade a plant's constituents and nutrients. If you do choose to use a heat mechanism like a dehydrator, use the lowest temperature setting possible and check the plants often.

Bundles should be hung in an area that is protected from direct sunlight and moisture, where there is good warm air circulation. Normally, bundles of herbs will dry in 1 to 2 weeks.

Hanging bundles of drying herbs can add a decorative touch to any space in your home that is warm and does not receive direct sunlight.

Screen and Basket Drying

When using screens to dry herbs, choose a nonmetal screening material, such as nylon. Metal screening can change the taste and fragrance of a plant as it dries, and there is also the potential that medicinal constituents will be altered. If you must use a metal screen, lay a barrier of cotton cloth or paper between the plant material and the screen. This will help protect your plants without preventing the movement of air.

Place the screen on blocks or hang it horizontally from the ceiling to allow air to move below, around, and above the screen. Place the screen out of direct sunlight and protect it from moisture. Plants will take from one to several weeks to dry on screens.

Basket drying is one of my favorite ways to dry small amounts of herbs. Choose a basket that is shallow and has a weave that will let air flow through it without allowing the plant material to fall out. Baskets must be tossed every day or so to redistribute the plants, allowing for even drying and air exposure.

Drying in Paper Sacks and Cardboard Boxes

If you're in a pinch and don't have any other way to dry your plants, or if you've gathered plants from a friend's garden and you will be traveling for a few days before returning home, it is possible to dry plants in paper sacks or cardboard boxes.

The key to success with this method is to avoid putting too much plant material in each sack or box, and to leave the top open so that air can flow into the container. Check plants often to make sure that they are not molding or mildewing. If you notice this happening, you probably have too much plant material in the sack or box.

Gently shake the sack or box every day or two to redistribute the plant material and assist the drying process. Plants will usually dry in 1 to 2 weeks.

An open basket works well to dry heads of garlic. Loosely woven fiber baskets are good for flowers.

Testing for Dryness

Most plants, when fully dry, will be brittle and make a snapping or crackling sound if they are crushed. When this happens, your plants are ready to store; it's best to do so promptly to lessen their exposure to air and dust, which will degrade them more quickly.

Another way to test for dryness is to gently tear a piece of the plant material. If you notice any moisture beads forming along the tear, the plant needs to dry a bit longer. You can also place the edge of the tear against your upper lip, the most sensitive part of your body. If you feel any moisture on your upper lip, allow the plant to dry a while longer before storing it.

Before storing a dried plant, crumble a piece in your hand to be sure there is no moisture in it.

Proper Storage Methods

Choosing the right container or location for storage can often affect how well your plants keep their potency, color, taste, and smell. Dried plants should be stored in clean, airtight glass jars or paper containers that can be taped closed. Plastic and most metal containers (except stainless steel) are unsuitable, although unchipped porcelain (also called enameled metal) can be used. Most jars come with metal lids (the canning-jar type), but these are worry-free because of the nonmetal coating. If you would like to store herbs in decorative tins, line them first with a paper bag or waxed paper to create a barrier between the plants and the metal.

Where to Store

Put your storage containers out of direct light and away from extreme heat. They should also be protected from moisture. Cabinets and pantries are good places to store herbs, but you can even place your jars on open shelves as long as the light and heat exposure is not too intense.

How Long Will It Last?

Properly dried and stored herbs will maintain their color; they should look vibrant and healthy. Their taste should be strong and their smell should resemble how the plant smelled when it was fresh. If your herbs do not meet these qualifications, they should be discarded.

When properly stored, dried herbs will generally keep for a year. Ground and powdered herbs may have a shorter shelf life, about 4 to 6 months, at which point they should be added to the compost pile.

Airtight glass storage jar.

Eight

making herbal preparations

 Few tasks in life are as rewarding as being in charge of your own health care. For me, a part of that means preparing my own botanical medicines. The recipes and directions in this chapter will allow you to make preparations in your own kitchen "pharmacy," from the plants you have harvested from your garden. These directions will apply as general guidelines; see chapter 10 for individual plant requirements.

Every plant will have its own special dosage recommendations and cautionary notes. I suggest you invest in one or two reliable resource books (see Recommended Reading) for information on effective and safe usage relevant to your particular health needs.

Fresh or Dried Herbs?

I am often asked if fresh plants are medicinally stronger than dried plants. I guess I view that question the same way I would if someone asked me if all people with brown hair have green eyes. Of course, every person has his or her own individual traits, and plants are really no different. Some plants are more effective when fresh, others are too strong and must be dried; some plants are equally good medicinally when used fresh *or* dried.

I do feel that fresh plants contain more vitality or essence of life than dried plants. I think this is very positive and adds a beneficial effect to the way a plant will work in our bodies. I compare it to eating freshly picked fruits and vegetables rather than dehydrated ones. Personally, I enjoy using plants in their fresh state to prepare my botanical medicines whenever it is possible and appropriate to do so.

Choosing Utensils and Equipment

Preparing medicinal remedies in your kitchen requires that you give a few moments' thought to the utensils you will be using. It isn't necessary to buy fancy or extra equipment, but you will want to be sure that you have utensils that are made from appropriate materials.

Materials

Plastic should not be used at all when preparing or packaging medicinal remedies. Only stainless steel or unchipped enamel is acceptable for metal containers. Avoid aluminum and copper pans at all costs; neither of those materials is conducive to good health. Glass or Pyrex containers and pans are the best. I like using wooden spoons, but stainless-steel spoons are also fine. Follow the same criteria for bowls and packaging containers.

Equipment and Utensils

You could stock your kitchen with a huge variety of pots, pans, spoons, and jars, but the truth is that you can make do with just a few items. Here are the equipment and utensils I like to keep on hand in my kitchen:

- Long-handled wooden spoons
- Several different-sized kitchen knives
- Different-sized strainers (at least three)
- One or two large kettles (I have one stainless steel and one Pyrex)
- A few saucepans, varying in size from 1- to 3-quart (.95 l to 2.84 l)
- A set of measuring cups and spoons
- Pint and quart canning jars
- Mortar and pestle
- Spice mill
  - Blender (good quality is essential)
  - Different-sized funnels
  - Glass and glazed pottery bowls
  - Wooden cutting board
  - Cotton napkins (for use as straining cloths)

Making Homemade Remedies

The decision of which type of remedy you should prepare will ultimately be based on the plant, the person who will be taking the preparation, and the condition for which the remedy is being used.

Infusions and decoctions are good for many types of herbs, but they require preparation time for each use. Vinegars, syrups, elixirs, and honey are all pleasant and effective ways to use herbs, but they have limited shelf life. Similarly, crystallized herbs and lozenges are easy to use, but have a shelf life of only several weeks to a few months. Tinctures, on the other hand, have nearly unlimited shelf life and are convenient to use. Topical preparations like salves and creams are neat, convenient methods of applying herbs, while poultices and compresses are very effective but not quite so tidy. Regardless of what type of remedy you prepare, you will find that each one can enhance your health and well-being.

The Golden Rule: Label *Everything*

Whenever you make your herbs into homemade medicines, it is absolutely essential to make sure the containers are fully labeled. My apprentices fondly call me the Label Police, and I wear that title with great honor. No one leaves class with an unlabeled preparation.

I cannot tell you how many times I have been contacted by the Poison Control Center because they have a call from someone who has ingested something and they don't know what it was. If you label your items completely, you will avoid this situation.

Label your preparations with the name of the remedy, every single ingredient it contains (include the plant parts in your ingredients), recommended dose, any cautionary information (such as pregnancy warnings) that may apply, and an expiration date if appropriate for the remedy. 🌿

A cup of potent herbal tea is one of the easiest and most versatile medicinal preparations you can make straight from the garden.

Infusions and Decoctions

Infusions and decoctions are medicinal-strength teas, rather than beverage teas. Whether you infuse or decoct the plants will be determined by the part of the plant that is used.

Infusions are prepared from leaves, stems, and flowers. They are covered with boiling water and allowed to steep.

Decoctions are prepared from roots and rhizomes, barks, and seeds, and are gently simmered in water.

As a general measurement, use 1 teaspoon of dried or 2 teaspoons of fresh herb per cup of water. Most herbal infusions and decoctions will keep for up to three days when stored in a tightly closed glass container in the refrigerator. Any tea left after that time should be discarded and a fresh batch made.

Many teas may be drunk either hot or cold. Occasionally it is preferable to drink a particular tea at one temperature only, so learn more about the individual herb you plan to use. I feel strongly that you should not use a microwave oven to make or reheat teas. Microwaves emit a small amount of radiation, and I don't think it's healthy to include that in your medicinal infusions or decoctions. It really takes only a short time to prepare these teas by a more traditional method (stove, electric coffeepot, French press, and so on).

To prepare an infusion: Measure the correct amount of herb into a heat-tolerant container. In a pan or teapot, bring the water to a boil, then pour the water over the herbs. Cover with a lid and allow the herbs to steep for 10 to 15 minutes. Strain out the herbs, and you're ready to enjoy your infusion.

To prepare a decoction: In a pan or teapot, bring the water to a boil. Add the measured herbs to the pan and reduce the temperature until the water is gently simmering. Allow the herbs to simmer for 15 to 20 minutes, strain, and enjoy.

Nothing could be simpler than making an herbal infusion. All that's needed is a bowl, the herbs, and boiling water.

 ## Great Herbs for Infusions and Decoctions

- **Peppermint–lemon balm** infusion will soothe an upset digestive tract
- **Burdock root** decoction is a wonderful support for the liver
- **Dandelion root–chicory root** decoctions will improve skin health
- **Oat straw** infusion is a fantastic support for the nervous system
- **Nettle** infusion can be used as a whole-body tonic
- **Red clover** blossom infusion helps boost the immune system ❦

Traditional Tinctures

Traditionally, tinctures have been made by a method called maceration. This method can be used to prepare both alcohol and vinegar tinctures, as well as topical liniments.

You will need the following components to prepare your menstruum (the maceration plant and solvent).

▸ 1 clean 1-pint (473 ml) glass jar with a tight-fitting lid (canning jars work great)

▸ Approximately 1 cup of chopped fresh herbs or 1/4 cup of coarsely ground dried herbs

▸ 1 pint of brandy or vodka (your choice; brandy is usually 75–80 proof, while vodka is generally 80–85 proof)

To prepare a tincture: Place the herb material in the jar. Pour the liquid over the top of the plant material until it reaches the shoulder of the jar. Put the lid on tightly and label the container with all of the ingredients and the date. This is the menstruum.

Store the menstruum at room temperature for four to six weeks. Shake it vigorously every couple of days. Keep out of direct light and heat.

After four to six weeks you will be ready to squeeze out the menstruum. Place a clean cotton cloth (I use cloth napkins or a piece of a cotton sheet) in the bottom of a colander or strainer. Put the colander into a pan or bowl. Slowly pour the liquid and herb material into the colander and let it drain for a minute or two, then pull up the corners of the cloth to form a bundle. Squeeze the bundle until all the liquid has been removed from the plant material. The squeezed plant material, called marc, can be discarded into the compost pile.

The strained liquid is your finished tincture. Store in a clean glass bottle, tightly closed and fully labeled. For convenience, I keep 1- or 2-ounce (30 ml to 60 ml) bottles of tinctures in my medicine cabinet (of course, they are also labeled), refilling them as needed from the larger bottles in my dispensary.

Storage. Tinctures with at least 25 percent alcohol content will keep indefinitely. They do not require an expiration date and can be used until they are gone. My friend Brigitte Mars is fond of saying that a tincture is something you give to your grandchildren and they can pass it on to their grandchildren, providing it has not been used up.

Tinctures are the preparation of choice for many people. They are simple to make and use and will keep indefinitely.

Terrific Traditional Tincture Herbs

- **Astragalus, milk thistle, and spilanthes** make an excellent combination tincture for immune system support
- **Skullcap and catnip** can be tinctured together for stress and anxiety
- **Thyme, echinacea, and mondarda** are a powerful trio for cold and flu symptoms
- **Dill and peppermint** are a perfect tummy-soothing blend
- **Echinacea and ginger** can be tinctured together as a virus fighter
- **Gotu kola, rosemary, and spearmint** are a great formula for clear thinking
- **California poppy and passionflower** tincture will help relieve pain 🌺

Vinegar Tinctures

To prepare a vinegar tincture, follow the same instructions for traditional tinctures, using organic apple cider vinegar in place of the alcohol. Do not use white vinegar to prepare vinegar tinctures. White vinegar is processed using harsh and toxic chemicals that you will not want in your botanical medicines or in your body.

Vinegar menstruums should sit for two to six weeks, after which you can squeeze them out and begin using your tincture. Vinegar tinctures have a shelf life of one year from the date the plant was put into the menstruum. Make sure the expiration date is listed on your label.

You can use dried or fresh herbs in tinctures. Just be sure to appropriately adjust the amount of herb to solvent.

Nourishing Vinegar Tinctures

- **Alfalfa** is fabulous for bone health
- **Ginger and peppermint** reduce flatulence
- **Chamomile and catnip** will help to alleviate grumpiness in kids
- **Thyme** tincture is a must for good intestinal function 🌿

Topical Liniments

Although they are prepared in the same fashion as traditional and vinegar tinctures, liniments are not taken internally but, rather, are applied topically.

Since they will be applied to the skin, I prefer not to use brandy or vodka to prepare liniments; both of those types of alcohol feel a bit sticky on the skin. Instead I use equal parts pure grain alcohol (the brand most readily available is called Everclear) and spring water as the menstruum. If pure grain alcohol isn't available in your area, substitute vodka; it will be a little tackier to the touch, but will have the same medicinal value. I don't use rubbing alcohol in my liniments because it isn't a pure solvent, and I prefer not to have it absorbed into the skin.

Liniments are made in exactly the same way as tinctures; allow the menstruum to sit for four to six weeks. Also like tinctures, liniments have an indefinite shelf life.

Liniments to Live By

- **Yucca** should be used for joint pain relief
- **Peppermint** is soothing to sore muscles
- **Lemon balm** will help heal cold sores
- **Lavender** is an excellent all-around soother
- **Echinacea** makes a great antiseptic liniment
- **Yarrow** liniment relieves itchy skin 🌿

Syrups and Elixirs

Syrups and elixirs are great ways to use botanical medicines. Since they taste good, they often become a parent's ally in administering herbal medicines to children. Picky adults are also more easily pacified with a syrup or elixir. These medicines are made from a traditional tincture base.

Blends for Syrups and Elixirs

- **Horehound and sage** syrup for coughs and irritated throats
- **Echinacea and ginger** syrup for colds and flus
- **St.-John's-wort, passionflower, and skullcap** elixir blended with peaches for nervous system support
- **Astragalus, burdock, licorice, and vanilla** extract for a winter-season elixir
- **Chaste berry, motherwort, and oatseed** with cherries elixir for women's health
- **Angelica, rosemary, and violet** syrup for respiratory support

To prepare a syrup: Warm 1 cup of honey in a pan over low heat. Add 1 to 2 ounces of traditional tincture and cook for 10 to 15 minutes. It isn't necessary to vigorously boil the syrup, just simmer it very gently. This process will blend the syrup and dissipate most of the alcohol.

Allow the syrup to cool to room temperature, then pour it into a glass bottle and label it with an expiration date (syrups will keep for six months). Store these preparations in the refrigerator. Syrups are usually administered by the teaspoonful.

To prepare an elixir: Combine ½ cup of honey, ½ cup of fresh or frozen fruit, and 1 ounce of traditional tincture in a blender. My favorite fruit choices are berries, peaches, and bananas, but you should experiment to see which fruits you like using best. I don't recommend using citrus fruits to make elixirs because they are too acidic and create an unpleasant taste. You can substitute ¼ cup fruit juice or fruit nectar for the actual fruit. Blend well until smooth and creamy.

Store elixirs in a properly labeled glass bottle in the refrigerator for up to two weeks. Always include an expiration date. Elixirs are normally administered by the tablespoonful.

Fresh fruits such as bananas, strawberries, and even kiwi make delicious flavorings for herbal elixirs.

CAUTION: Syrups

Never leave a pan of herbal syrup cooking unattended, even for a moment. Syrups are notorious for boiling over in the blink of an eye, and they can easily catch fire when that happens. Always heat syrups gently, and keep a careful watch over them until they are finished cooking.

Medicinal Honey

Medicinal honey is sort of a syrup, I suppose, but it is infused with the herbs themselves rather than with a traditional tincture. I especially enjoy using medicinal honey for throat conditions and when I am working with children. They also make a great medicinal food.

I definitely think that fresh herbs make a superior medicinal honey, but if fresh herbs are unavailable, you can use dried.

To prepare a medicinal honey: In a pan, heat 1 quart of wildflower honey (available at helath-food stores) over low heat until it is just warmed through. Add ½ cup of chopped fresh herbs or ¼ cup of dried herbs and continue heating for 15 to 20 minutes, then pour the mixture into a heat-tolerant jar (canning jars work well) and close tightly. Label properly with an 18-month expiration date.

I don't strain the herbs from my honey. The preparation will be stronger if the herbs continue to infuse in the honey during the storage time. At the time you use the honey, you may either warm it and strain out the herbs or just use the honey, as I do, with the herbs included. Use medicinal honey by the teaspoon or tablespoon.

Crystallized Herbs

This is a delicious way to use therapeutic herbs. It's like having a sweet treat that's truly good for you. My favorites are crystallized ginger and angelica roots.

To prepare crystallized herbs: Start by preparing a medicinal honey. Once the honey is cooked, pour the mixture into a glass baking pan. Cover with plastic wrap and allow it to sit for two to three days at room temperature.

Strain out the herbs and place them in a single layer on a baking sheet lined with waxed paper. Cover them loosely with another piece of waxed paper to protect from dust, but without preventing good air circulation. The excess honey may be poured into a jar and used as an herbal honey for cooking or sweetening beverages. Allow the herbs to sit for one week.

Dust the honey-covered herbs with table sugar — a light coating is all that's needed. Spread out the herbs in a single layer on a piece of butcher paper or wax paper and allow them to dry for one to two days. Store them in a glass jar until ready to use. Crystallized herbs will usually keep for two to four weeks at room temperature or for several months in the refrigerator. Eat one or two pieces at a time.

Delicious and Healthy Crystallized Herbs

- **Rosemary** flowers are wonderful for healthy circulation.
- **Gingerroot** is great for digestive-tract health.
- **Violet** flowers will enhance the skin and heart function.
- **Angelica** stalks are terrific for the respiratory system and female reproductive system.
- **Spearmint** leaves help support the nervous system.
- **Borage** flowers are fabulous for skin health.

Honey-covered leaves, flowers, stalks, and roots can be transformed into tasty crystallized herbs.

Lozenges

You'll appreciate having herbal lozenges when the winter season comes around or if you are an avid sports fan who likes to cheer for your favorite team. Lozenges are wonderful for soothing a painful, irritated throat, so be sure to choose herbs for your lozenges that have appropriate actions.

Excellent Lozenge Herbs

- **Astragalus** for immune support
- **Ginger** for heartburn relief
- **Blue vervain** for colds and flus
- **Echinacea** for fighting bacterial and viral infections
- **Sage** for irritated throats ✿

To prepare herbal lozenges: Make ½ cup of a decoction or infusion (see directions on page 122) from the herb of your choice. Pour the tea into a glass bowl and add 1 cup of powdered marsh mallow root. Stir in additional marsh mallow root until you have mixed a thick paste. Add ½ to 1 ounce of traditional tincture (I like to use a tincture that has antiviral or antibacterial properties) and blend well. Finally, add 1 to 3 drops of peppermint or spearmint food-grade essential oil (available at health-food stores). Mix well.

When just cool enough to handle comfortably, take a pea-size amount of the paste and smooth it with your fingers, shaping it into a small oval or ball. Lay your lozenges on a piece of waxed paper and allow them to air-dry for several hours. Store the lozenges in a covered dish in the refrigerator until you are ready to use them.

Lozenges will normally keep for several weeks in the refrigerator. Suck on a lozenge whenever needed to soothe a painful throat, but do not exceed 12 lozenges daily unless otherwise directed by a health-care professional.

Honey is one of the most pleasant mediums in which to take medicinal herbs. Herbal honeys are especially good for children.

Favorite Medicinal Honeys

- **Lavender** promotes restful sleep
- **Ginger** encourages good circulation
- **Monarda** soothes irritated throats
- **Lemon balm** calms upset stomachs
- **Chamomile** relieves headaches ✿

Compresses and Poultices

Compresses and poultices are applied topically to an injury or wound. They should be prepared fresh each time they are needed. The herbs used for the compress or poultice will be determined by the condition being addressed.

To prepare a compress: Make a decoction or infusion (see directions on page 122) with the selected herb. The herb and the condition being treated will determine whether a cool or hot compress is necessary; consult your reference books for information on temperature. Soak a clean cotton cloth in the strained liquid and gently squeeze out the excess. Apply the cloth over the affected area. Reapply fresh compresses as recommended, depending on the herbs used.

To prepare a poultice: Place 1 cup of the chosen herb in a heat-tolerant bowl or pan and pour 2 cups of boiling water over it. Cover the bowl and allow the herb to steep in the water until it is cool enough to be tolerated by the skin; use caution, because hot liquids will cause burning. Lay a clean cotton cloth over the affected area and then use a ladle or spoon to apply the hot, wet herb material on top of the cloth. Keep the poultice in place until it has cooled completely and then discard it to the compost pile. Never reuse a poultice, and always launder the cloth before using it again. Poultices are usually applied 1 to 3 times daily, depending on the herb and the condition. Again, be sure to consult your reference books for more in-depth information.

Soothing Herbs for Compresses and Poultices

- **Comfrey** for sports injury healing
- **Plantain** for insect bite and bee sting relief
- **Spearmint** for a skin antiseptic
- **St.-John's-wort** for soothing nerve endings
- **Chamomile** for cramp relief
- **Rosemary** for muscle pain relief

A compress is an easy-to-make, effective remedy that can be used to treat different types of cuts, abrasions, and injuries.

Many herbs make excellent poultices, which can be applied topically to sprains, strains, bruises, and wounds.

Infused Oils

Many types of skin conditions will benefit from an herbal infused oil. Oils are normally applied topically to the affected area. Infused oils also become the base used to prepare salves, ointments, balms, and creams. Calendula flowers make a wonderful infused oil.

To prepare an infused oil: You will need a clean glass quart jar that is completely dry inside. Make sure all of your utensils are also clean and dry; the least bit of moisture can spoil your oil. Place ⅓ cup of dried plant material in the jar and add enough good-quality olive oil to fully cover the plant material.

Check the jar after several hours to make sure the plant material has not absorbed all of the oil. If all the oil has been absorbed, add another inch or so. Cover the jar with a clean piece of cotton cloth or an unbleached coffee filter and secure it with a rubber band or canning jar lid ring. Do not cover with a lid yet, because the herb will sometimes release gases that could blow a lid right off the jar. (I have had mullein flower oil on my kitchen ceiling on more than one occasion. This is not a fun thing to clean up!) Let the oil infuse in a sunny window or on the kitchen counter for about 10 days.

Strain out the plant material and discard it into your compost pile. The remaining oil may be kept in a glass bottle at room temperature for up to one year.

Incredible Infused Oils

- **Mullein** flowers are wonderful for ear pain
- **Calendula** flowers will soothe the skin
- **St.-John's-wort** makes a great first-aid oil
- **Basil** oil will aid digestion
- **Thyme** can be used for stress relief ❧

These jars of St.-John's-wort oil will be allowed to sit for about 10 days before being strained and then used as an infused oil.

Your herbal creations, such as salves, can be produced in bulk and sold commercially.

Ointments, Salves, and Balms

The difference between an infused oil and these preparations is simply the addition of a solidifying agent, such as beeswax or cocoa butter. Making the preparation more solid allows you to apply it to the skin more easily and keep it in place longer.

Ointments have only a small amount of beeswax or cocoa butter added; they are almost the consistency of pudding and are easily spread onto the skin. A salve is made firmer by the addition of more beeswax and it "seals" better; it protects the skin from drying out or having excess moisture enter. Balms have even more beeswax and are firmer than salves; they are usually used on the lips or temples.

You can purchase from mail-order suppliers small metal tins that are fantastic for these prepa-

rations. These tins often have a paper-covered lid that makes labeling a snap. They range in size from ¼ ounce (perfect for a lip balm) to 2 ounces (good for ointments). I often clean and reuse ½-ounce glass baby food jars for ointments, salves, and balms. Always label each jar completely.

To prepare an ointment: Warm, but don't boil, 1 cup of infused oil of choice. (See directions on page 129 for making an infused oil.) In a separate saucepan, heat ½ ounce of beeswax or cocoa butter just until melted. Pour the wax into the warmed oil. Test the consistency by putting a drop of the mixture onto a glass plate. Put the plate into the freezer for a minute or so, until the mixture cools completely. Once it's cooled, try it out on your skin; it should be easy to spread. If it is too thin, add another small chip of wax and stir gently until melted. If it's too thick, add a bit more oil. Pour the finished ointment into a jar or tin. Allow it to cool completely before covering. These preparations have a shelf life of one year.

To prepare a salve or balm: Follow the guidelines for making an ointment, but increase the amount of beeswax to 1 ounce. Adjust to your desired consistency.

 Wonderful Herbs for Salves, Ointments, and Balms

- **Calendula** should be used for scrapes, cuts, and abrasions
- **Lemon balm** heals cracked lips
- **Lavender** is an excellent headache reliever
- **Self-heal** soothes sore feet
- **Comfrey** salve will prevent scarring
- **Marsh mallow** is antibacterial and will also soothe skin irritation
- **Oatseed** makes a great salve for itchy skin conditions

Using Solidifier

I recommend purchasing a quart-size saucepan at a secondhand shop for preparing ointments and salves. It's difficult to fully remove wax residues from pots and utensils, so a special pan reserved for the purpose will ensure that you don't end up with wax in your dinner.

Do not add a lot of beeswax or cocoa butter to your salve, ointment, or balm at one time. The preparation can easily become too firm, and then you will have to add more oil to fix the consistency. It's more efficient to proceed slowly and conservatively when adding your solidifying agents.

For salves, I usually add approximately 1 ounce of beeswax or cocoa butter per cup of oil, and just a bit more for balms. Since there are no precise measurements for solidifying agents, you must approach this task as an art, not an exact science. Adjust as you go until the consistency is to your liking. After you prepare a batch or two of salve or ointment, you will get a knack for the process and won't have any trouble at all in preparing these items. 🌿

Creams

The key to success in making creams is to have a really good electric mixer, which will help make the cream smooth. If you live in a hot climate, you may have more trouble holding your creams (they may turn moldy) unless they are refrigerated. I find that making smaller batches more often works well with creams.

To prepare a cream: In a chilled mixing bowl, combine 1 cup of room-temperature infused oil (see page 129) with ½ cup of melted cocoa butter and begin whipping the mixture at high speed. With the mixer running, add ½ cup of coconut oil and continue to whip the mixture, which should begin to take on a creamy consis-

tency. It may be necessary to cool the bowl with the mixture in it several times during the process. When you have a rich and creamy consistency, spoon it into glass containers with tight-fitting lids; label the containers. Expiration dates will vary, but my creams usually hold nicely for one to two months. They may last longer if they are stored in a refrigerator; this is especially important if you live in a hot climate.

Create a soothing first-aid cream by adding calendula, mullein, or self-heal. For sore muscles, try cayenne or rosemary.

Butters and Suppositories

Medicinal butters are used topically to treat various skin conditions, from rashes to cuts and abrasions. Herbal suppositories, also called pessaries, are used vaginally or rectally, depending on the circumstance. Both suppositories and butters are stored frozen until an hour or so before use.

To prepare a medicinal butter: Heat 1 ounce of cocoa butter in a small saucepan over very low heat. Add ¼ to ½ teaspoon of each powdered herb of choice. Mix well and remove from heat.

Once the mixture has cooled enough to handle, shape small pieces of the mixture into balls the size of a marble. After you have shaped all the mixture into balls, put them in a labeled freezer bag or labeled tin and store them in the freezer until an hour before needed. Butters will keep nicely in the freezer for up to 18 months.

To use a butter, first allow one marble-sized piece to soften at room temperature in a covered container. Once softened, apply the butter topically to the affected area; massage in gently. Dosages will depend on the health concern that is being addressed.

To prepare suppositories: Heat 1 ounce of cocoa butter in a small saucepan over very low heat. Add ¼ to ½ teaspoon of each of the powdered herbs of choice. Mix well and remove from heat.

After the mixture has cooled enough to handle, shape small pieces of the mixture into marble-size balls or bullet shapes. Place the suppositories in a labeled freezer bag or tin and store them in the freezer. Suppositories, like butters, will keep in the freezer for up to 18 months.

Allow suppositories to warm to room temperature in a covered container before using. Once the suppository has reached a comfortable temperature, insert it either rectally or vaginally depending on the condition being addressed. Dosages will depend on the health concern that is being addressed.

Selling Your Creations

If you decide to make a medicinal product line from your garden surplus, you will need to call your local health department to learn what requirements your kitchen must meet. It is also mandatory that you design labels that meet FDA labeling regulations, even if you have only have a very small business. The FDA requires label compliance for all products sold that are prepared for health or food use. Contact the FDA's Washington, D.C., office (see Resources for more information); ask for a list of product regulations. You must also obtain information on sales tax licenses and other business regulations from your city, state, and county government offices.

▶ tammi's pessary

This formula is useful as a suppository for vaginal infections or as a butter for infected minor cuts.

- 1 ounce melted cocoa butter
- ½ teaspoon powdered echinacea root
- ¼ teaspoon powdered marsh mallow root
- ¼ teaspoon powdered yerba mansa root
- 1–2 drops pure tea tree essential oil

Follow the directions above for making a suppository or butter. Use as directed above, depending on the health concern.

A common muslin drawstring bag is the perfect way to contain herbs for an herbal bath.

Baths and Foot Soaks

Few things in life can compare with how good an herbal bath or foot soak will make you feel. Both treatments are easy to do and can be used for all types of ailments — from hives and stress relief, to more serious conditions like respiratory infections and sinus conditions.

To prepare an herbal bath: Put a large handful (approximately ½ cup) of dried herbs in the center of a washcloth. Pull up the corners and secure into a bundle with a string or rubber band. Alternatively, you can place the herbs in a drawstring muslin bag. Throw the bundle into the tub while the water is running. You are basically making a giant tea out of the bathwater. Adjust the water temperature to make it comfortable, and climb in. Soak for at least 20 minutes, longer if you have the time. When you're finished with your bath, discard the herbs into the compost pile and launder the washcloth.

To prepare a foot soak: Foot soaks are more concentrated than herbal baths. Place a generous handful (approximately ½ cup) of herbs in a large washbasin and pour in 2 quarts (1.9 l) of boiling water. (In a pinch, I have been known to use a large roasting pan for foot soaks. They work great for bigger feet!) Allow the herbs to steep for 10 minutes, then add enough cold water to make the temperature comfortably hot. Soak your feet until the water is cool. Dry your feet and massage them with an herbal infused oil. Put on clean cotton socks, and you will no doubt feel much better.

For a foot soak, combine herbs and boiling water in a basin. Add some cool water, then soak your feet.

 Super Soaks

- **Peppermint** foot soak for increased circulation
- **Sage, echinacea, and ginger** foot soak for colds and flus
- **Passionflower and lemon balm** foot soak for stress relief
- **California poppy** foot soak for pain relief
- **Chamomile** bath soak for calming and soothing
- **Lavender and roses** bath soak for promoting restful sleep
- **Spearmint and lemon verbena** bath soak for lifting the spirits
- **Oat straw** bath soak for relieving itchy skin

Your sleep pillow can be made of a simple piece of cloth, or you can jazz it up with colorfully patterned materials.

Sleep Pillows

Sleep pillows — little herb-filled pillows that have aromatherapeutic effects — are used for concerns like chronic insomnia and headaches. They are even appropriate for individuals who are feeling a lot of anxiety and stress. Part of the therapeutic effect of using an herbal sleep pillow comes from making the pillow; they are fun to create!

To prepare a sleep pillow: Cut one 6- by 8-inch (15 by 20 cm) piece of cloth. (Any natural fiber cloth will do.) Fold the cloth in half, with the wrong sides together, and stitch up two sides of the cloth (leaving one end open). Turn the sewn cloth right side out. Put approximately ¼ cup of dried crushed herbs into the cloth pillow and stitch the open side closed. Slip the sleep pillow into your pillowcase on the side that will be next to your face. As you sleep, you will smell the herbal aromas, which will have a therapeutic effect on you.

 Sandman's Favorite Sleep Pillows

- **Hops and chamomile** are a good combination for restful sleep
- **Mugwort and rosemary** blend for vivid dreams
- **Lavender** prevents insomnia
- **Coyote** mint relieves sinus congestion ❧

Herbal Powder

This is the simplest preparation I know. Powders are dusted on topically to treat skin conditions like rashes and chafing. Powdered herbs are sometimes made into a paste with a bit of water and then taken internally. You can also make your own capsules (empty size 00 capsules are available at health food stores). However, herbs taken as a paste will be more fully absorbed than if they are in a capsulated form.

To prepare an herbal powder: Powder your herbs in a flour mill, spice mill, or blender. I usually don't prepare more than I can use in a short period of time, because once an herb has been powdered, it will lose its potency more quickly. Store powdered herbs in a glass jar with a tightly sealed lid. Place the jar in a location where it is out of direct sunlight and away from excessive heat (in other words, don't set a container next to your cooking stove). Label the jar and use the herbs within a week.

Herbs can be ground into a powder in a blender, spice mill, or even with a mortar and pestle.

 Herbs for Powders

- **Echinacea** has strong antibacterial properties
- **Rosemary** is a great antiseptic
- **Comfrey** promotes skin tissue regeneration
- **Plantain** removes the itch from insect bites
- **Goldenseal** relieves minor burns
- **Yerba mansa** has excellent antimicrobial properties ❧

Insect Repellent

The only part of the gardening season that I really dread is the mosquitoes and gnats that are out in full force. I prepare my own insect repellents to combat this problem, and they work very nicely without the added chemical ingredients that you'll find in commercial repellents. Here is the recipe that I use, but there are many variations; I enjoy creating a different version each time. Feel free to experiment to find the right ingredient combination for you.

To prepare an insect repellent: In a 2-ounce glass spray bottle, add 1 ounce of lavender infused oil, 1 ounce of aloe vera juice, and 3 to 4 drops of lemon verbena or pennyroyal essential oil (see caution box). Shake well before using. Spray onto the skin as needed, being careful to avoid the eye, ear, nose, and mouth areas. Insect repellents will last at least six to eight months.

Other essential oils that help repel insects include eucalyptus, rose geranium, and atlas cedarwood. Dried herbs and essential oils can also be used to help protect your pets from insects such as fleas and ticks. A combination of equal amounts of lavender flowers, cedarwood chips, and pennyroyal herb (*not* essential oil) can be added to the stuffing of an herb-repellent pillow for a cat or dog.

CAUTION: Essential Oil

Essential oils are highly concentrated botanicals and should not be used undiluted. Even a few drops of some oils can burn or irritate the skin. Pennyroyal essential oil is not appropriate for use by pregnant women or young children. It should also not be applied to cats as a flea repellent, since they clean themselves so often and can ingest the oil.

Empower Yourself with a Kitchen "Pharmacy"

As you become efficient at preparing your own remedies, you will find countless different ways to utilize the medicinal plants from your garden. There really is no end to the possibilities. You may decide that you enjoy making these items so much that you want to begin preparing them as gifts for friends and family. Or perhaps you'll want to make products to add income to your life. Whatever your reason for learning home medicine preparation, I am sure you will enjoy it and the feeling of empowerment you get from preparing your own botanical medicines.

Whatever preparation you choose to make, you'll no doubt find plenty of useful herbs in your garden.

Nine

enjoying
medicinal foods

As I have gotten older, I have thought more and more about the concept of incorporating my plant medicines into my foods. I am forever questioning the patterns that my generation grew up with, particularly the belief that a pill can cure anything and everything. Pills certainly have a small place in health care, but that place should be kept in perspective. It makes much more sense to use our daily whole foods as a source for not only nutrition, but also therapeutic healing.

It's my experience that using medicinal plants can be done in a tasty way more times than not. Tinctures and teas are fantastic and I rely on them daily, but isn't it wonderful to think of eating your medicines as a delicious part of your salad or spaghetti sauce? 🌿

Using Herbs Is Simple

In my quest to incorporate medicinal plants into our foods, I have discovered that this is really very easy to accomplish. The fact to remember is that each individual portion of the meal must include a therapeutic amount of the herb. We are very accustomed to using herbs as culinary seasonings — relying on those spunky herbs and spices to zest up our food — and little else. Now I would like to challenge you to think a bit differently about your cooking habits. Why not have a parsley salad instead of a lettuce salad? And who is to say that a pot roast cannot be made with burdock and dandelion roots combined with the carrots and potatoes? Just consider the possibilities!

The Japanese believe that color and presentation are as important to the meal as the taste of the food. I agree with them 100 percent. People in South America often make beans and rice a core part of their meals. I happen to love beans and rice and these are super foods for kidney health. However, these people also create the most amazing sauces to go with their bean dishes. Tomatoes, cilantro, epazote, and onions are all common ingredients in their cuisine. Healthy, healing, and yummy! The possibilities are endless and all that is required is a stroll through the garden to harvest fresh ingredients or a look through your dried-herb stores to see what treasures are waiting for you to find them.

While using medicinal herbs as food may seem strange, you'll soon discover their ability to turn an ordinary meal into an extraordinary treat.

Which Herbs to Use?

Your medicinal plant dishes will be delicious, of course, but they should also be specific to a health concern of yours, a family member, or perhaps friends. Someone who is working on urinary tract health will most certainly wish to incorporate therapeutic amounts of parsley and nettles into his or her diet. People who are thinking about a strong and healthy heart will be harvesting violet leaves and adding them to their salads. Stress-related health concerns absolutely should include a daily dose of oats — no exceptions.

Now you see what I mean. Just start thinking about which plants have which properties and then ponder how they can go into a meal in a therapeutic way. Also take into account the particular herb's flavor; some herbs are not very tasty to begin with. It's really easy to incorporate medicinal herbs into your meals, and here are some starting ideas to get you cooking.

Creative Ways to Use Edible Flowers

- Nasturtiums, violets, lavender blossoms: sprinkle in or on salads
- Calendula flowers: float in soups
- Roses, strawberry flowers, pinks (dianthus): decorate cakes and cookies
- Mint flowers, violets: add to tea or lemonade
- Raspberry flowers, roses, pinks (dianthus), calendula flowers: freeze in ice cubes for drinks
- Chive blossoms, violets, cilantro flowers, dill flowers: add to butter or cream cheese spreads
- Chive blossoms, nasturtiums: add to sandwiches
- Nasturtiums, chive flowers, dill flowers, squash blossoms: use in a flower omelet
- Red clover blossoms: add to oatmeal

Medicinal Salads

Many of our daily meals include a salad. Sometimes the main part of the meal is focused on a salad. Either way, this is a great way to use freshly harvested medicinal greens. It's also a lovely way to enjoy edible and medicinal flowers.

Choosing Ingredients

Prepare your green salad using herbs like dandelion leaves and flowers, parsley, and chicory leaves. There are many possibilities. Once you have prepared the green part of the salad, add other vegetables, such as celery, tomatoes, green peppers — whatever you like. Top off the salad with a generous portion of edible flowers and a sprinkling of sunflower seeds and wow! — just wait till you taste it. It's fabulous.

Here are some good herbal salad ingredients:

▸ **Alfalfa and sedum** provide nutrients for a whole-body tonic effect.

▸ **Basil, peppermint, spearmint, and parsley** promote good digestive function.

▸ **Borage, gotu kola, and dandelion** are fantastic for skin concerns.

▸ **Chicory and dandelion** support the liver, gallbladder, and urinary tract.

▸ **Marsh mallow, hollyhock, plantain, and peppermint** are valuable for intestinal issues.

▸ **Violets** support cardiovascular health.

▸ **Sunflowers** are excellent for reproductive health and respiratory conditions.

▸ medicinal salad

This tasty salad will support heart and urinary tract health, making it a wonderful spring, summer, or fall tonic treat. Many vinegar tinctures could be used to prepare a dressing for this salad. Serves 4–6.

1	pound baby salad greens
1	cup each violet leaves, marsh mallow leaves, and dandelion leaves
1	tomato, chopped
12–15	violet flowers
1/4	cup raw sunflower seeds

Toss together gently all ingredients and serve with an herbal vinegar and oil dressing of your choice.

▸ cottage cheese–gotu kola lunch salad

This salad is a great digestive aid, and it's also very good for supporting milk production in nursing moms. Serves 1.

1/2	cup cottage cheese
1/2	teaspoon dill seeds
4–6	gotu kola leaves
1 or 2	sprigs lemon thyme

In a bowl, stir together the cottage cheese and dill seeds. Allow the mixture to sit for 15 to 30 minutes; the cheese will soften the seeds, and the seeds will infuse the cheese with a delicious flavor. Just before serving, top the mixture with gotu kola and lemon thyme leaves.

▸ flower power salad

Rich in antioxidants, this salad will benefit the entire circulatory system. Serves 2.

2	tomatoes, sliced
1	green bell pepper, thinly sliced
4	fresh basil leaves
2	strawberry flowers
2	violet flowers
2	nasturtiums

Lay the tomato slices on two salad plates. Spread the pepper slices on top of the tomatoes. On top of the peppers, place one end of each basil leaf in the center of the plate to form a crosslike shape. Sprinkle the flowers on top of all, and add a tablespoon of herbal vinegar to flavor.

Add medicinal plants to your regular salad for a boost in flavor as well as nutrients.

Cooking with Medicinal Roots

Medicinal roots benefit many body systems, but they are especially good for the liver, gallbladder, pancreas, and urinary tract. Remember to wash the roots well before adding them to your dishes. Also keep in mind that roots often require a longer cooking time than do other vegetables.

Choosing Ingredients

We have all grown up eating carrots and turnips, but have you ever considered using dandelion or burdock roots instead? Dandelions are rich in iron and potassium; they also support good liver function and help balance blood sugar levels. Burdock is excellent for helping clear infections out of the bloodstream; it also promotes good skin health. Every teenager would appreciate the clear skin that burdock can facilitate. I cook both of these roots with chicken, roasts, and baked vegetables.

Fennel root is very good for the digestive tract; parsley roots help support urinary tract health. These hearty roots make wonderful additions to any stir-fry dish.

Enliven your stir-fries with an array of delicious fruits, vegetables, and herbs such as gingerroot.

▶ **ginger, rice, and everything nice**

A warming dish for people who often feel cold, this recipe is also good for relieving the sinus congestion, cough, and sore throat that accompany cold and flu season. Besides these benefits, it's absolutely delicious! Serves 2.

- 1 cup uncooked brown rice
- 3 cups water
- 2 tablespoons powdered vegetable broth (available at health-food stores)
- 2–3 tablespoons butter
- 1 onion, quartered and sliced
- 1 celery stalk, thinly sliced
- 3 mushrooms, sliced
- 4 cloves garlic, minced
- 1 red bell pepper, thinly sliced
- 1 tablespoon freshly grated ginger
- 2 tablespoons tamari or soy sauce

1. *In a 2-quart saucepan, place the rice, water, and powdered vegetable broth. Bring the ingredients to a boil over medium heat. Reduce the temperature and continue to simmer gently until the rice is tender and most of the liquid is absorbed.*

2. *In a saucepan, heat the butter over medium heat. Sauté the onion, celery, mushrooms, garlic, and pepper until tender and translucent.*

3. *Add the ginger and sauté for 3–5 minutes longer. Add the tamari or soy sauce and mix.*

4. *Serve the vegetables on top of the rice for a spicy meal.*

▸ roast beef

This hearty dish will make your liver happy and add a warm glow to your skin. If you'd prefer to have a rooty, all-vegetable celebration, simply substitute another potato and some mushrooms for the beef. Serves 6–8.

- 1 large roast from range-fed beef
- 2 onions, peeled and chopped
- 8 cloves of garlic, peeled and chopped
- 6–8 dandelion roots, chopped or sliced
- 1–3 burdock roots, chopped or sliced
- 2–4 hollyhock or marsh mallow roots, sliced
- 3–4 potatoes, chopped
- 4–6 carrots, sliced

1. *Preheat the oven to 400°F (205°C).*
2. *Place all ingredients in a large baking pan or roasting pan, with 1 to 2 inches of water in the bottom. Bake for 1 hour.*
3. *Lower temperature to 325°F (160°C); continue to cook 1½ to 2 hours longer, or until roast is tender, juicy, and done as desired.*

Fresh vegetables from the garden are the perfect companion for health-giving herbs.

▸ mashed potatoes, turnips, and parsley

Strengthen your kidneys and bladder with this fantastic recipe. Serves 4–6.

- 4 parsley roots
- 1 turnip
- 3 potatoes
- ½ stick butter (do not substitute margarine)
- ¼ teaspoon garlic powder
  Pinch of celery seed
- 1 cup sour cream
- ½ cup Parmesan cheese

1. *Wash the fresh vegetables and herbs. In a large saucepan boil the parsley roots, turnip, and potatoes until tender. Drain.*
2. *In a large bowl, mash the roots and potatoes with a potato masher. Add butter, garlic powder, and celery seed. Stir in the sour cream and cheese. Mix well.*
3. *Serve the mixture topped with sautéed vegetables of choice (my favorites are squash and carrots). Or serve as a side dish for a holiday dinner.*

Glorious Soups and Stews

I am a big fan of soups and stews. Just chop up all the ingredients, simmer for the better part of a day, and serve hot with a loaf of homemade bread. That's some version of heaven, by my standards.

Choosing Ingredients

Soups and stews are an easy way to incorporate medicinal herbs into the picture. A soup to help someone with a bladder infection might include delicious parsley, dandelion, nettles, and hollyhock. A person who is undergoing allopathic cancer treatments will surely appreciate a soothing soup prepared with astragalus and red clover to help support and nourish the body through the rigors of chemotherapy or radiation.

Soups and stews are extremely versatile. You can serve them at any time of the year, and make them with a multitude of fresh-from-the-garden ingredients.

 ## Super Soup Herbs

For variety, try some of these supreme soup and stew medicinal herbs:

- **Burdock** often gives welcome relief for joint conditions.
- **Calendula** acts a broth-coloring agent that is also a good astringent herb for the intestinal tract.
- **Marsh mallow and plantain** can soothe irritated mucous membranes.
- **Cilantro and lemongrass** are nice "coolers" for people who always feel overheated.
- **Dill** is a priority for digestive discomforts like flatulence and belching.
- **Lovage** may be substituted for celery and will be beneficial for a respiratory tract condition. It also aids digestion. 🌾

▶ gingered pumpkin soup

I love cooking this soup for a warming circulatory- and digestive-supporting meal. Winter squash may be substituted for the pumpkin. Serves 4–6.

1	tablespoon butter
3–4	whole marsh mallow plants, chopped
1	tablespoon chopped gingerroot
4	cups vegetable or chicken broth
4–6	cups baked pumpkin
½	cup cow's or soy milk

1. *Melt the butter in a skillet and sauté the marsh mallow and ginger until tender. Transfer to a large cooking pot, add the vegetable broth, and simmer gently for about 5 minutes, until the marsh mallow and ginger are softened.*

2. *In a blender, combine approximately 1 cup pumpkin, 1 cup broth mixture, and ⅛ cup milk. Puree until smooth.*

3. *Pour pureed soup into another large cooking pot; repeat the blending step until all the pumpkin has been pureed. Heat soup until just warmed through; do not boil.*

Herbs added to soups create the perfect nourishing meal for a cold winter evening.

▸ dilly potato soup

This is a good, nourishing soup for anyone recovering from illness, surgery, or exhaustion. It's also valuable for people who would like to decrease their amount of flatulence and belching. Serves 8–10.

        6 potatoes, cubed
        1 stalk celery, chopped
        1 cup fresh or frozen peas
        2 carrots, sliced
        1 onion, chopped
      3–4 cloves garlic, minced
     8–10 cups water
        3 tablespoons dill seed
        2 cups cow's or soy milk

1. *In a large soup pot, place the potatoes, celery, peas, carrots, onion, garlic, and water. Boil gently until the vegetables are tender.*

2. *Mix in dill seed. Pour soup into a blender, add the milk, and puree.*

3. *If necessary, rewarm the soup over low heat. Do not boil; it will easily scorch. Serve hot with salad or bread.*

▸ hearty vegetable soup

Perfect for the flu season, this soup helps relieve congestion of the sinuses and lungs. It also supports the immune system and helps relieve diarrhea. Serves 8–10.

     8–10 cups water
      6–8 teaspoons powdered vegetable broth
            (available at health-food stores)
        8 cloves garlic, peeled and chopped
        8 carrots, chopped
        2 potatoes, chopped
        2 onions, chopped
      1/4 cup fresh lovage root, chopped
        2 fresh burdock roots, chopped
      1/2 cup barley
      1/4 cup quinoa
    10–12 calendula flowers, crushed

1. *In a large soup pot, mix the water, powdered vegetable broth, vegetables, and roots. Bring to a boil over medium heat. Gently boil for 2–3 hours, adding more water if necessary to keep the soup consistency.*

2. *Reduce heat to simmering. Add the barley, quinoa, and calendula. Cook for 45–60 minutes.*

3. *When cooked well, serve the soup with fresh, warm bread with whipped or herbal honey.*

Dried herbs and spices add flavor and healing qualities to all of your favorite dishes.

Hearty Cereals, Whole Grains, and Breads

Whole grains and cereals nourish and support the nervous and immune systems. Despite their longer preparation time, breads are easier to prepare than most people imagine. Nurture yourself with these foods — you deserve it.

▸ blueberry-cinnamon muffins

For healthy eyes and better vision, add blueberries to your diet. With the addition of cinnamon, which will support vision through enhanced circulation, these muffins are a terrific choice for breakfast or snacking. Makes 12 muffins.

> 2½ cups whole wheat flour
> 3 teaspoons baking powder
> 1 teaspoon sea salt (optional)
> 1½ teaspoons ground cinnamon
> ⅓ cup honey
> 1 egg
> ¼ cup milk
> ¼ cup melted butter
> 1 cup fresh or frozen blueberries

1. *Grease or line muffin cups and preheat oven to 400°F (205°C). In a bowl, sift together the flour, baking powder, sea salt, and cinnamon.*

2. *In a separate bowl, beat together the honey, egg, and milk. Stir in the butter and dry ingredients and beat all just until moistened.*

3. *Fill muffin cups two-thirds full and bake for 20–25 minutes. Serve with honey or enjoy the muffins plain.*

Choosing Ingredients

Oats are certainly one of my favorite herbs, and daily consumption is absolutely necessary. High in calcium and protein, oats nourish the nervous system and the skin and support good bone health. They relieve itchy skin conditions, check stress levels, and act as an excellent reproductive-organ tonic. Eat your oatmeal and oatmeal cookies — that is my advice to every person on this planet!

Milk thistle and plantain seeds are both great when ground up and added to hot cereals, rice dishes, and homemade breads. Whenever you prepare a pan of quinoa or bulgur, toss in a handful of red clover blossoms, sunflower seeds, and a pinch of sage for a delicious extra touch.

What could be more delicious — and nutritious — than breads infused with fabulous herbs such as dill, fennel, and garlic?

Bread Winners

Enhance those whole grains and homemade breads with these herbs:

• **Dill and fennel** added to breads are delicious, promote good digestion, and relieve discomfort associated with heartburn.

• **Lovage** is a fantastic addition to rice and lentil dishes and the perfect ticket when someone is recovering from a respiratory infection.

• **Blueberries** contribute to good vision and are a sweet addition to breads and cereals.

• **Cinnamon,** a delicious spice, also helps improve digestion and circulation. ❦

▸ licorice and banana oatmeal

Perfect for the flu season, this soup helps relieve congestion of the sinuses and lungs. It also supports the immune system and helps relieve diarrhea. Serves 1.

½ ripe banana, mashed well
1–2 pinches of powdered licorice root
1 bowl of well-cooked oatmeal (use regular or organic uncooked oats, not the quick-cooking or pre-cooked variety)
Organic milk (optional)

Blend the banana and licorice into the bowl of oatmeal. Add a little organic milk, if desired, and enjoy.

Medicinal Seasonings

Throughout your cooking experiences you will find that you'll sometimes need to season a dish in a more traditional way. But can medicinal herbs be used in this way? Absolutely! Herbs can be used either fresh or dried as spices. The more you use fresh herbs, the more you will spoil yourself! I prefer fresh over dried herbs when both are available.

Consider filling a pepper mill with chaste berry seeds. These have a spicy black pepper taste and have been used as a seasoning in Europe since the Middle Ages. Chaste berry is considered a reproductive tonic herb for both women and men.

Try garnishing a baked potato with a tablespoon of fresh, chopped rosemary. Rosemary is known to bring oxygen to the brain and support memory function. Best of all, it's very tasty!

Of course, we are all familiar with Greek oregano as a seasoning, but did you know that it is also a strong antioxidant herb? Use it regularly for this benefit.

▸ whole grains/poultry seasoning

Add a little zing with this blend. Makes 1¾ cups.

¼ cup dried marjoram
¼ cup dried basil
¼ cup dried parsley leaf
¼ cup dried lemon peel
⅓ cup dried sage
¼ cup dried savory
¼ cup dried celery leaves or ⅛ cup celery seed

Combine all herbs and blend well. Powder in a spice grinder or blender. Store in a glass jar with tight-fitting lid.

▸ hearty quinoa-bean chili

Quinoa and beans both offer a great source of protein. The beans also support kidney health, while the cumin, garlic, and chili powder improve digestion and circulation. Serves 6–8.

  1 cup dry pinto or adzuki beans
  2 tablespoons olive oil
  1 red or green bell pepper, chopped
  1 medium onion, chopped
  2 cloves garlic, minced
  1 teaspoon cumin seeds
10 cups water
  1 (6-inch) piece of kelp
2–3 teaspoons chili powder
 ⅔ cup quinoa
  1 cup fresh or frozen corn

1. *Place beans in a bowl; cover with water, and allow to soak 8–10 hours or overnight. Drain and rinse.*
2. *In a large soup pot, heat the olive oil over medium. Sauté the pepper, onion, garlic, and cumin seeds until the vegetables are tender.*
3. *Add the water, beans, kelp, chili powder, quinoa, and corn and mix well. Cook 1–2 hours, or until beans are tender.*
4. *Just before serving, remove the kelp. Top the chili with a sprinkling of cheese, if desired. Serve with freshly baked cornbread or tortillas.*

Other Ways to Create Therapeutic Dishes

So you've got some vegetables or perhaps a side dish or appetizer that needs a little something extra. What can you do to incorporate your medicinal herbs into these dishes? Here are a few easy tips.

Epazote is a traditional Mexican medicinal herb that is used in food preparation. This herb is added conservatively to bean dishes during the long cooking time. It is considered helpful in preventing parasites and worms when used in this way on a fairly regular basis.

▸ refreshing mint- and fruit-infused water

One of the nicest treats I can make is a sparkling glass pitcher filled with this delicious flavored water. It is excellent for the digestive tract, but more important, it's fabulous for lifting the spirits and cooling off on a hot summer gardening afternoon.

 ½ gallon spring, well, or good-quality tap water
  Several sprigs fresh peppermint or spearmint
2–3 strawberries, sliced
 ½ orange, sliced

1. *Fill a pitcher almost to the top with water. Add the mint sprigs and fruit. Let the water infuse in the refrigerator for at least 30 minutes.*
2. *To serve, pour the water into a tall glass over ice. Sip and enjoy!*

Prickly pear has been studied as a medicinal food for diabetic people because it is so effective at balancing blood sugar levels. Native American people of the Southwest and Latin America have been cooking it as a vegetable for years. I find it very delicious when prepared with onions, garlic, peppers, and potatoes.

Feverfew is a highly researched herb that relieves migraine headache. British folk prepare feverfew-and-butter sandwiches as a way to take their daily dose of feverfew leaves.

Catnip pesto is a wonderful way to calm down and relax. Simply substitute catnip for half the basil in your favorite pesto recipe.

▶ dandelion fritters

These fritters have earned quite a reputation around our house with friends, family, and students. They taste like breaded spinach rolls, and while your taste buds are enjoying the flavors, your liver is enjoying the tonic support of the dandelion flowers. Makes 1 large fritter.

> 1–2 tablespoons olive oil or butter
> 1 onion, chopped
> ½ red, green, or yellow bell pepper, chopped
> Seasoning herbs of choice (I like celery seed, garlic, and onion powder)
> ½ cup flour
> 2 cups dandelion flowers, stemmed and rinsed (leave them moist)

1. *Heat the butter or oil in a large cast-iron skillet. Add the onion and bell pepper and sauté until translucent, about 5 minutes.*

2. *While the onion and pepper are cooking, mix your favorite seasoning herbs, to taste, into the flour.*

3. *Gently toss the moist dandelion flowers in the flour mixture until they are well coated. Add them to the skillet as flavoring and sauté until the dandelions are golden brown. Serve dandelion fritters plain or dip in ranch dressing.*

Try infused oil and herbal vinegars on your next salad, or use them as a dip for breads and fresh vegetables.

Be creative! Combine fresh fruits and herbs in salads, beverages, and even desserts. Taking your medicine will never be the same.

▸ hot ginger–echinacea lemonade

This drink is excellent as an expectorant tea, a sore throat soother, or a warming beverage on a cold winter day. Serves 2.

> 2 cups boiling water
> 1 teaspoon dried echinacea flowers or roots
> 1 teaspoon finely chopped fresh gingerroot
> Juice of 1 freshly squeezed lemon
> 1 teaspoon honey

In a bowl or teapot, pour the boiling water over the echinacea and gingerroot. Cover and steep for 10–15 minutes. Add the lemon juice and honey and stir. Serve warm.

▸ hot spiced apple juice

An excellent drink to support good digestion and circulation, this spicy take on an old favorite is great for sipping when diarrhea is a problem. It's also a wonderful beverage for holidays and other festive occasions. Serves 2.

> 2 cups organic apple juice
> 1 cinnamon stick, broken into pieces
> 3–6 whole cloves
> 3–6 whole allspice berries

In a saucepan, warm the juice over low heat. Add the spices and continue to heat to just below boiling, 10–15 minutes. Strain out the spices. Serve hot.

Ten

a gardener's materia medica

The purpose of this chapter is to help you get better acquainted with the individual medicinal herbs. Every plant will have its own specific growing needs, as well as harvesting and processing requirements. Each of them has a unique health gift for us; there just cannot be a blanket rule for all of them. Take some time to review this chapter and then keep it handy for future reference.

A *materia medica* is a type of literature that contains written descriptions and pictures of medicinal plants. One of the earliest herbal texts, called *Materia Medica,* was written by the ancient Roman physician Dioscorides around A.D. 77. You won't find that many plants here, but take this opportunity to learn about the plants that interest you. 🌾

Get Acquainted

Knowing just a bit about where a certain plant would live in nature helps me when I am trying to decide where to place it. Understanding plant personality traits will help you design a garden with plants that are appropriate to your land, climate, and personal health needs.

Be familiar with both growing and propagation requirements of your herbs; they may be more involved than you think, and it's never fun to find out the hard way. I present here information gleaned from my personal experiences and information shared with me by other growers. Keep in mind that plants often have a will of their own and each time you grow them you're bound to find that something is slightly different. Be flexible and respectful, and you will achieve success.

You'll also find here information on the best times to harvest, as well as market potential. Of course, demand changes over time; always do your research before making major commitments.

I've included a guide to what types of medicinal preparations are most suitable for each herb. To find more detailed information on usage, dosage, and cautions, be sure to consult a reliable reference book (see Recommended Reading).

Now, let me introduce you to 101 of my dearest friends. You may know some by other common names, listed as A.K.A. (also known as).

If you live in North America, use this map to determine which growing zone you are in. It will be much easier to grow perennials if you know in what zones they are considered hardy.

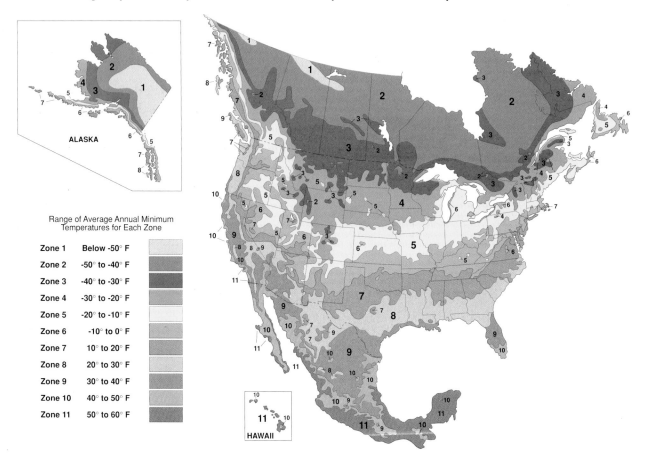

Range of Average Annual Minimum Temperatures for Each Zone

Zone 1	Below -50° F
Zone 2	-50° to -40° F
Zone 3	-40° to -30° F
Zone 4	-30° to -20° F
Zone 5	-20° to -10° F
Zone 6	-10° to 0° F
Zone 7	10° to 20° F
Zone 8	20° to 30° F
Zone 9	30° to 40° F
Zone 10	40° to 50° F
Zone 11	50° to 60° F

ALASKA

HAWAII

Achillea millefolium

Yarrow

Native American people call the yarrow plant chipmunk tail because the leaf looks just like the tail of the tiny creatures. The lacy texture of yarrow leaves can add a charming look to a garden. Although some varieties of yarrow have yellow flowers, these flowers should *not* be used medicinally. ✿

✾ Yarrow at a Glance

- ▸ **Plant Cycle:** Perennial
- ▸ **Type of Growth:** Herbaceous
- ▸ **Light Requirements:** Full sun, partial shade
- ▸ **Water Requirements:** Low to moderate

- ▸ **Parts Used:** Aerial
- ▸ **Home Pharmacy Uses:** Infusion, traditional tincture, cider vinegar tincture, syrup, compress, poultice, elixir, lozenge, ointment, salve, cream, balm, foot soak, bath herb, infused oil, honey, liniment

Personality: Perennial; herbaceous (Zones 3–9)

Height: 2 to 3 feet (.6 to .9 meter)

Bloom Traits: White flowers appear in mid- to late summer.

Likes/Dislikes: Yarrow can be found growing in open, grassy areas such as mountain meadows and prairies. It prefers disturbed soil areas and grows only in temperate climates.

Propagation/Maintenance: Stratify seeds for a month before sowing. Sow indoors and transplant outside in mid- to late spring, or sow directly outdoors in early spring. Germination is around 70 percent; sprouting occurs in 7 to 14 days. Root divisions are another easy way to propagate yarrow. Take divisions in spring or fall for ideal results. Yarrow will spread, and needs to be spaced 12 inches (30 centimeters) apart. Provide plants low to moderate amounts of water.

Sun/Soil: Full sun or partial shade; prefers well-drained soil

Harvesting: Harvest the aerial parts in mid- to late summer, preferably while the plant is in full flower. Snips or scissors work well.

Market Potential: Moderate; because flowers are more labor-intensive to harvest and command a higher price, be sure to discuss whether your buyer wants just flowers or flowering aerial parts

Medicinal Benefits: Yarrow is used for women's and children's health concerns, winter illnesses and respiratory conditions, the throat and the skin, and for gastrointestinal health. It is also considered beneficial for circulation and muscle aches.

Parts Used: Flowering aerial parts, fresh or dried

Home Pharmacy Uses: Infusion, traditional tincture, cider vinegar tincture, syrup, compress, poultice, elixir, lozenge, ointment, salve, cream, balm, foot soak, bath herb, infused oil, honey, liniment

Agastache foeniculum
Anise Hyssop

The beautiful anise hyssop will draw admiring looks from all your friends. It will attract butterflies, hummingbirds, and honeybees, all excellent pollinators. At dusk it is irresistible to the hummingbird moth. 🐝

Personality: Perennial; herbaceous (Zones 6–10)

Height: 2 to 3 feet (.6 to .9 meter)

Bloom Traits: Spikes of rich purple flowers bloom off and on throughout the summer.

Likes/Dislikes: Anise hyssop, like other members of the *Agastache* genus, grows in sunny areas. It prefers the lower mountain elevations.

Propagation/Maintenance: Sow the seeds out in late spring or start early in a greenhouse and transplant out after the danger of frost has passed. Expect 70 to 80 percent germination, in about 2 weeks. Anise hyssop grows as a clump, but readily reseeds itself to the surrounding area. Provide light to moderate water, and space plants 15 inches (38 centimeters) apart.

Sun/Soil: Full sun, partial shade; grows well in poorer clay, gravelly, or sandy soils

Companion/Complementary Planting: Horehound, chamomile; festive when planted next to spilanthes

Harvesting: Harvest all the aerial parts, preferably while in flower, using a pair of snips or scissors.

Market Potenial: Low to moderate

Medicinal Benefits: Supports digestion, soothes lower respiratory tract irritation, and helps lower fevers

Parts Used: Flowering aerial parts, fresh or dried

Home Pharmacy Uses: Infusion, traditional tincture, cider vinegar tincture, syrup, elixir, lozenge, balm, foot soak, bath herb, honey

Alcea rosea
Hollyhock

Many people grow hollyhock in their gardens, but not many folks realize that this plant has edible flowers as well as medicinal properties in the flowers, leaves, and roots. Enjoy both its beauty and health benefits. 🐝

Personality: Perennial; herbaceous (Zones 3–9)

Height: 6 to 8 feet (1.8 to 2.4 meters)

Bloom Traits: Flowers mainly in pinks, reds, whites, and yellows. Blooming begins in midsummer and often continues until early fall.

Likes/Dislikes: A garden plant only, hollyhocks are grown throughout the temperate parts of the world.

Propagation/Maintenance: You'll get more consistent results if you stratify seeds for a few weeks and then sow indoors. Germination is usually about 70 percent, and sprouting takes place in about 2 weeks. Transplant outside after danger of frost is past. I germinate them at a nighttime temperature of 70°F (21°C). Space 15 inches (38 centimeters) apart; plants will grow in clumps. Water moderately.

Sun/Soil: Prefers full sun and loamy soil; adaptable

Companion/Complementary Planting: Grow with licorice, lemon balm, and feverfew

Harvesting: Leaves are handpicked or snipped at any time during the growing season. Flowers are handpicked when in bloom. Roots are dug up with a needle-nose spade in late summer or early fall.

Market Potenial: Poor; marsh mallow is preferred

Medicinal Benefits: Used for the gastrointestinal tract and as a soothing herb for throat conditions

Parts Used: Leaves, flowers, and roots, fresh or dried

Home Pharmacy Uses: Decoction, traditional tincture, compress, poultice, medicinal food, ointment, salve, cream, balm

Personality: Tender perennial; woody (Zones 8–11)

Height: 3 to 4 feet (.9 to 1.2 meters)

Bloom Traits: Delicate, fragrant white flowers bloom in mid- to late summer.

Likes/Dislikes: A tropical plant that is only a garden guest for subtropical and temperate regions, it is also an extensive farm crop in some tropical regions.

Propagation/Maintenance: Take softwood tip cuttings and use liquid or powder rooting hormone. Cuttings require extra heat; we keep night temperatures at 65 to 70°F (18 to 21°C) and daytime temperatures in the high 80s and 90s (30 to 37°C). Provide good air circulation, and keep cuttings consistently moist. Rooting percentage varies greatly with sunlight exposure and temperature. Put cuttings under lights for 14 to 20 hours per day while rooting. Transplant outdoors only after weather is warm and well settled in temperate climates. Bring indoors before fall frost. In tropical climates, lemon verbena is grown year-round. It grows in clumps; plants should be spaced 12 to 15 inches (30 to 38 centimeters) apart. Provide it with moderate to high amounts of water.

Sun/Soil: Sun, partial shade; prefers rich soil, but will tolerate poor soil if given enough water and fish emulsion fertilizer

Harvesting: Cut aerial parts, with snips, in mid- to late summer. Dry, then strip leaves from stems. Discard stems. Leaves may be handpicked; use immediately after harvest.

Market Potential: High

Medicinal Benefits: Used as a calming digestive tea and as a calming sleep herb, it is also a common ingredient in herbal insect repellents.

Parts Used: Leaves and flowers, fresh or dried

Home Pharmacy Uses: Infusion, cider vinegar tincture, elixir, sleep pillow, honey, insect repellent

Aloysia triphylla

Lemon Verbena

Certified organic lemon verbena will be in great demand, as long as it is harvested and dried properly to preserve the high levels of volatile oils. This is a primary ingredient in herbal teas; tea companies would be good places to solicit if you can successfully grow this herb without synthetic chemicals. 🌿

Lemon Verbena at a Glance

▸ **Plant Cycle:** Tender perennial

▸ **Type of Growth:** Woody

▸ **Light Requirements:** Sun, partial shade

▸ **Water Requirements:** Moderate to heavy

▸ **Parts Used:** Leaves, flowers

▸ **Home Pharmacy Uses:** Infusion, cider vinegar tincture, elixir, sleep pillow, honey, insect repellent

Althaea officinalis
Marsh Mallow

In the late 1800s, a confection called marshmallow was made from the roots of this herb. The roots were cooked with sugar and whipped until they were light and airy. Although the resulting sweet treat is different from the modern-day marshmallow (which is made up mostly of corn syrup), this is where that campfire favorite originated. 🌿

Personality: Perennial; herbaceous (Zones 5–8)

Height: 3 to 4 feet (.9 to 1.2 meters)

Bloom Traits: Very pale pink flowers bloom up the stalk from mid- to late summer.

Likes/Dislikes: Marsh mallow prefers open meadows near streams, lakes, or ponds.

Propagation/Maintenance: Stratify seeds for several weeks. Seeds may be planted outside as soon as the soil can be worked. They can also be sown indoors and transplanted outside in mid- to late spring. Expect good germination of 70 to 80 percent. Sprouting takes 2 to 3 weeks. Marsh mallow will grow in clumps, and should be spaced 12 inches (30 centimeters) apart. Water moderately.

Sun/Soil: Sun, partial shade, shade; prefers a loamy soil

Harvesting: Harvest the roots in the spring or fall. They are large and deep, so use a needle-nose spade or a garden fork. Leaves and flowers may be handpicked at any time during the growing season.

Market Potential: Moderate

Medicinal Benefits: A soothing herb for the gastrointestinal tract, urinary tract, and throat, marsh mallow is often used for winter illnesses and to alleviate skin conditions.

Parts Used: Roots, leaves, and flowers, fresh or dried

Home Pharmacy Uses: Infusion, decoction, traditional tincture, cider vinegar tincture, syrup, elixir, lozenge, compress, poultice, medicinal food, ointment, salve, cream, balm, infused oil, honey, powder

---

⚘ Marsh Mallow at a Glance

- **Plant Cycle:** Perennial
- **Type of Growth:** Herbaceous
- **Light Requirements:** Sun, partial shade, shade
- **Water Requirements:** Moderate to high

- **Parts Used:** Roots, leaves, flowers
- **Home Pharmacy Uses:** Infusion, decoction, traditional tincture, cider vinegar tincture, syrup, elixir, lozenge, compress, poultice, medicinal food, ointment, salve, cream, balm, infused oil, honey, powder

Anemopsis californica

Yerba Mansa

Yerba mansa is enjoying good market demand due to the fact that it can often be substituted for goldenseal, an at-risk herb. There is concern about yerba mansa being overharvested from wild populations, and cultivation is strongly encouraged. It is tricky to grow, however, and may not be the right plant for everyone. ✺

✺ Yerba Mansa at a Glance

▶ **Plant Cycle:** Perennial

▶ **Type of Growth:** Herbaceous

▶ **Light Requirements:** Full sun, partial shade

▶ **Water Requirements:** Moderate to high

▶ **Parts Used:** Whole plant, roots

▶ **Home Pharmacy Uses:** Decoction, traditional tincture, syrup, elixir, lozenge, ointment, salve, balm, foot soak, infused oil, suppository, powder, liniment

Personality: Perennial; herbaceous (Zones 5–10)

Height: 12 inches (30 centimeters)

Bloom Traits: Conical flowers with white petals bloom in late spring to early summer.

Likes/Dislikes: This is a desert plant that is native to the southwestern parts of North America. It prefers hot climates and chooses to grow near water sources, like ponds, streams, and lakes.

Propagation/Maintenance: Seeds often benefit from a 3 percent hydrogen peroxide soak for 10 minutes or a gibberellic acid (growth hormone) treatment just before sowing. Sow indoors in a very warm greenhouse. Seeds require daytime temperatures of 90 to 104°F (32 to 40°C) for 1 to 2 weeks and constant nighttime temperatures between 60 and 70°F (15 to 21°C). Keep seeds well watered before and after sprouting. Sprouting takes place in 4 to 6 weeks, at a germination rate of 70 to 80 percent. Transplant outside, 12 inches (30 centimeters) apart, in early summer when temperatures are well settled and warm. Yerba mansa will spread, and requires moderate to heavy watering.

Sun/Soil: Full sun, partial shade; prefers a moist, alkaline soil that is reasonably high in organic matter

Harvesting: If it has been a very hot growing season with abundant water available, harvest the roots or whole plants in the fall of the first year. If growing under normal conditions, harvest in the spring or fall of the second year. I prefer to allow the plants to go to seed before harvesting them. Use a garden fork to lift the plants from the soil. Any runners that were attached to harvested plants should be replanted in the field.

Market Potential: High

Medicinal Benefits: Used for acute stages of winter illnesses and respiratory conditions, and for lymphatic support

Parts Used: Whole plant and roots, fresh or dried

Home Pharmacy Uses: Decoction, traditional tincture, syrup, elixir, lozenge, ointment, salve, balm, foot soak, infused oil, suppository, powder, liniment

Anethum graveolens
Dill

Have you ever wondered why pregnant women or people who have the flu crave dill pickles? Dill is calming and soothing to an upset stomach, and eating dill pickles is one easy way to get the much-needed herb into our bodies. You can prepare dill tincture to use for the same effect. 🌿

Personality: Annual; herbaceous

Height: 3 to 5 feet (.9 to 1.5 meters)

Bloom Traits: Large umbels of small yellow flowers bloom from mid- to late summer.

Likes/Dislikes: A traditional garden herb, dill prefers not to compete for space with weeds or other plants.

Propagation/Maintenance: Dill is easily grown from seed and can be sown directly into the garden. It may also be started indoors and transplanted outside after all danger of frost is past. Seeds germinate within 1 to 3 weeks at a rate of 50 to 60 percent. Germination is usually very consistent. Space these plants 10 to 12 inches (25 to 30 centimeters) apart. Water moderately.

Sun/Soil: Full sun; prefers well-drained soil

Companion/Complementary Planting: Tomatoes, chilies, sweet peppers, strawberries, and thyme

Harvesting: Harvest seeds and leafy parts with a small pair of scissors in mid-July to late August.

Market Potential: Low to moderate; widely used in the culinary market, but rarely used medicinally

Medicinal Benefits: Dill is often recommended for discomforts associated with poor digestive function.

Parts Used: Seeds and leaves, fresh or dried

Home Pharmacy Uses: Infusion, traditional tincture, cider vinegar tincture, syrup, elixir, medicinal food, honey

Angelica archangelica
Angelica

Angelica is gaining recognition as a substitute herb for the environmentally at-risk osha plant *(Ligusticum porteri)*. It is often combined with herbs like rosemary and yerba mansa for optimum benefit. 🌿

Personality: Biennial or monocarpic perennial; herbaceous (Zones 4–9)

Height: 4 to 6 feet (1.2 to 1.8 meters)

Bloom Traits: Umbels have clusters of yellowish green flowers.

Likes/Dislikes: Angelica grows in moist soil and partial shade, usually near streams in sandy/loamy soil.

Propagation/Maintenance: Sow seeds immediately upon ripening or store in the freezer until ready to sow. Expect between 30 and 50 percent germination, depending on seed freshness. Sprouting usually occurs in 3 to 4 weeks. Transplant outdoors 1 to 2 weeks before the last frost. Space plants 15 inches (38 centimeters) apart. Angelica grows in clumps with a large taproot system. It needs moderate to heavy watering.

Sun/Soil: Shade, partial shade, full sun; prefers a richer loam soil, but is tolerant of clay or sandy soils that are rich in organic matter

Harvesting: First-year roots may be harvested in late fall, whereas second-year roots should be dug in early spring; use a needle-nose spade or fork. Harvest stalks with snips any time during the growing season.

Market Potential: Moderate to high

Medicinal Benefits: A circulatory-enhancing herb, angelica is also a mild expectorant.

Parts Used: Roots and stalks, fresh or dried

Home Pharmacy Uses: Decoction, traditional tincture, cider vinegar tincture, syrup, crystallized, elixir, honey

Arctium lappa

Burdock

Burdock or gobo, as it is also called, has long been considered a mainstay vegetable in Asian cultures. Burdock is also widely used in herbal products. The difficulty is convincing consumers that they should buy organically grown burdock rather than wild-harvested plants. But as more concern is raised, many buyers are beginning to appreciate the reliability that comes with organic certification. 🌿

Burdock at a Glance

- ▸ **Plant Cycle:** Biennial
- ▸ **Type of Growth:** Herbaceous
- ▸ **Light Requirements:** Full sun, partial shade, shade
- ▸ **Water Requirements:** Moderate

- ▸ **Parts Used:** Roots, seeds
- ▸ **Home Pharmacy Uses:** Decoction, traditional tincture, cider vinegar tincture, syrup, compress, poultice, elixir, medicinal food, ointment, salve, cream, balm, foot soak, bath herb, infused oil

A.K.A.: Gobo, great burdock

Personality: Biennial; herbaceous

Height: 3 to 4 feet (.9 to 1.2 meters)

Bloom Traits: Green immature burs with a pink center do not occur until late in the summer of the second year. As they become mature, they form seed and turn a tannish color.

Likes/Dislikes: Burdock is commonly found along rivers and streams in the shade or partial shade of big old trees. It also likes open waste ground with slightly alkaline soil.

Propagation/Maintenance: Sow seeds direct into the garden early in spring. Seeds will germinate at nearly 80 to 90 percent if stratified first. If the seeds are not stratified, germination will be slightly less, but only marginally so. Burdock can be started indoors and transplanted out, but it grows very fast in a pot and will need to be transplanted within a very short time. Space 18 inches (45 centimeters) apart and water moderately. Burdock plants themselves do not spread, but they readily self-sow, and one plant can easily become a colony in the third year.

Sun/Soil: Full sun, partial shade, shade; loamy soil is preferred, but nearly any type of soil will do

Harvesting: The roots are harvested either in the fall of the first year's growth or in the spring of the second year's growth. These deep taproots will require a needle-nose spade or a garden fork to lift them out of the soil. The seed burs may be picked in the late fall of the second year's growth. Do not harvest burs that are left over from the previous year's plants in the spring; they will most certainly be full of bugs.

Market Potential: Moderate to high

Medicinal Benefits: Burdock is a great medicinal food that offers excellent support to the liver, urinary tract, and skin.

Parts Used: Roots and seeds, fresh or dried

Home Pharmacy Uses: Decoction, traditional tincture, cider vinegar tincture, syrup, compress, poultice, elixir, medicinal food, ointment, salve, cream, balm, foot soak, bath herb, infused oil

Artemisia species
Wormwood

Wormwood has a strong tradition of use as a remedy for many ailments. Historically, it was used to treat seasickness, gout, intoxication, and food poisoning. This is a very strong herb, and it's best to seek the advice of a healthcare professional before using. 🌿

Personality: Perennial; herbaceous (Zones 4–9)

Height: 12 inches (30 centimeters) and taller

Bloom Traits: White to yellow flowers that are not usually very showy bloom in late summer or fall.

Likes/Dislikes: Native to open, grassy areas of mountain meadows and prairies, wormwoods often grow in very hot, dry conditions and disturbed soil areas.

Propagation/Maintenance: Stratify seeds for several weeks. Then sow directly outdoors in early spring, or plant indoors and transplant outside in mid- to late spring. Germination is around 50 percent, but varies among species. Root divisions, done in the spring or fall, are the easiest way to propagate. Cuttings tend to be less successful; they are very susceptible to botrytis and overwatering. Space this spreader 12 to 15 inches (30 to 38 centimeters) apart and water lightly.

Sun/Soil: Full sun; well-drained soil

Companion/Complementary Planting: Penstemon, thyme, yucca, and brickellia. It repels most insects.

Harvesting: Harvest aerial parts with snips or scissors at any time during the growing season.

Market Potential: Low

Medicinal Benefits: Primarily for gastrointestinal and women's health concerns, wormwood should be used only with the supervision of an experienced herbalist.

Parts Used: Aerial parts, fresh or dried

Home Pharmacy Uses: Infusion, traditional tincture, cider vinegar tincture

Artemisia vulgaris
Mugwort

During the Middle Ages, people believed that putting a leaf of mugwort in their shoes would prevent them from becoming weary. The herb was reputed to allow the traveler to walk 40 miles before noon! 🌿

A.K.A.: Cronewort

Personality: Perennial; herbaceous (Zones 4–8)

Height: 4 to 5 feet (1.2 to 1.5 meters)

Bloom Traits: Spikes of whitish green flowers pale in comparison to the stunning purple stems and green leaves with silvery undersides.

Likes/Dislikes: Mugwort comes from Mediterranean mountain regions, where it is commonly found growing in disturbed areas.

Propagation/Maintenance: Stratify the seeds for several weeks and then sow indoors. Germination takes about 2 weeks and sprouting is near 70 percent. Without stratification, you can expect closer to 50 percent germination. Transplant outdoors in mid- to early spring. Mugwort does stay in a clump, but it grows quite large; space plants 15 to 20 inches (38 to 50 centimeters) apart. Water lightly to moderately.

Sun/Soil: Full sun, partial shade; no special soil needs

Harvesting: Aerial parts may be harvested with snips or scissors at any time during the growing season.

Market Potential: Low

Medicinal Benefits: Mugwort is primarily used for menopause symptoms in women and digestive tract support.

Parts Used: Aerial parts, fresh or dried

Home Pharmacy Uses: Infusion, traditional tincture, cider vinegar tincture, syrup, elixir, ointment, salve, cream, balm, foot soak, sleep pillow, bath herb, infused oil, honey, liniment

Asclepias asperula

Inmortal

At this point, inmortal is not heavily burdened in the wild, but only because its medicinal use does not go broadly beyond the regions to which it is native. It is not being cultivated, to my knowledge, except at our farm, and there are several herbal product lines that use this herb as an ingredient. I would like to see more farms grow this plant, and I would like for product manufacturers to use inmortal only from certified organically grown sources to prevent wild harvesting. 🌿

🌿 Inmortal at a Glance

- ▸ **Plant Cycle:** Perennial
- ▸ **Type of Growth:** Herbaceous
- ▸ **Light Requirements:** Full sun
- ▸ **Water Requirements:** Low
- ▸ **Parts Used:** Roots
- ▸ **Home Pharmacy Uses:** Decoction, traditional tincture, syrup, powder

A.K.A.: Antelope horns

Personality: Perennial; herbaceous (Zones 4–6)

Height: 12 to 15 inches (30 to 38 centimeters)

Bloom Traits: Beautiful mauve and cream-colored clusters of flowers bloom in the spring.

Likes/Dislikes: Inmortal grows in the high desert regions of the southwestern parts of North America. It can be found growing in dry, poor soil, but often in wash areas or on slopes that receive adequate spring moisture.

Propagation/Maintenance: Root divisions are one way to propagate inmortal. They are best done in early spring. Inmortal can also be grown by seed. Seeds benefit from stratification and scarification. I also do a warm-water soak for 1 hour before sowing them. Sow seeds indoors and transplant outside in late spring, or sow outdoors directly in the very early spring. Germination takes 2 to 3 weeks and is considered marginal at 30 to 40 percent. Space 24 inches (60 centimeters) apart; this herb will spread. Water lightly.

Sun/Soil: Full sun; prefers a poorer soil that is somewhat dry

Harvesting: The roots can be harvested in spring or fall. I prefer the fall, so that the plant has an opportunity to self-seed before the root is dug up. Use a needle-nose spade or a garden fork to lift the roots out of the soil.

Market Potential: Low

Medicinal Benefits: Inmortal is beneficial as a cardiovascular and respiratory tract herb.

Parts Used: Roots, dried

Home Pharmacy Uses: Decoction, traditional tincture, syrup, powder

Asclepias tuberosa

Pleurisy Root

Pleurisy root is not in high demand within the natural products industry, but it is used in several product lines. Wild harvesting is sometimes done before the herb has self-propagated by seed, and often identification is not done properly. The result is contamination of the roots with other plants, and contaminated roots must be discarded. The process of wild harvesting this herb can cause damage to the surrounding delicate ecosystems. As a result, United Plant Savers has put pleurisy root on its at-risk list for close monitoring. ✿

Pleurisy Root at a Glance

▸ **Plant Cycle:** Perennial

▸ **Type of Growth:** Herbaceous

▸ **Light Requirements:** Full sun

▸ **Water Requirements:** Low to moderate

▸ **Parts Used:** Roots

▸ **Home Pharmacy Uses:** Traditional tincture, elixir, syrup, honey

A.K.A.: Butterfly weed

Personality: Perennial; herbaceous (Zones 4–9)

Height: 24 inches (60 centimeters)

Bloom Traits: Vibrant fans of orange flowers bloom from midsummer on.

Likes/Dislikes: Pleurisy root is native to the prairies and common in wide open areas or in grassy mountain meadows, especially in the foothills.

Propagation/Maintenance: Stratify seeds for a minimum of 1 month and then sow indoors. Expect 40 percent germination in 2 to 3 weeks. Seedlings do not appreciate being held in pots for more than several weeks, so transplant them outside in mid- to late spring. Pleurisy root can also be direct sown outside in late winter or early spring. This herb grows in clumps; space plants 12 inches (30 centimeters) apart. Provide light to moderate amounts of water.

Sun/Soil: Full sun; well-drained soil

Companion/Complementary Planting: Pleurisy root grows well with penstemons, goldenrod, hyssop, and dill. It attracts monarch butterflies, so do not plant it next to a birdbath or bird feeder, or the birds may have lunch on the butterfly caterpillars.

Harvesting: Harvest the roots in the fall after the plant has had an opportunity to go to seed. These taproots will come out easily with a garden fork. A needle-nose spade also works well.

Market Potential: Low to moderate

Medicinal Benefits: Pleurisy root is often recommended for winter illnesses and respiratory conditions. Consult a qualified healthcare professional for dosage guidelines.

Parts Used: Roots, dried; do not ingest other parts of the plant

Home Pharmacy Uses: Traditional tincture, elixir, syrup, honey

Astragalus membranaceus
Astragalus

Astragalus is considered an important tonic herb in traditional Chinese medicine. It is gaining popularity in Western medicine for its fantastic ability to support the immune system. Although seed was not formerly available in the United States, gardeners are now growing this plant on North American soil. 🌿

A.K.A.: Huang qi

Personality: Perennial; herbaceous (Zones 6–11)

Height: 3 to 4 feet (.9 to 1.2 meters)

Bloom Traits: Pretty, pale yellow, pea flower–shaped blooms occur from midsummer until frost.

Likes/Dislikes: A native to northeastern China, astragalus seems to prefer sun to partial shade. It grows in open areas or along the margins of treed places, often in dry, sandy soils.

Propagation/Maintenance: Stratify seeds for at least 3 weeks before sowing. Then scarify them and soak in warm water for 1 hour before you plant them. Sow seeds directly into the ground in early spring or start them early indoors and transplant them out at the last frost date. Space plants 15 inches (38 centimeters) apart and water moderately. Although astragalus grows as a single plant, it has a tendency to sprawl a bit as it gets older.

Sun/Soil: Partial shade to full sun; well-worked soil

Harvesting: The roots of astragalus are harvested in the fall after they are at least 2 years old. The average harvesting time is between the third and fifth year of growth, but this can vary depending on where you live and how much growth the roots produce each year. The taproots will require a needle-nose spade or a fork to dig them fully and easily.

Market Potenial: High; included in many Western and Chinese herbal formulas

Medicinal Benefits: Astragalus is recognized for its ability to offer deep immune system support.

Parts Used: Roots, fresh or dried

Home Pharmacy Uses: Medicinal food, decoction, traditional tincture, cider vinegar tincture, syrup, elixir, lozenge, honey, powder

---

🌿 Astragalus at a Glance

- ▸ **Plant Cycle:** Perennial
- ▸ **Type of Growth:** Herbaceous
- ▸ **Light Requirements:** Partial shade to full sun
- ▸ **Water Requirements:** Moderate
- ▸ **Parts Used:** Roots
- ▸ **Home Pharmacy Uses:** Medicinal food, decoction, traditional tincture, cider vinegar tincture, syrup, elixir, lozenge, honey, powder

Avena sativa

Oat

The ancient Egyptians were known to cultivate oats, which they used for food and medicine. They knew that harvesting oatseed at the milky stage would provide the highest level of nutritional and medicinal benefit. This wise culture also regarded oats as a very important skin herb. 🌿

Oat at a Glance

- **Plant Cycle:** Annual
- **Type of Growth:** Herbaceous
- **Light Requirements:** Full sun
- **Water Requirements:** Moderate
- **Parts Used:** Seeds, grains, aerial

- **Home Pharmacy Uses:** Infusion, traditional tincture, cider vinegar tincture, syrup, compress, poultice, elixir, medicinal food, ointment, salve, cream, bath herb

A.K.A.: Oatseed, oat straw

Personality: Annual; herbaceous

Height: 4 to 5 feet (1.2 to 1.5 meters)

Bloom Traits: This grass sports light green grain spikelets that turn golden upon full maturity. Flowering will occur approximately 1 month after planting, depending on weather conditions.

Likes/Dislikes: Like many grasses, oats grow in open, sunny areas. They have been cultivated in nearly every temperate climate around the world.

Propagation/Maintenance: Sow seeds directly outdoors in mid- to late spring. No special treatments are needed. Oats will grow in clumps and should be spaced about 8 inches (20 centimeters) apart. Water moderately.

Sun/Soil: Full sun; prefers a soil with good organic matter content (4 to 5 percent is ideal)

Harvesting: To harvest oatseed, pick in the milky stage (when the green grains get very plump and spurt out a milky juice when squeezed). Strip the grains off the spikelets by pulling them through your fingertips. Have a bucket or bag ready to catch the oat grains as you move through the patch. If you are harvesting oatstraw, cut and dry the aerial parts (stems, leaves, grains) of the plant when it is in the milky stage. If you want oats for cooking, allow the grains to come to full maturity and then harvest them.

Market Potential: Moderate (oat straw) to high (oatseed); although the market for oatseed is better, harvesting it is very labor intensive and dollar return is marginal

Medicinal Benefits: Oats are a whole-body tonic for all ages, but are especially useful for the nervous system, skin, and bone health. Oats are also quite good for male and female reproductive health.

Parts Used: Milky-stage seeds, grains, and aerial parts, fresh or dried; if used in tinctures, the seeds should be used fresh

Home Pharmacy Uses: Infusion, traditional tincture, cider vinegar tincture, compress, poultice, elixir, medicinal food, ointment, salve, cream, bath herb

Betonica officinalis

Betony

Sometimes called wood betony because it prefers a woodland setting, betony is often confused with a North American plant *(Pedicularis canadensis)* that is known by the same common name. However, this European herb, a glorious member of the Mint family, is much easier to grow. ❀

A.K.A.: Wood betony

Personality: Perennial; herbaceous (Zones 5–8)

Height: 12 inches (30 centimeters)

Bloom Traits: Purple, and very occasionally pink or white, blooms from midsummer on

Likes/Dislikes: Betony is a woodland plant that prefers a moist and shady growing habitat.

Propagation/Maintenance: Betony seeds should be stratified for several weeks before starting them indoors. Transplant them outdoors 10 to 12 inches (25 to 30 centimeters) apart in mid- to late spring. Each year the clump of plants will gradually become larger, but this is not a rapid spreader. Be sure to give it moderate to high amounts of water.

Sun/Soil: Shade, partial shade; rich garden soil is best, but it will also grow in clay soil

Harvesting: The aerial parts are harvested at any time during the growing season. I prefer to harvest betony when it is in flower, but this is not mandatory. Use scissors or snips for this task.

Market Potential: Poor to moderate

Medicinal Benefits: A fantastic pain-relieving herb, betony is also often used to address stress and disrupted sleep patterns.

Parts Used: Aerial parts, fresh or dried

Home Pharmacy Uses: Infusion, traditional tincture, syrup, ointment, salve, cream, balm, foot soak, bath herb, liniment

Borago officinalis

Borage

The gorgeous, star-shaped flowers are a lovely violet in color. They taste like cucumbers; add them to your salad or sandwich for a delectable and beautiful treat. ❀

Personality: Annual; herbaceous

Height: 3 feet (.9 meter)

Bloom Traits: Intensely blue, star-shaped flowers bloom all summer.

Likes/Dislikes: Borage is a Mediterranean native that prefers a sunny to dappled sunlight environment.

Propagation/Maintenance: Plant seeds directly outdoors in late spring or sow early indoors and transplant out in late spring. Seeds are easy and require no special treatments. Borage forms a fairly large plant over the course of the summer months, so space seedlings 15 inches (38 centimeters) apart. Water moderately.

Sun/Soil: Sun, partial shade; no special soil needs

Companion/Complementary Planting: I find that borage is a grasshopper magnet, but it is very hardy. I sometimes place it next to plants that can be badly damaged by grasshoppers, like lemon balm. The grasshoppers will then eat the borage (which has a tolerance level for this) instead of the other plants.

Harvesting: Borage leaves, stems, flowers, and seeds are best harvested when the plant is in flower with green seed beginning to form. Cut using snips or scissors.

Market Potential: Moderate

Medicinal Benefits: Borage is a good medicinal food and a remedy for skin and women's reproductive concerns.

Parts Used: Flowering aerial parts, fresh or dried

Home Pharmacy Uses: Infusion, traditional tincture, cider vinegar tincture, syrup, crystallized, elixir, lozenge, honey

Brickellia grandiflora

Brickellia

The use of brickellia is rich among the northern regions of Mexico and throughout the southwestern parts of the United States. Although Native peoples have traditionally used it in the treatment of diabetes, brickellia is becoming popular among other herbalists and naturopaths.

Brickellia at a Glance

▸ **Plant Cycle:** Perennial

▸ **Type of Growth:** Herbaceous

▸ **Light Requirements:** Sun

▸ **Water Requirements:** Low

▸ **Parts Used:** Aerial

▸ **Home Pharmacy Uses:** Infusion, traditional tincture, cider vinegar tincture

A.K.A.: Prodigiosa, tassel flower

Personality: Perennial; herbaceous (Zones 4–9)

Height: 2 to 3 feet (.6 to .9 meter)

Bloom Traits: Smallish, cream-colored flowers bloom from mid- to late summer.

Likes/Dislikes: Brickellia grows in high desert environments. It is usually found where spring runoff is abundant but later in the season water is marginal. It is a native of southern Colorado and grows in many of the southwestern states.

Propagation/Maintenance: To start brickellia, take from tender tip cuttings. Use a liquid rooting hormone to encourage more rapid rooting. Start cuttings indoors and transplant outdoors, 15 to 20 inches (38 to 50 centimeters) apart, when weather is fully settled and cuttings have developed a strong root structure. Extra heat — constant nighttime temperature of 70°F (21°C), day temperatures between 80 and 95°F (26 to 32°C) — will help along the rooting process. Brickellia will grow in clumps and needs only light watering.

Sun/Soil: Sun; poorer and somewhat sandy soil is preferred, but it is adaptable

Companion/Complementary Planting: Plant in community with penstemons, California poppies, and coyote mint.

Harvesting: Aerial parts are harvested at any point during the summer. Snips or scissors work great.

Market Potential: Low; brickellia is mainly used by peoples of the southwestern United States

Medicinal Benefits: Intensely bitter, brickellia is used to regulate blood sugar levels.

Parts Used: Aerial parts, fresh

Home Pharmacy Uses: Infusion, traditional tincture, cider vinegar tincture

Calendula officinalis

Calendula

Calendula may be used as an herbal food coloring for broth, rice, and even frosting, where it imparts a rich golden color. King Henry VIII of England reputedly liked his food highly seasoned and brightly colored, and his cooks relied heavily on calendula to meet his demands. The plant is often called pot marigold, a tribute to its early culinary uses.

Calendula at a Glance

- **Plant Cycle:** Annual
- **Type of Growth:** Herbaceous
- **Light Requirements:** Full sun
- **Water Requirements:** Moderate
- **Parts Used:** Flowers

- **Home Pharmacy Uses:** Infusion, traditional tincture, compress, poultice, medicinal food, ointment, salve, cream, balm, foot soak, bath herb, infused oil, liniment, insect repellent

A.K.A.: Pot marigold

Personality: Annual; herbaceous

Height: 12 to 15 inches (30 to 38 centimeters)

Bloom Traits: Bright yellow and orange flowers bloom from early summer until a killing frost. They close up at night and reopen in early to midmorning.

Likes/Dislikes: Calendula is now considered a garden plant only. Its origin is not known, but it is a common choice for nearly all types of gardens.

Propagation/Maintenance: Propagate calendula from seeds. They are easy and require no pretreatments. They are best sown directly into the ground, but may be started indoors and transplanted out at a later time. Germination is normally very reliable, around 80 percent. Seeds take 1 to 2 weeks to sprout. This plant, which grows in clumps, does not spread by roots or runners, but it does self-sow vigorously. Space 10 inches (25 centimeters) apart and provide light to moderate amounts of water.

Sun/Soil: Full sun; will grow in nearly every type of soil, as long as it isn't overly moist

Companion/Complementary Planting: Calendulas tend to attract aphids, whiteflies, and thrips. You can use them as a magnet plant, by putting them around other plants that are troubled by those pests.

Harvesting: Only the flowers of calendula are harvested; pick by hand when they are just fully opened. Avoid picking flowers that have already begun to form seed; these will not be as medicinally active. Remove spent blossoms to promote blooming throughout the summer and early fall. Once all the flowers are allowed to go to seed, calendula will die.

Market Potenial: Moderate to high; usually preferred in dried form

Medicinal Benefits: Excellent for skin health, but also appropriate for gastrointestinal tract concerns

Parts Used: Flowers, fresh or dried

Home Pharmacy Uses: Infusion, traditional tincture, compress, poultice, medicinal food, ointment, salve, cream, balm, foot soak, bath herb, infused oil, liniment, insect repellent

Callirhoe involucrata
Callirhoe

According to Kelly Kindscher, author of *Medicinal Wild Plants of the Prairie*, callirhoe is traditionally used by several Native American tribes. Many herbalists, including me, like to work with callirhoe medicinally. The plant is best grown in its native environment, where it is easier to cultivate. 🌿

A.K.A.: Poppy mallow, wine cup

Personality: Perennial; herbaceous (Zones 4–6)

Height: 8 to 10 inches (20 to 25 centimeters)

Bloom Traits: Hot pink flowers begin to bloom in late spring and continue into the fall.

Likes/Dislikes: Callirhoe grows in open areas that are grassy and usually fairly dry. It prefers a moist spring to get it started and then enjoys hot temperatures.

Propagation/Maintenance: Callirhoe is tricky to propagate. I have found that the best method is seed, but even that can be difficult. Stratify the seeds for at least 3 months, then scarify them and soak them in 3 percent hydrogen peroxide for 20 to 30 minutes. Sow immediately. Transplant outdoors, 12 to 15 inches (30 to 38 centimeters) apart, in mid- to late spring. Callirhoe is a spreading plant, and prefers light watering.

Sun/Soil: Full sun, partial shade; prefers a dry soil that is not overly rich in nutrients

Harvesting: The roots can be harvested with a garden fork or needle-nose spade in the early spring, but late fall is preferable since it allows the plant to form seed before the roots are dug up.

Market Potential: Low

Medicinal Benefits: Like other types of mallows, it is used for the gastrointestinal tract and for skin health.

Parts Used: Roots, fresh or dried

Home Pharmacy Uses: Decoction, compress, poultice, ointment, salve, cream, balm, infused oil

Capsella bursa-pastoris
Shepherd's purse

Fresh shepherd's purse is a medicinal herb used in first aid. It is also a spicy and tasty medicinal food. Added to salads and sandwiches, it is sure to perk up any meal. 🌿

Personality: Annual; herbaceous

Height: 8 to 24 inches (20 to 60 centimeters)

Bloom Traits: Delicate, little white flowers blossom on this Mustard family member in late spring to early summer.

Likes/Dislikes: Shepherd's purse is an early-spring herb that pops up in disturbed areas across North America.

Propagation/Maintenance: Sow directly outdoors in late fall (and let winter do the stratifying for you) or stratify seeds for at least 4 weeks and sow directly outdoors in early spring. Do not start shepherd's purse indoors. Space these clumping plants 10 inches (25 centimeters) apart. Water moderately.

Sun/Soil: Full sun; well-drained soil

Harvesting: When the plant is in full flower, harvest aerial parts. I find the easiest way is simply to pull up the plants and trim off the roots with a pair of snips or scissors.

Market Potential: High, especially with tincture companies. The plant must be shipped overnight because it loses potency when it is not freshly processed.

Medicinal Benefits: Used to treat bleeding associated with the urinary tract, gastrointestinal tract, women's reproductive organs, and the circulatory system

Parts Used: Flowering aerial parts, fresh

Home Pharmacy Uses: Traditional tincture

Capsicum species

Cayenne

Cayenne is a member of the Solonaceae family, which includes potatoes, eggplant, and bell peppers. Never eat the leaves, stems, or flowers of the cayenne pepper plant; they can be toxic. The fruits are perfectly safe, however. Be conservative in how much cayenne you add to your remedies; these peppers are hot! 🌿

🌿 Cayenne at a Glance

- ▸ **Plant Cycle:** Annual
- ▸ **Type of Growth:** Herbaceous
- ▸ **Light Requirements:** Full sun
- ▸ **Water Requirements:** Low
- ▸ **Parts Used:** Fruits
- ▸ **Home Pharmacy Uses:** Traditional tincture, cider vinegar tincture, medicinal food, ointment, salve, cream, balm, foot soak, infused oil

Personality: Annual; herbaceous

Height: To 24 inches (60 centimeters)

Bloom Traits: White and somewhat star-shaped flowers bloom in early to midsummer, followed by the formation of green chili fruits. The fruits will turn bright red upon maturity.

Likes/Dislikes: Cayennes are probably native to South America. They are only a cultivated plant at this time, although there are some types of chilies that still can be found growing in the wild. Cayennes prefer to grow in hot and somewhat dry areas, where there are long seasons and bright sunny days.

Propagation/Maintenance: Start cayenne in late winter or early spring, indoors in a bright, sunny, warm location. Seeds require no special treatment, but seedlings appreciate very warm temperatures to grow well. Expect good germination in about a week. We reliably get 80 to 90 percent germination if all growing conditions are right. Transplant cayenne outdoors, 12 inches (30 centimeters) apart, after all danger of frost has past. The plant grows in clumps and requires little watering.

Sun/Soil: Full sun; prefers dryish soil, but is tolerant

Companion/Complementary Planting: Grow near basil and cilantro to enhance each herb's flavor.

Harvesting: Pick the bright red fruits (chilies) in late summer or even in early fall before the frost hits. The chilies are handpicked and gloves are recommended; capsicum resins on the skin can cause burning, especially for people who have fair or sensitive skin.

Market Potential: Moderate; cayenne is a great farmer's market product and many chefs are interested in it as flavoring

Medicinal Benefits: An excellent medicinal food and preparation for heart and circulatory health, cayenne is also used for pain relief, especially of the joints and muscles.

Parts Used: Fruits, fresh or dried

Home Pharmacy Uses: Traditional tincture, cider vinegar tincture, medicinal food, ointment, salve, cream, balm, foot soak, infused oil

Centella asiatica

Gotu Kola

Have you ever heard that elephants have an incredibly long and sharp memory? Is it a coincidence, then, that elephants often favor the memory- and brain-enhancing gotu kola as a food? 🌿

🌿 Gotu Kola at a Glance

- **Plant Cycle:** Annual; perennial
- **Type of Growth:** Herbaceous
- **Light Requirements:** Full sun, partial shade
- **Water Requirements:** High
- **Parts Used:** Aerial

- **Home Pharmacy Uses:** Infusion, traditional tincture, cider vinegar tincture, elixir, compress, poultice, medicinal food, ointment, salve, cream, balm, foot soak, bath herb, infused oil, honey

Personality: Annual in North America, perennial in tropical climates; herbaceous (Zones 8–11)

Height: 6 to 8 inches (15 to 20 centimeters)

Bloom Traits: Greenish flowers that sit underneath the leaves are barely visible. They bloom in early spring.

Likes/Dislikes: Gotu kola is grown as a garden plant in temperate climates. In tropical climates or where it grows wild, it is found along open ditches with good exposure to moisture.

Propagation/Maintenance: Gotu kola is difficult to grow from seed; greater success is had when grown from layerings or root divisions. Layerings will be easier and most successful (see chapter 4). Cuttings must be kept moist but not overly wet. Night temperatures should be near 70°F (21°C), with daytime temperatures in the high 80 to 90°F (26 to 36°C) range. Root divisions are the easiest way to propagate gotu kola. Simply separate the parent into several divisions and plant. Gotu kola also grows very nicely as a hanging houseplant. This herb is sprawling and roots every place its stems make contact with the soil. Space 10 inches (25 centimeters) apart and water very well and often.

Sun/Soil: Partial shade to full sun; prefers a rich garden loam, but will grow in almost any well-worked soil

Harvesting: Harvesting may be done at any time during the hot growing season for outdoor plants. If plants are being grown indoors or in a greenhouse, harvesting can take place year-round. Use small snips or scissors to harvest the aerial parts of this plant.

Market Potential: Moderate to very high

Medicinal Benefits: Traditionally used as an adaptogenic herb, gotu kola benefits the skin, promotes good memory and concentration, and is being researched for its anticancer properties.

Parts Used: Aerial parts, fresh or dried

Home Pharmacy Uses: Infusion, traditional tincture, cider vinegar tincture, syrup, elixir, compress, poultice, medicinal food, ointment, salve, cream, balm, foot soak, bath herb, infused oil, honey

Chenopodium ambrosioides

Epazote

Epazote is an unassuming garden plant that gets your attention primarily with its fragrance. Every time it is lightly brushed or touched, epazote releases a resinous, creosote-like scent. Despite its unusual smell, this herb makes a wonderful addition to the beanpot as a medicinal food. ✿

Personality: Annual or short-lived perennial; herbaceous

Height: 12 to 15 inches (30 to 38 centimeters)

Bloom Traits: Greenish spikes grow from early summer through late summer, depending on heat; hot weather causes earlier flowering.

Likes/Dislikes: Epazote is a desert plant native to the southwestern United States and Mexico. It prefers growing in disturbed areas that are hot and dry.

Propagation/Maintenance: Sow seeds indoors for transplanting outside in late spring, or sow directly in garden soil in mid- to late spring. No special treatments are required. Epazote comes up easily from seed in 1 to 2 weeks; germination is 60 to 70 percent. The herb grows in clumps, so space the plants 10 to 12 inches (25 to 30 centimeters) apart. Water lightly.

Sun/Soil: Full sun; no special soil needs

Harvesting: Harvest the aerial parts anytime between early and late summer. Snips or scissors work nicely for this task.

Market Potential: Low

Medicinal Benefits: Epazote is used as a medicinal food in southwestern and Mexican cultures. It is considered beneficial for treating parasites, although it should be used carefully for this purpose. Epazote should not be used by pregnant woman.

Parts Used: Aerial parts, fresh or dried

Home Pharmacy Uses: Infusion, traditional tincture, medicinal food

✤ Epazote at a Glance

- ▸ **Plant Cycle:** Annual; perennial
- ▸ **Type of Growth:** Herbaceous
- ▸ **Light Requirements:** Full sun
- ▸ **Water Requirements:** Low
- ▸ **Parts Used:** Aerial
- ▸ **Home Pharmacy Uses:** Infusion, traditional tincture, medicinal food

Cichorium intybus
Chicory

Chicory has a long history of use as a coffee-type beverage. The roots are roasted, and sometimes blended with coffee beans, to create a delicious and healthful drink. 🌿

Personality: Perennial; herbaceous (Zones 3–10)

Height: 15 to 24 inches (38 to 60 centimeters)

Bloom Traits: Beautiful periwinkle blue flowers bloom from mid- to late summer.

Likes/Dislikes: Chicory is likely to be found growing in open grassy areas and in disturbed areas. It is a common roadside plant, adding a cheerful face to the miles of pavement.

Propagation/Maintenance: Seeds germinate best if they are stratified before sowing. Sow indoors or directly outdoors. Transplant outdoors, 10 inches (25 centimeters) apart, in mid- to late spring. Expect excellent germination in 5 to 7 days. Chicory requires low to moderate watering, and will grow in clumps.

Sun/Soil: Full sun; no special soil needs

Companion/Complementary Planting: Chicory grows very well with red clover, alfalfa, and plantain.

Harvesting: Harvest roots in the spring or fall with a needle-nose spade or a garden fork. Leaves may be handpicked at any time during the growing season, but will be best in the early summer months. Flowers are edible and can be harvested by hand when in bloom.

Market Potential: Low

Medicinal Benefits: Similar to dandelion, chicory is beneficial to digestive tract and urinary tract health.

Parts Used: Roots, leaves, and flowers, fresh or dried

Home Pharmacy Uses: Decoction, traditional tincture, cider vinegar tincture, syrup, medicinal food

Coriandrum sativum
Cilantro/ Coriander

The leafy parts of this herb are known as cilantro; the seeds are called coriander. Both are recognized in cooking circles, but few people think of this plant as a medicinal herb. Restaurants and farmer's markets are both good outlets for fresh cilantro, and coriander is sold as a spice. 🌿

Personality: Annual; herbaceous

Height: 10 to 12 inches (25 to 30 centimeters)

Bloom Traits: Small, delicate white flowers appear as temperatures warm and the plant bolts.

Likes/Dislikes: Considered a garden herb, cilantro grows in moist gardens from tropical to temperate climates, during the cooler parts of the growing season. It does not tolerate hot temperatures and will rapidly bolt.

Propagation/Maintenance: Sow untreated seeds outdoors in early to mid-spring or start indoors and transplant out in mid- to late spring. Seeds do not germinate well in the heat of summer. You can also sow in late summer or very early fall for a fresh supply before the frost hits. Space plants 8 to 10 inches (20 to 25 centimeters) apart, and provide moderate to high amounts of water. This herb will grow in clumps.

Sun/Soil: Full sun, partial shade, shade; no special soil needs

Harvesting: Harvest aerial parts with snips or scissors before it goes to flower. Handpick seed clusters and gently rub the golden brown seeds from the stems.

Market Potential: Low to moderate

Medicinal Benefits: Good for digestive health

Parts Used: Aerial parts and seeds, fresh

Home Pharmacy Uses: Cider vinegar tincture, medicinal food, honey

Cymbopogon citratus

Lemongrass

Lemongrass is a plant of strong economic value in Guatemala. However, much of the plant material grown and exported from this country is sprayed heavily with toxic chemicals. Grow your own lemongrass to be sure it is free of unhealthy chemical residues. 🌸

Lemongrass at a Glance

▸ **Plant Cycle:** Tender perennial
▸ **Type of Growth:** Herbaceous
▸ **Light Requirements:** Full sun, partial shade, shade
▸ **Water Requirements:** Moderate to high

▸ **Parts Used:** Aerial
▸ **Home Pharmacy Uses:** Infusion, cider vinegar tincture, medicinal food, foot soak, sleep pillow, bath herb, infused oil, honey

Personality: Tender perennial; herbaceous (Zones 8–11)

Height: 3 to 4 feet (.9 to 1.2 meters)

Bloom Traits: No specific blooms

Likes/Dislikes: Lemongrass is a tropical plant native to Sri Lanka and Seychelles that is used primarily for farming and gardening. It prefers a climate that is moist and hot, but will tolerate warm, dry climates only if it is watered regularly.

Propagation/Maintenance: Root divisions work fairly well but require a lot of mother plants. I have found that lemongrass is best grown from seed. It does beautifully in our hot greenhouse, providing it is kept well watered. Germination is about 90 percent; seeds take only a few days to sprout. In temperate climates, transplant outdoors after all frost danger has passed and bring back indoors early in fall before frost hits. Lemongrass is a perennial in tropical climates. It grows in clumps and should be given moderate to high amounts of water. Space plants 12 to 15 inches (30 to 38 centimeters) apart.

Sun/Soil: Full sun, partial shade, shade; prefers a moist loamy or sandy soil

Companion/Complementary Planting: Lemongrass complements lemon verbena, passionflower, and gotu kola in a garden environment.

Harvesting: All of the aerial parts may be harvested from mid- to late summer. The summer heat concentrates the oils and increases the intensity of its flavor. I harvest with scissors, but snips would also work.

Market Potential: Moderate; chefs who cook with medicinal foods are a great market

Medicinal Benefits: A medicinal food used to support a healthy digestive tract, lemongrass also has some anti-inflammatory benefits.

Parts Used: Aerial parts, fresh or dried

Home Pharmacy Uses: Infusion, cider vinegar tincture, medicinal food, foot soak, sleep pillow, bath herb, infused oil, honey

Echinacea angustifolia, E. pallida,
E. purpurea

Echinacea

Echinacea has become at risk of endangerment in its wild habitat, as the direct result of overharvesting. Many states are taking action to protect what remaining echinacea populations they have, and organizations like United Plant Savers are trying to encourage the proper cultivation of this medicinal plant. Fortunately, we know how to grow echinacea. Proper cultivation is a must, and understanding the buyer's requirements will save a lot of headaches. Be clear about the customer's needs and ask for a written contract for roots especially, since this is a three-year-out harvesttime. 🌺

Echinacea at a Glance

▸ **Plant Cycle:** Perennial

▸ **Type of Growth:** Herbaceous

▸ **Light Requirements:** Full sun

▸ **Water Requirements:** Low to moderate

▸ **Parts Used:** Whole plant

▸ **Home Pharmacy Uses:** Infusion, decoction, traditional tincture, syrup, compress, poultice, elixir, lozenge, ointment, salve, cream, balm, foot soak, bath herb, infused oil, honey, butter, suppository, powder, liniment

A.K.A.: Purple coneflower

Personality: Perennial; herbaceous (Zones 3–9, depending on the species)

Height: *E. angustifolia,* 24 inches (60 centimeters); *E. pallida,* 2 to 3 feet (.6 to .9 meter); *E. purpurea,* 3 to 4 feet (.9 to 1.2 meters)

Bloom Traits: Pinkish purple flowers bloom from mid- to late summer.

Likes/Dislikes: Echinacea is a prairie wildflower that grows in wide open, grassy areas.

Propagation/Maintenance: All echinacea species do better from seeds artificially stratified for at least 3 months. Or stratify naturally, by sowing seeds directly in the late fall or early spring; this is reliable only in areas that have consistently cold winters. If sown indoors, transplant outside in late spring. Seeds germinate sporadically and average around 50 percent. They take anywhere from 2 to 6 weeks to sprout. Echinacea grows in clumps; space 12 inches (30 centimeters) apart. Provide moderate water for *E. purpurea,* light water for the other species.

Sun/Soil: Full sun; *E. angustifolia* and *E. pallida* require poorer soil that is not overly moist, while *E. purpurea* requires richer soil and regular watering

Harvesting: Roots are harvested in the fall or spring, when they reach 2½ to 3 years old. *E. purpurea* has a tricky-to-harvest taproot, while *E. angustifolia* and *E. pallida* have fibrous roots that are easier to harvest. Harvest aerial parts, flowers, and seeds with snips from the second growing season on. Whole plants are harvested when in peak flower. Use a garden fork or needle-nose spade to dig roots and whole plants.

Market Potential: Moderate to very high

Medicinal Benefits: Great for colds and flus, immune support, and respiratory and skin conditions

Parts Used: Whole plant, fresh or dried

Home Pharmacy Uses: Infusion, decoction, traditional tincture, syrup, compress, poultice, elixir, lozenge, ointment, salve, cream, balm, foot soak, bath herb, infused oil, honey, butter, suppository, powder, liniment

Ephedra nevadensis, E. viridis

Mormon Tea

This plant takes its name from the early Mormon settlers in Utah, who used the herb to make a beverage. The settlers also prepared medicines from the plant. It grows abundantly in the desert regions as well as other parts of the southwestern United States. ❧

☘ Morman Tea at a Glance

- ▸ **Plant Cycle:** Perennial
- ▸ **Type of Growth:** Herbaceous
- ▸ **Light Requirements:** Full sun
- ▸ **Water Requirements:** Low
- ▸ **Parts Used:** Aerial
- ▸ **Home Pharmacy Uses:** Infusion, traditional tincture

Personality: Perennial; herbaceous (Zones 5–9)

Height: 12 to 24 inches (30 to 60 centimeters)

Bloom Traits: Golden yellow blooms appear all along the stalk in late spring or early summer.

Likes/Dislikes: Mormon tea is a desert dweller. It prefers hot and dry climates, often choosing its shelter in canyon cliffs.

Propagation/Maintenance: Even though Mormon tea is a desert plant, the desert can get very cold in the winter. Simulate this by stratifying the seed for 1 to 2 weeks. Just before sowing, soak seeds for 15 minutes in 3 percent hydrogen peroxide. This improves germination to 75 to 80 percent. Sow seeds indoors, in a sandy soil mix, and expect germination in about 2 weeks. Extra-warm temperatures enhance both sprouting and the growing process. Plant outdoors in hot, dry climates after spring weather is well settled. Mormon tea grows in clumps and generally should be spaced 12 to 15 inches (30 to 38 centimeters) apart; in the hottest southwestern climates, it will need 24 to 36 inches (60 to 90 centimeters). Water lightly.

Sun/Soil: Full sun; prefers a poorer soil that is well drained

Companion/Complementary Planting: Combine with yerba de la negrita, white sage, inmortal, and prickly pear cactus in a very dry and sunny area.

Harvesting: Mormon tea is harvested at any point during the growing season. Aerial parts are gathered using snips.

Market Potential: Low; Chinese ephedra (*Ephedra sinensis*) is the ephedra of choice for most manufacturers. This variety has a higher level of ephedrine alkaloids that can create health risks, however, whereas Mormon tea, with its lower ephedrine levels, does not produce side effects.

Medicinal Benefits: Primarily used for its urinary tract healing properties, ephedra is also considered appropriate for some respiratory conditions.

Parts Used: Aerial parts, fresh or dried

Home Pharmacy Uses: Infusion, traditional tincture

Eschscholzia californica

California Poppy

Few plants have as stunning an appearance as a mass planting of California poppies. Their grayish-green, feathery foliage and dramatic orange flowers never fail to stop people in their tracks. Use the edible flowers to decorate a cake or create a confetti effect in a cream cheese spread. 🌸

Personality: Annual; herbaceous

Height: 12 inches (30 centimeters)

Bloom Traits: Vibrant, bright orange flowers bloom from late spring until a killing frost.

Likes/Dislikes: These plants prefer to grow in wide open, grassy areas, where they are quite happy to intermix with native grasses and other wildflowers. They are native to the California Sierras.

Propagation/Maintenance: Stratify seeds for a week or so and then sow them directly into the garden soil, or start them early indoors and transplant out in late spring. Space 10 to 12 inches (25 to 30 centimeters) apart and provide light to moderate amounts of water. Germination is usually around 70 percent and occurs in 7 to 14 days. Although the individual plants do not spread, they are vigorous self-sowers and can easily fill in a given space in 1 to 2 years.

Sun/Soil: Sun, partial shade; no special soil needs

Harvesting: The entire plant is harvested when the poppies are in bloom. At this stage you will have both poppy flowers and seedpods present. Simply pull up the entire plant or use a garden fork if the ground is not moist enough to extract them. They have a large orange taproot that is usually easy enough to pull out by hand.

Market Potential: Moderate

Medicinal Benefits: A wonderful nervine that is excellent for relieving stress and anxiety, it also offers pain relief and is a helpful sleep aid.

Parts Used: Whole plant in flower, fresh or dried

Home Pharmacy Uses: Infusion, traditional tincture, syrup, compress, poultice, elixir, ointment, salve, cream, balm, foot soak, bath herb, infused oil, honey, liniment

🌿 California Poppy at a Glance

- ▸ **Plant Cycle:** Annual
- ▸ **Type of Growth:** Herbaceous
- ▸ **Light Requirements:** Sun, partial shade
- ▸ **Water Requirements:** Low to moderate

- ▸ **Parts Used:** Whole plant
- ▸ **Home Pharmacy Uses:** Infusion, traditional tincture, syrup, compress, poultice, elixir, ointment, salve, cream, balm, foot soak, bath herb, infused oil, honey, liniment

Foeniculum vulgare

Fennel

The uncrushed seeds of the fennel plant taste sweet. Crushing the seeds releases more medicinal oils, and the taste becomes strong and slightly bitter. Fennel is widely known as a culinary herb, but it is also excellent for several medicinal uses.

Fennel at a Glance

▸ **Plant Cycle:** Perennial

▸ **Type of Growth:** Herbaceous

▸ **Light Requirements:** Full sun

▸ **Water Requirements:** Low to moderate

▸ **Parts Used:** Seeds, leaves, roots

▸ **Home Pharmacy Uses:** Infusion, traditional tincture, cider vinegar tincture, syrup, compress, elixir, medicinal food, bath herb, infused oil, honey

Personality: Perennial; herbaceous (Zones 6–9)

Height: 4 to 5 feet (1.2 to 1.5 meters)

Bloom Traits: Umbels of yellow flowers bloom late July until frost.

Likes/Dislikes: Fennel is native to the Mediterranean part of the world and prefers disturbed soil areas.

Propagation/Maintenance: Easily grown from seed that has been stratified for at least 2 weeks (up to several months), fennel may be sown directly into the garden after the last frost date. It can also be planted indoors for transplanting outside in late spring. Fennel seeds sprout in about 2 weeks and have a 70 percent germination rate. The herb grows in clumps; plants should be spaced 12 to 15 inches (30 to 38 centimeters) apart. Provide low to moderate amounts of water for fennel.

Sun/Soil: Full sun; prefers well-worked and -drained soil with 4 to 5 percent organic matter, but grows in nearly all types of soil

Companion/Complementary Planting: Fennel complements sunflowers, calendulas, and nasturiums, and attracts butterflies and hummingbirds.

Harvesting: Harvest the large, deep roots in spring or fall, using a needle-nose spade or garden fork. Handpick leaves at any time during the growing season. Harvest seeds with snips or scissors either in the green seed umbel stage or fully ripened, depending on medicinal recommendations. Green seed umbels may be prepared whole. Gently rub ripened seed off the umbel stems.

Market Potential: Moderate; fully ripe, dried and cleaned seeds are preferred

Medicinal Benefits: A medicinal food, fennel promotes milk production in nursing mothers, good digestion, and respiratory tract and throat health. It is excellent for children.

Parts Used: Seeds, leaves, and roots, fresh or dried

Home Pharmacy Uses: Infusion, traditional tincture, cider vinegar tincture, syrup, compress, elixir, medicinal food, bath herb, infused oil, honey

Geranium caespitosum, G. fremontii,
G. richardsonii, G. maculatum

Wild Geranium

All species of wild geranium show potential for becoming at risk. Although not currently being harvested in great quantities for manufacturing, it is a slow-growing native plant in many regions of North America that is feeling the effects of wild harvesting. Since it grows much more quickly in a cultivated environment, wild geranium can be grown and sold in quantity relatively simply. 🌿

Wild Geranium at a Glance

- ▸ **Plant Cycle:** Perennial
- ▸ **Type of Growth:** Herbaceous
- ▸ **Light Requirements:** Full sun, partial shade, shade
- ▸ **Water Requirements:** Moderate to high

- ▸ **Parts Used:** Aerial, roots, whole plant
- ▸ **Home Pharmacy Uses:** Infusion, decoction, traditional tincture, powder, ointment, salve, cream, balm, foot soak, bath herb, infused oil

Personality: Perennial; herbaceous (Zones 4–8 for *G. maculatum*, Zones 3–9 for others)

Height: 6 to 24 inches (15 to 30 centimeters)

Bloom Traits: Pink or purple flowers bloom early to late summer.

Likes/Dislikes: Wild geranium often grows at higher elevations, in disturbed soil of meadows, pastures, and along mountain roadsides.

Propagation/Maintenance: Propagate by cuttings and root or crown divisions. Seeds may develop but are rarely viable. Cuttings require several weeks to develop a strong root structure. Rooted cuttings taken in early spring should be ready to transplant in late spring. If possible, make divisions and replant each directly into the ground. Keep well watered until the roots have settled. Divisions that do not have good root systems should be planted in pots and allowed to grow strong roots before transplanting. Geraniums grow in clumps; space 12 to 15 inches (30 to 38 centimeters) apart. Water moderately to heavily.

Sun/Soil: Shade, partial shade, full sun (not preferred); prefers well-drained soil but will tolerate some gravel or well-worked clay with 4 to 5 percent organic matter

Harvesting: If only the roots are used, dig them with a needle-nose spade or garden fork when the ground is not frozen in spring, autumn, or winter months. Aerial parts may be harvested with snips throughout the summer. If the whole plant is being used, harvest anytime during the active growing season.

Market Potential: Low; although an important medicinal, demand is low in the herbal products industry

Medicinal Benefits: Internally and externally used as an astringent for gastrointestinal complaints, and for skin and throat conditions, wild geranium is also considered an excellent antiseptic herb.

Parts Used: Aerial parts, roots, whole plant, fresh or dried

Home Pharmacy Uses: Traditional tincture, powder, infusion, decoction, ointment, salve, cream, balm, foot soak, bath herb, infused oil

Glycyrrhiza glabra

Licorice

Licorice has traditionally been available only from outside the United States. Buyers are pleased to find good certified organic growers of licorice who can supply this rhizome either fresh or dried. ❧

⚘ Licorice at a Glance

- ▸ **Plant Cycle:** Tender perennial
- ▸ **Type of Growth:** Herbaceous
- ▸ **Light Requirements:** Full sun, partial shade
- ▸ **Water Requirements:** Moderate
- ▸ **Parts Used:** Rhizome
- ▸ **Home Pharmacy Uses:** Decoction, traditional tincture, syrup, elixir, lozenge, medicinal food, honey, powder

Personality: Tender perennial; herbaceous (Zones 9–11)

Height: 4 to 5 feet (1.2 to 1.5 meters)

Bloom Traits: Gorgeous lavender and white flowers bloom in mid- to late summer.

Likes/Dislikes: Licorice is a Mediterranean plant by nature and prefers a hot and somewhat arid climate.

Propagation/Maintenance: Seeds must be stratified for several weeks. Just before sowing, scarify them and then soak for 2 hours in warm water. Sow immediately, preferably indoors, and then transplant outside in mid- to late spring. Outdoor sowing is possible, but results are much less predictable. My experience is that treated seed will germinate at about 70 to 80 percent, while untreated seed brings about only a 20 percent success rate. Sprouting normally takes about 2 weeks. Each year licorice will die back in the winter and come up vigorously in late spring. The plant will gradually get larger over time; space 24 inches (60 centimeters) apart. I usually harvest older licorice and start over with a small plant. Water moderately.

Sun/Soil: Full sun, partial shade; well-drained soil is preferred

Harvesting: Harvest licorice rhizomes in the third year of growth. Use a needle-nose spade to lift them out of the soil. They are normally quite large, even in our clay soil, and require a fair amount of energy to dig. Harvest in the spring or fall.

Market Potential: High; U.S. buyers are usually pleased to find domestic, organic sources of this herb

Medicinal Benefits: Licorice is a wonderful tonic herb for winter illnesses and immune, digestive tract, respiratory tract, and adrenal gland support. It is also excellent for children's health. Some people will be advised to avoid licorice; consult a reliable herbal reference for specific details.

Parts Used: Rhizome, fresh or dried

Home Pharmacy Uses: Decoction, traditional tincture, syrup, elixir, lozenge, medicinal food, honey, powder

Grindelia species
Grindelia

Grindelia buds must be Mother Nature's version of a ready-made cough drop. They have a menthol-like flavor, and produce a quick expectorant result. 🌺

A.K.A.: Gumweed, rosin weed

Personality: Perennial; herbaceous (Zones 6–10)

Height: 24 inches (60 centimeters)

Bloom Traits: Yellow flowers and resinous round buds appear from mid- to late summer.

Likes/Dislikes: Grindelia is common in disturbed areas along roadsides, prairies, and mountains.

Propagation/Maintenance: Sow untreated seeds directly in the garden soil, or start early indoors and transplant outside in mid- to late spring. Space this clump-growing plant 12 inches (30 centimeters) apart and provide light to moderate water.

Sun/Soil: Full sun; prefers soil that isn't too rich

Companion/Complementary Planting: Grows well in community with brickellia, penstemons, and mullein

Harvesting: Harvest flowers and resinous buds with snips or scissors when there are more buds than flowers. Gather only the upper 3 to 4 inches of the stalks.

Market Potential: Low to moderate

Medicinal Benefits: A good respiratory and mild heart-supporting herb

Parts Used: Flowers, buds, and leaves, fresh or dried

Home Pharmacy Uses: Infusion, traditional tincture, syrup, lozenge, honey

Helianthus annuus
Sunflower

Few plants are identified with the midwestern region of the United States as much as sunflower. In this area, sunflower is used to make food, oil, medicinal preparations, and birdseed. 🌺

Personality: Annual; herbaceous

Height: 2 to 12 feet (.6 to 3.6 meters)

Bloom Traits: Bright yellow flowers with chocloate brown centers bloom from early summer until fall.

Likes/Dislikes: Native to North America, sunflowers are commonly found in undisturbed sunny areas, mountains, grasslands, and drier tropical regions.

Propagation/Maintenance: Sow untreated seeds indoors in mid- to late spring and transplant outside when frost danger is past. Seeds may also be planted directly in the garden soil in late spring. Germination is about 80 percent and takes place in 1 to 2 weeks. They grow in clumps; space 12 to 15 inches (30 to 38 centimeters) apart. Water lightly to moderately.

Sun/Soil: Full sun; well-drained soil

Companion/Complementary Planting: Very nice with fennel, angelica, and calendula

Harvesting: Harvest seed heads, with a pair of strong snips, when fully ripe in late summer or early fall.

Market Potential: Low; competition is fierce

Medicinal Benefits: Good for the urinary, respiratory, and digestive tracts, and useful for winter illnesses

Parts Used: Seeds, dried

Home Pharmacy Uses: Medicinal food

Heracleum sphondylium
Cow Parsnip

Growing your own cow parsnip is a good "insurance policy" that you will be getting the correct plant. In the wild, cow parsnip often grows in similar habitats to water hemlock. The two plants are cousins and even resemble each other, but while cow parsnip is a very useful medicinal plant, water hemlock is extremely poisonous. 🌾

Personality: Perennial; herbaceous (Zones 3–9)

Height: 3 to 4 feet (.9 to 1.2 meters)

Bloom Traits: White flowers appear in midsummer and eventually develop into great umbels of seeds.

Likes/Dislikes: Cow parsnip grows in shady river and streamside locations. It likes having its roots moist.

Propagation/Maintenance: Stratify seeds for 2 to 3 months and then sow indoors in mid-spring or directly outdoors in early spring. Transplant indoor plants outside, 24 inches (60 centimeters) apart, in late spring. Expect 60 to 70 percent germination. Cow parsnip will grow in clumps, and requires moderate to high amounts of water.

Sun/Soil: Partial shade, shade; prefers a rich loamy or sandy soil

Harvesting: Harvest the roots in the spring or fall with a needle-nose spade or garden fork Seeds may be picked in late summer or early fall when they are fully mature. Handpick entire seed umbels or use scissors. Gently rub off the seeds and discard stems.

Market Potential: Low

Medicinal Benefits: Used primarily for the digestive tract and occasionally for nervous system concerns. Only the roots and seeds should be used.

Parts Used: Roots and seeds, fresh or dried

Home Pharmacy Uses: Decoction, traditional tincture, foot soak, bath herb, infused oil, liniment

Humulus lupulus
Hops

Resins in hops are strong; after a morning of picking, enough of them may be absorbed through the skin to make you feel very relaxed, perhaps even ready for a nap. High-quality, insect-free, certified organic hops are difficult to find. Because of this, there is great market potential for this herb. 🌾

Personality: Perennial; herbaceous, vining (Zones 4–8)

Height: 8 feet (2.39 meters) and taller

Bloom Traits: Green strobiles are abundant by late summer.

Likes/Dislikes: Hops are found growing in disturbed soil, vining onto structures, trees, and fences.

Propagation/Maintenance: Root divisions are best. Seed germinates very poorly and sporadically over 6 to 8 weeks, often with only a 5 to 10 percent success rate. Stratifying seeds for 3 to 6 months and then soaking them overnight in warm water before sowing may help. Hops can also be propagated by cuttings; tip cuttings are less successful than layerings. Hops spread easily by root runners, and stems root every place they make contact with the soil. Space plants 6 to 8 feet (1.8 to 2.4 meters) apart; a strong trellis system will be required. Do not plant with less vigorous herbs. Water moderately to heavily.

Sun/Soil: Sun, partial shade; prefers normal to rich garden soil, but will tolerate poorer soils

Harvesting: Strobiles are handpicked when they are fully developed, but still goldish green (not tan).

Market Potential: Moderate to very high

Medicinal Benefits: Used as a sleep aid and to relieve pain, hops are strong and should be used carefully.

Parts Used: Strobiles, fresh or dried

Home Pharmacy Uses: Infusion, traditional tincture, sleep pillow, bath herb, foot soak

Hydrastis canadensis

Goldenseal

Goldenseal is classified as an at-risk plant in the United States by the Convention of International Trade of Endangered Species (CITES). Its wild harvesting is strictly governed for export sales. Still, goldenseal needs more help! Much of the wild rhizomes are harvested for domestic use in the United States, and that is not nearly so closely controlled. Groups like United Plant Savers are working very hard to help protect this medicinal plant from extinction in the wild. Certified organic cultivation is greatly encouraged. ❧

Goldenseal at a Glance

▸ **Plant Cycle:** Perennial

▸ **Type of Growth:** Herbaceous

▸ **Light Requirements:** Shade, partial shade

▸ **Water Requirements:** Moderate

▸ **Parts Used:** Rhizome

▸ **Home Pharmacy Uses:** Decoction, traditional tincture, syrup, compress, elixir, ointment, salve, cream, balm, foot soak, bath herb, infused oil, butter, suppository, powder, liniment

Personality: Perennial; herbaceous (Zones 3–9)

Height: 10 to 15 inches (25 to 38 centimeters)

Bloom Traits: Greenish white flowers occur in the spring. Bright red berries form from the flowering parts later in the summer.

Likes/Dislikes: Goldenseal is a woodland plant that grows in fairly dense shade and moist humus soil.

Propagation/Maintenance: Goldenseal is often propagated by root divisions in the fall. It is also grown from seeds, although this is more difficult. Buy seeds from a reliable source, and when they arrive, stratify them in moist sand in the refrigerator. Sow seeds in late fall or very early in spring, in seedbeds that are well shaded and not too hot. Allow seedlings to grow in seedbeds until the following year, when they can be transplanted, 8 to 10 inches (20 to 25 centimeters) apart, into their permanent garden home. Goldenseal will grow in clumps, and requires moderate watering.

Sun/Soil: Shade, partial shade; prefers a humus soil that is rich in composting hardwood tree leaves, but is remarkably adaptable to different soils

Harvesting: Rhizomes are usually harvested between 4 and 6 years of age. They may be carefully dug using a garden fork. Dig rhizomes in the fall rather than in the spring, so that the plant has a chance to propagate itself from seed first.

Market Potential: Very high

Medicinal Benefits: Goldenseal is used for the acute stages of winter illnesses and respiratory conditions. It is also helpful for some skin conditions. It has been improperly used for many years as a tonic and detoxification herb, and that has seriously contributed to its threatened extinction.

Parts Used: Rhizome, fresh or dried

Home Pharmacy Uses: Decoction, traditional tincture, syrup, compress, elixir, ointment, salve, cream, balm, foot soak, bath herb, infused oil, butter, suppository, powder, liniment

Hypericum perforatum

St.-John's-Wort

Demand for St.-John's-wort is very good right now, and the certified organically grown plant is sought after. Many growers, however, are cultivating St.-John's-wort, which will cause a decrease in market value. This herb is very labor intensive to harvest and the harvesting window is limited to a couple of weeks. Plan to have extra help available during the St.-John's-wort harvest. 🌿

🌿 St.-John's-Wort at a Glance

- ▸ **Plant Cycle:** Perennial
- ▸ **Type of Growth:** Herbaceous
- ▸ **Light Requirements:** Full sun, partial shade
- ▸ **Water Requirements:** Low to moderate

- ▸ **Parts Used:** Flowering tops
- ▸ **Home Pharmacy Uses:** Traditional tincture, syrup, compress, elixir, ointment, salve, cream, balm, foot soak, bath herb, infused oil, lini-ment

Personality: Perennial; herbaceous (Zones 3–8)

Height: 24 to 30 inches (60 to 75 centimeters)

Bloom Traits: Bright yellow, star-shaped flowers bloom profusely around the summer solstice.

Likes/Dislikes: St.-John's-wort grows abundantly in disturbed areas, especially in mountain meadows and along roadsides.

Propagation/Maintenance: Seeds should be stratified for 3 to 4 weeks to improve germination. Germination occurs in about 2 weeks and is approximately 70 percent. Seeds may be sown indoors and then transplanted outside in mid- to late spring, or sown directly outdoors in early spring. St.-John's-wort may be propagated by root divisions in spring or fall. This herb will spread; space plants 12 inches (30 centimeters) apart. Provide low to moderate amounts of water.

Sun/Soil: Full sun, partial shade; well-drained soil

Harvesting: Harvest only the flowering tops when the plant is in peak bloom and bud stage. This is the time when the levels of hypericin — one of the primary constituents responsible for the action of St.-John's-wort — are highest in the plant. Use snips or scissors to harvest the upper 3 to 4 inches (7.5 to 10 centimeters) of flowering leafy tops. Do not harvest nonflowering plants.

Market Potential: High

Medicinal Benefits: Unfortunately, St.-John's-wort has been pigeonholed as *only* an antidepressant herb. Nothing could be farther from the truth. This herb is also extremely beneficial for other nervous system ailments, immune support and winter illnesses, conditions related to the muscles, and as a topical skin treatment.

Parts Used: Flowering tops, fresh

Home Pharmacy Uses: Traditional tincture, syrup, compress, elixir, ointment, salve, cream, balm, foot soak, bath herb, infused oil, liniment

Inula helenium
Elecampane

This herb was often used by the ancient Romans for indigestion. Roman scholar Pliny also recommended elecampane to lift the spirits. Elecampane is becoming more widely recognized as a substitute for at-risk herbs like osha and lomatium. As this information becomes more accessible, the market viability for elecampane should become stronger.

Personality: Perennial; herbaceous (Zones 4–9)

Height: 4 to 6 feet (1.2 to 8 meters)

Bloom Traits: Bright yellow, daisylike flowers bloom from mid- to late summer.

Likes/Dislikes: Elecampane is most happy growing along edges of woodland or forest environments. It will often be found near streams, ponds, or other moist places.

Propagation/Maintenance: Stratify the seeds for several weeks and then sow indoors for transplanting in late spring. Elecampane will also do well sown directly outdoors in mid-spring. Germination takes about 2 weeks and success is approximately 50 percent. Space these herbs 12 inches (30 centimeters) apart, and provide light to moderate amounts of water.

Sun/Soil: Full sun, partial shade; prefers rich, loamy soil but is very adpatable

Harvesting: Harvest the roots of elecampane in the spring or fall. Use a needle-nose spade or a garden fork to lift these very big and deep taproots.

Market Potential: Moderate; often used as a substitute for the at-risk osha and lomatium

Medicinal Benefits: Elecampane is a very beneficial herb for the respiratory tract, and specifically for winter illnesses that affect that system of the body.

Parts Used: Roots, fresh or dried

Home Pharmacy Uses: Decoction, traditional tincture, syrup, elixir, foot soak, honey

Elecampane at a Glance

- ▶ **Plant Cycle:** Perennial
- ▶ **Type of Growth:** Herbaceous
- ▶ **Light Requirements:** Full sun, partial shade
- ▶ **Water Requirements:** Low to moderate
- ▶ **Parts Used:** Roots
- ▶ **Home Pharmacy Uses:** Decoction, traditional tincture, syrup, elixir, foot soak, honey

Lavandula angustifolia

Lavender, English

Most of us are familiar with the fragrance of lavender. But this is a fantastic medicinal plant that can be used in a multitude of ways. The leaves, stems, and flowers are all medicinally valuable, making the lavender plant available for harvesting throughout the growing season.

English Lavender at a Glance

▶ **Plant Cycle:** Perennial

▶ **Type of Growth:** Herbaceous

▶ **Light Requirements:** Full sun

▶ **Water Requirements:** Low

▶ **Parts Used:** Aerial

▶ **Home Pharmacy Uses:** Infusion, traditional tincture, cider vinegar tincture, syrup, compress, poultice, elixir, ointment, salve, cream, balm, foot soak, sleep pillow, bath herb, infused oil, honey, butter, suppository, liniment, insect repellent

Personality: Perennial; herbaceous (Zones 5–8)

Height: 24 inches (60 centimeters)

Bloom Traits: Varieties of English lavender have purple to deep blue flowers that bloom from early summer to the end of the season.

Likes/Dislikes: Lavender prefers dry soil and a sunny, hot environment similar to its native Mediterranean region.

Propagation/Maintenance: Seeds should be stratified for 1 to 2 weeks and then sown indoors. Transplant outdoors in mid- to late spring. Germination usually takes 2 to 3 weeks and is about 50 percent. Lavender may be propagated by cuttings, but use care to avoid overwatering. Liquid or powder rooting hormone helps speed up the rooting process. Warm nighttime temperatures of about 70°F (21°C) and good air circulation will help them root more quickly as well. Lavender grows in clumps and should be spaced 12 to 15 inches (30 to 38 centimeters) apart. Water lightly.

Sun/Soil: Full sun; well-drained soil is mandatory

Companion/Complementary Planting: Grow with *Echinacea angustifolia*, penstemon, hyssop, and yarrow.

Harvesting: Aerial parts should be harvested with snips at any point during the summer months. Cut to about 3 inches (7.5 centimeters) above the ground. Occasionally a buyer will want flowers only. These must be harvested carefully with a small pair of scissors to avoid including stem and leaves.

Market Potential: Moderate to high; dried flowers are in the highest demand, while aerial parts draw a smaller market

Medicinal Benefits: Lavender is versatile and recommended for many health concerns, including women's and children's health, nervous system conditions, and pain relief. It is also a very good skin herb.

Parts Used: Aerial parts, fresh or dried

Home Pharmacy Uses: Infusion, traditional tincture, cider vinegar tincture, syrup, compress, poultice, elixir, ointment, salve, cream, balm, foot soak, sleep pillow, bath herb, infused oil, honey, butter, suppository, liniment, insect repellent

Leonurus cardiaca
Motherwort

Wort is an old English word meaning "to heal," and when attached to mother we get a picture of how this plant has been used; it is often given to women just after childbirth to facilitate the recovery process. The Latin name comes from the words for "lion" and "heart," appropriate for an herb that is considered a good heart supporter. ✣

Personality: Perennial; herbaceous (Zones 4–8)

Height: 2 to 4 feet (.6 to 1.2 meters)

Bloom Traits: Motherwort has small whorls of lavender flowers from mid- to late summer.

Likes/Dislikes: This herb is commonly found in disturbed areas in temperate climates. It grows abundantly near streams and rivers.

Propagation/Maintenance: Stratify seeds for several weeks. Sow directly outdoors or start indoors and transplant outside in mid- to late spring. Seeds germinate in about 2 weeks at a rate of 75 to 80 percent. This clump-growing herb should be spaced 15 to 20 inches (38 to 50 centimeters) apart. Water moderately.

Sun/Soil: Full sun, partial shade, shade; no special soil needs

Harvesting: Harvest the aerial parts of motherwort from spring through fall. Snips or scissors will work nicely for the task.

Market Potential: Moderate

Medicinal Benefits: Motherwort is used for women's ailments, as a heart tonic herb, and for some nervous system and digestive tract conditions.

Parts Used: Aerial parts, fresh or dried

Home Pharmacy Uses: Infusion, traditional tincture, cider vinegar tincture, elixir, syrup, honey

Leucanthemum vulgare
Oxeye Daisy

Oxeye daisy is often grown in gardens as a perennial plant, and it is much favored by gardeners as a fresh-cut flower. But few people realize that this cheerful plant also has a variety of medicinal uses. ✣

Personality: Perennial; herbaceous (Zones 3–8)

Height: 2 to 4 feet (.6 to 1.2 meters)

Bloom Traits: White flower with a yellow center blooms from early to midsummer.

Likes/Dislikes: Native to Eurasia, oxeye daisy has adapted to nearly every temperate climate. It is found growing in high mountain meadows, prairie grasslands, and disturbed areas.

Propagation/Maintenance: Root divisions may be done in the spring or fall. Seeds are easy, but benefit from a stratification of at least 1 week. Germination is around 70 percent and sprouting occurs within 1 to 2 weeks. Sow indoors and transplant out in the mid- to late spring, or sow directly outdoors in early spring. Clumps will become larger each year. Oxeye daisy reseeds easily. Space plants 12 to 15 inches (30 to 38 centimeters) apart and water moderately.

Sun/Soil: Full sun, partial shade; no special soil needs

Companion/Complementary Planting: Quite lovely planted with licorice, santolina, and rosemary

Harvesting: Harvest flowering aerial parts with snips in midsummer.

Market Potential: Low

Medicinal Benefits: Used for gastrointestinal, throat, skin, women's, circulatory, and urinary concerns

Parts Used: Flowering aerial parts, fresh or dried

Home Pharmacy Uses: Infusion, traditional tincture, ointment, salve, foot soak, bath herb

Levisticum officinale

Lovage

The market for lovage is not currently very great, but this may change as more manufacturers realize that this plant holds some of the same properties — respiratory and digestive support — as its cousin, osha. 🌿

A.K.A.: Garden osha; it is not true osha (*Ligusticum porteri*)

Personality: Perennial; herbaceous (Zones 5–8)

Height: 2 to 3 feet (.6 to .9 meter)

Bloom Traits: Umbels of white flowers appear in late spring to early summer.

Likes/Dislikes: Native to mountainous regions of southern Europe and common in the Mediterranean

Propagation/Maintenance: Stratify seeds for 1 to 2 weeks and then sow indoors. Expect near 50 percent germination, which takes about 2 weeks. Transplant this clump-grower outdoors, 24 inches (60 centimeters) apart, in mid- to late spring. Water moderately.

Sun/Soil: Sun, shade, partial shade; needs well-drained soil

Harvesting: Harvest the roots in spring or fall with a needle-nose spade or garden fork. Handpick or snip the leaves and stems at any point during the growing season. With a pair of snips or scissors, cut off the seed umbel when fully ripened (late summer or early fall). Gently rub off the seeds between your palms.

Market Potential: Low to moderate

Medicinal Benefits: Excellent for treating winter illnesses and respiratory tract concerns

Parts Used: Roots, leaves, stems, and seeds, used fresh or dried

Home Pharmacy Uses: Infusion, decoction, traditional tincture, cider vinegar tincture, syrup, elixir, lozenge, medicinal food, foot soak, bath herb, honey

Liatris species

Gayfeather

Native American peoples of at least 11 different tribes have used gayfeather as a medicinal plant. Some tribes even relied on this plant as a food source. 🌿

Personality: Perennial; herbaceous (Zones 3–9)

Height: 10 to 12 inches (25 to 30 centimeters)

Bloom Traits: Bright purple spikes of flowers bloom from midsummer through early fall.

Likes/Dislikes: Gayfeather is a prairie plant that enjoys growing among native grasses and other wildflowers.

Propagation/Maintenance: Stratify seeds for a minimum of 3 months and then soak in 3 percent hydrogen peroxide for about 15 minutes. Sow immediately. Start seeds either outdoors in a sandy seedbed or indoors for transplanting outside in late spring. Seed germination varies greatly and is usually not high, around 30 to 50 percent. Seeds typically take between 3 and 4 weeks to germinate. Space plants 8 to 10 inches (20 to 25 centimeters) apart. They grow in clumps and require light to moderate watering.

Sun/Soil: Full sun; no special soil needs

Harvesting: Harvesting gayfeather should be done in the spring or the fall, preferably in the fall so that the plant has a chance to develop seeds first. Use a garden fork or a needle-nose spade for this job.

Market Potential: None; mainly used by people in its native habitat

Medicinal Benefits: A diuretic for mild urinary concerns, it also makes a valuable syrup for persistent tickly coughs.

Parts Used: Roots, fresh or dried

Home Pharmacy Uses: Infusion, traditional tincture, syrup, elixir, lozenge, honey

Lobelia cardinalis

Cardinal Flower

Lobelia inflata, or Indian tobacco, is the species of *Lobelia* generally used in the natural products industry, is currently classified as at-risk. It is much more difficult to grow than *L. cardinalis*, which is an acceptable alternative to *L. inflata* if formulas are adjusted to accommodate the difference in potency. It would be nice to see more herbalists and companies taking this approach to lessen the burden on the *inflata* species. 🐝

A.K.A.: Lobelia, red lobelia

Personality: Perennial; herbaceous (Zones 3–9)

Height: 15 to 30 inches (38 to 76 centimeters)

Bloom Traits: Shocking scarlet flowers bloom from mid- to late summer.

Likes/Dislikes: Cardinal flower prefers to grow alongside streams, lakes, and ponds. It is a water-lover and will be found growing where its roots can stay moist.

Propagation/Maintenance: Stratify seeds for 8 to 10 weeks and then sow indoors 6 to 8 weeks befor transplanting outside in late spring. Space 12 inches (30 centimeters) apart and provide constant moisture. Cardinal flower grows in clumps.

Sun/Soil: Shade, partial shade; prefers moist loamy or sandy soil that is slightly acid to slightly alkaline

Harvesting: Harvest the aerial parts with snips or scissors when the plant is in full flower.

Market Potential: Low

Medicinal Benefits: Beneficial internally for bronchial conditions and externally for tense muscles

Parts Used: Aerial parts, fresh or dried

Home Pharmacy Uses: Infusion, traditional tincture, vinegar tincture, syrup, foot soak, bath herb, infused oil, liniment

Marrubium vulgare

Horehound

This plant, often an ingredient in old-fashioned cough syrups and cough drops, is excellent bee fodder, especially in high mountain desert climates. Of course, bees are welcome creatures because they are fantastic crop pollinators. 🐝

Personality: Perennial; herbaceous (Zones 3–8)

Height: 12 to 24 inches (30 to 60 centimeters)

Bloom Traits: Blooms from July till frost, with small white flowers

Likes/Dislikes: Commonly found in grasslands, prairies, pastures, and meadows, horehound grows in dry, sandy wash areas, in rocky soil, and in juniper forests.

Propagation/Maintenance: Horehound is easily propagated from seed. No special treatments are required and seeds germinate in 2 to 3 weeks consistently at 70 to 80 percent. Transplant outdoors in mid- to late spring. Tip cuttings and root divisions (see chapter 4) can also be used to propagate horehound. Use care in watering; horehound will not grow well if overwatered. Horehound grows in clumps and readily reseeds. Space plants 12 inches (30 centimeters) apart.

Sun/Soil: Full sun; poorer soil is preferred

Companion/Complementary Planting: Horehound grows nicely with thyme, rosemary, feverfew, and oxeye daisy.

Harvesting: Horehound may be harvested any time during the growing season. Aerial parts are harvested with snips.

Market Potential: Moderate

Medicinal Benefits: This herb is used for relief of symptoms of winter illnesses.

Parts Used: Aerial parts, fresh or dried

Home Pharmacy Uses: Traditional tincture, syrup, lozenge, infusion, honey, elixir

Matricaria recutita and
Chamaemelum nobile

Chamomile

Chamomile is widely used in the herb industry, but harvesting the flowers is very labor intensive and it is often difficult to compete with foreign markets. The market will be excellent for those willing to harvest only the flowers and dry them. ❦

✿ Chamomile at a Glance

▸ **Plant Cycle:** Annual/perennial

▸ **Type of Growth:** Herbaceous

▸ **Light Requirements:** Full sun, partial shade

▸ **Water Requirements:** Low to moderate

▸ **Parts Used:** Flowers, flowering tops

▸ **Home Pharmacy Uses:** Infusion, traditional tincture, cider vinegar tincture, syrup, compress, poultice, elixir, ointment, salve, cream, balm, foot soak, bath herb, sleep pillow, infused oil, honey, liniment

Personality: German chamomile (*Matricaria recutita*), annual; Roman chamomile (*Chamaemelum nobile*), perennial; herbaceous (Zones 4–9)

Height: German, to 24 inches (60 centimeters); Roman, 8 to 10 inches (20 to 25 centimeters)

Bloom Traits: White, daisylike flowers bloom from June through frost.

Likes/Dislikes: These two species are considered garden dwellers.

Propagation/Maintenance: German chamomile is easy to grow from seed, and can be direct-sown in garden or field. Keeping the tiny seeds moist for germination can be very difficult, so try starting plants indoors and transplanting after frost danger has passed. Allow 3 to 5 weeks before transplanting outdoors. Space 10 inches (25 centimeters) apart. Seeds consistently germinate at 50 to 70 percent in about 2 weeks. This species grows as a single plant and needs light to moderate watering. Roman chamomile is also easy from seed, but the germination rate is 40 to 60 percent. Instead, propagate by divisions. Roman chamomile spreads by rhizomatous roots. Space the plants 8 inches (20 centimeters) apart, allowing room for plants to fill in as a ground cover. Provide light to moderate amounts of water.

Sun/Soil: Full sun, partial shade; grows best in well-drained soil

Harvesting: Harvest during the blooming season. If only flowers are used, pick by hand or with the help of a chamomile rake (a special tool designed for the purpose). If the flowers with 2 to 3 inches (5 to 7.5 centimeters) of stems are harvested, use a pair of snips.

Market Potential: High to very high

Medicinal Benefits: A sedative and nervine herb, chamomile has calming, soothing, and anti-inflammatory actions. It is an excellent digestive herb, sleep aid, children's herb, and skin aid.

Parts Used: Flowers and flowering tops, fresh or dried

Home Pharmacy Uses: Infusion, cider vinegar tincture, traditional tincture, syrup, compress, poultice, elixir, ointment, salve, cream, balm, foot soak, bath herb, sleep pillow, infused oil, honey, liniment

Medicago sativa

Alfalfa

The Arabs have called alfalfa the Father of All Foods because it is packed with nutrition. Alfalfa, for hay, is cut at 20 percent bloom and is harvested all the way to the ground. This includes the woody portions of the stem rather than just the tender flowering stalks. When correctly harvested for medicinal use, alfalfa will yield a superior product preferred by manufacturers. ✿

Alfalfa at a Glance

- **Plant Cycle:** Perennial
- **Type of Growth:** Herbaceous
- **Light Requirements:** Full sun
- **Water Requirements:** Moderate
- **Parts Used:** Aerial
- **Home Pharmacy Uses:** Infusion, traditional tincture, cider vinegar tincture, syrup, medicinal food, honey

A.K.A.: Lucerne

Personality: Perennial; herbaceous (Zones 5–8)

Height: 15 to 18 inches (38 to 45 centimeters)

Bloom Traits: Bright purple flowers begin to bloom in early summer. Repeat cuttings will result in several blooming cycles per growing season.

Likes/Dislikes: Alfalfa, often planted as a pasture crop, has escaped and is found growing along roadsides and in open fields. Wherever disturbed soils exist, alfalfa may be found. It is an often forgotten but beautiful garden plant.

Propagation/Maintenance: Direct-sow seed into the garden or field where you would like it to grow. About 80 percent of the seed will sprout in 2 to 4 weeks. Because alfalfa develops an extensive root structure quickly and sends its roots deep into the earth, it prefers not to grow in a pot and is best direct-sown rather than transplanted. Space plants 12 inches (30 centimeters) apart and water moderately for the highest yield. This herb grows in clumps with deep nitrogen-fixing roots that nourish the soil.

Sun/Soil: Full sun; prefers soil high in organic matter (4 to 5 percent)

Companion/Complementary Planting: Plant with red clover, chicory, narrow-leaf plantain, and dandelion.

Harvesting: Cut when the plant is in full bloom. The upper half of flowering plants only are cut with snips, unlike alfalfa harvested for livestock fodder.

Market Potential: Moderate to high

Medicinal Benefits: An excellent source of vitamins and minerals, alfalfa is a whole-body tonic herb.

Parts Used: Flowering aerial parts, fresh or dried

Home Pharmacy Uses: Infusion, traditional tincture, cider vinegar tincture, syrup, medicinal food, honey

Melissa officinalis
Lemon Balm

Lemon balm was the first herb I ever grew. A neighbor gave me a plant as a gift, and I had no idea what an impact it would have on my life. This wonderfully versatile medicinal plant has been used for centuries. 🌿

Personality: Perennial; herbaceous (Zones 4–9)

Height: 24 inches (60 centimeters)

Bloom Traits: Lemon balm has small white flowers that are not especially showy; it blooms on and off throughout the summer months.

Likes/Dislikes: Lemon balm is Mediterranean in origin. It prefers a warm climate that is not too wet.

Propagation/Maintenance: Easiest grown from seed that has been stratified at least 1 week. Start indoors and then transplant outside in late spring. Seed germination is 60 to 70 percent and takes about 14 days. Tip cuttings may also be done using a liquid or powder rooting hormone. Lemon balm grows in clumps and should be spaced 12 inches (30 centimeters) apart. This herb reseeds vigorously. Water moderately.

Sun/Soil: Full sun, partial shade; well-drained soil

Harvesting: Harvest aerial parts at any time during the growing season. Snips or scissors will work great. If you cut only the upper half of the plant, it will quickly regenerate, giving you several harvest cuts over the course of the summer.

Market Potential: Moderate

Medicinal Benefits: Used for the entire body, lemon balm is beneficial for the digestive tract, children's health, winter illnesses, and to strengthen the immune system. It is recommended for pain relief and nervous system health, and is considered a great stress reliever.

Parts Used: Aerial parts, fresh or dried; note that the dried plant loses some of its potency after 6 months

Home Pharmacy Uses: Infusion, traditional tincture, cider vinegar tincture, syrup, compress, poultice, elixir, lozenge, ointment, salve, balm, cream, foot soak, bath herb, infused oil, honey, liniment

🌿 Lemon Balm at a Glance

- **Plant Cycle:** Perennial
- **Type of Growth:** Herbaceous
- **Light Requirements:** Full sun, partial shade
- **Water Requirements:** Moderate
- **Parts Used:** Aerial
- **Home Pharmacy Uses:** Infusion, traditional tincture, cider vinegar tincture, syrup, compress, poultice, elixir, lozenge, ointment, salve, balm, cream, foot soak, bath herb, infused oil, honey, liniment

Mentha × piperita

Peppermint

Few plants are as diverse in their uses as peppermint. Familiar to all of us as an ingredient in chewing gum, candy, toothpaste, and even cleaning products, peppermint can be used medicinally to address nearly every body system. 🌿

Peppermint at a Glance

- **Plant Cycle:** Perennial
- **Type of Growth:** Herbaceous
- **Light Requirements:** Full sun, partial shade, shade
- **Water Requirements:** Moderate to heavy
- **Parts Used:** Aerial

- **Home Pharmacy Uses:** Infusion, traditional tincture, cider vinegar tincture, syrup, compress, elixir, lozenge, medicinal food, ointment, salve, cream, balm, foot soak, sleep pillow, bath herb, infused oil, honey, butter, liniment

Personality: Perennial; herbaceous (Zones 5–9)

Height: 24 inches (60 centimeters)

Bloom Traits: Spikes of purple flowers bloom in mid- to late summer.

Likes/Dislikes: Peppermint is often found as a garden escapee in disturbed soil areas near streams and ponds. It is also common in city alleys.

Propagation/Maintenance: Propagate peppermint from root divisions or cuttings. Both methods are easy and foolproof. Do not grow peppermint from seed if you wish to have a good, strong plant; seed crops of peppermint have very little smell or taste to them. This is a vigorous spreading herb; plants should be spaced 12 inches (30 centimeters) apart. Peppermint requires moderate to heavy watering, but if you grow the herb on the drier side, it will behave itself better in the garden.

Sun/Soil: Full sun, partial shade, shade; no special soil needs

Companion/Complementary Planting: Grow peppermint next to other aggressive plants like yarrow and wormwood to keep each one in its place.

Harvesting: Aerial parts are cut, with snips or scissors, at any point during the growing season. Harvesting peppermint just before it flowers will yield a sweeter taste. Flowering peppermint often has a very strong, burning, and even slightly bitter taste.

Market Potential: Moderate to high; properly dried peppermint is in demand by herbal tea companies

Medicinal Benefits: Useful for nearly every part of the body, including the digestive tract, muscular system, respiratory tract, and women's reproductive system. It is also useful for pain relief, skin concerns, winter illnesses, and children's concerns.

Parts Used: Aerial parts, fresh or dried

Home Pharmacy Uses: Infusion, traditional tincture, cider vinegar tincture, syrup, compress, elixir, lozenge, medicinal food, ointment, salve, cream, balm, foot soak, sleep pillow, bath herb, infused oil, honey, butter, liniment

Mentha pulegium
Pennyroyal

Pennyroyal has an unwarranted reputation for being dangerous. It is true that pregnant women should not use this plant, but many other herbs should be avoided during pregnancy. Pennyroyal essential oil, however, does have some cautions attached to it and should be used externally only and with extreme care. Market demand for pennyroyal has decreased drastically, although it is often included in herbal pet products to repel fleas and ticks (do not use on cats). 🌿

Personality: Perennial; herbaceous (Zones 7–9)

Height: 10 to 12 inches (25 to 30 centimeters)

Bloom Traits: Graceful lavender whorls bloom in mid- to late summer.

Likes/Dislikes: Pennyroyal is native to the hot Mediterranean regions of the world.

Propagation/Maintenance: Root divisions and cuttings are easy propagation methods. Seed can be sown indoors and then transplanted out in mid- to late spring. Germination rates are near to 65 percent and sprouting occurs in about 2 weeks. Pennyroyal has a spreading nature; plants should be spaced 12 inches (30 centimeters) apart. Water moderately.

Sun/Soil: Full sun, partial shade, shade; needs well-drained soil

Harvesting: Aerial parts are harvested at any point during the growing season. Cut with snips or scissors.

Market Potential: Low

Medicinal Benefits: Good for women's health (avoid if pregnant), winter illnesses, and digestive support

Parts Used: Aerial parts, fresh or dried

Home Pharmacy Uses: Infusion, traditional tincture, syrup, compress, foot soak, bath herb, honey, insect repellent

Mentha spicata
Spearmint

Most of us recognize the taste of spearmint in chewing gum. The flavor is distinct, pleasant, and uplifting. Spearmint is great for relieving depression and brightening stressful days. 🌿

Personality: Perennial; herbaceous (Zones 5–9)

Height: 24 inches (60 centimeters)

Bloom Traits: Lovely lavender flowers bloom in mid- to late summer.

Likes/Dislikes: Grows, as a garden escapee, near streams, rivers, lakes, and ponds, and in disturbed areas.

Propagation/Maintenance: Root divisions are a good way to propagate spearmint; divide in the spring or fall. Cuttings are also very easy and successful. They may be taken at any point during the growing season. Do not grow spearmint from seed, as it will not have the same high amounts of volatile oils. This spreader should be spaced 12 inches (30 centimeters) apart. It requires moderate to heavy watering.

Sun/Soil: Full sun, partial shade, shade; no special soil needs

Harvesting: Harvest aerial parts at any point during the growing season. Snips work best for this job.

Market Potential: Moderate; generally not as strong as peppermint, but great if you dry the spearmint

Medicinal Benefits: Useful for women's and children's health, nervous system, and respiratory and digestive tract conditions. It is also valuable for pain relief, winter illnesses, and throat and skin conditions.

Parts Used: Aerial parts, fresh or dried

Home Pharmacy Uses: Infusion, traditional tincture, cider vinegar tincture, syrup, compress, elixir, lozenge, medicinal food, ointment, salve, cream, balm, foot soak, sleep pillow, bath herb, infused oil, honey, liniment

Monarda didyma, M. fistulosa, M. fistulosa var. menthifolia, M. punctata

Monarda

Monarda is a very tasty, spicy herb. It is wonderful as a culinary seasoning. Good substitute for Greek oregano. 🌾

A.K.A.: Bee balm, wild oregano, bergamot, Oswego tea

Personality: Perennial; herbaceous (Zones 4–9)

Height: 2 to 3 feet (.6 to .9 meter)

Bloom Traits: Red, lavender, pinkish lavender, yellow, or pink- and purple-spotted flowers bloom early to late summer in most regions.

Likes/Dislikes: Monarda prefers sunny meadows and gardens and is often found growing near waterways.

Propagation/Maintenance: Seeds are best stratified for 3 months before sowing. Expect sporadic, 60 to 70 percent germination in 2 to 3 weeks. Tender tip cuttings have a lower success rate. Transplant seedlings or rooted cuttings outdoors in late spring. Root divisions propagate well. Space 12 inches (30 centimeters) apart. Plants grow in clumps and require moderate watering.

Sun/Soil: Full sun, partial shade; *M. fistulosa* var. *menthifolia* and *M. didyma* prefer rich soil and fair moisture, while *M. fistulosa* likes dry, well-drained soil and *M. punctata* prefers loose, sandy, drier soil.

Harvesting: Harvest aerial parts at any time during the growing season. Use a pair of snips.

Market Potential: Low to moderate; increasing

Medicinal Benefits: Excellent for treating winter illnesses, respiratory conditions, and the digestive tract

Parts Used: Aerial parts, fresh or dried

Home Pharmacy Uses: Infusion, compress, lozenge, ointment, salve, cream, balm, foot or bath soak, infused oil, liniment, honey, syrup, elixir, traditional or cider vinegar tincture

Monardella odoratissima

Coyote Mint

Coyote mint is a spunky little plant that looks something like a miniature version of monarda. They are distant cousins within the Mint family. 🌾

Personality: Perennial; herbaceous (Zones 6–9)

Height: 10 to 12 inches (25 to 30 centimeters)

Bloom Traits: Pale lavender flowers bloom from early to midsummer.

Likes/Dislikes: Coyote mint is native to the dry, high mountain desert areas of the southwestern states.

Propagation/Maintenance: When propagating by cuttings, use liquid rooting hormone and do not overwater. I prefer to grow this plant from seed. Stratify the seeds for 3 months before sowing and then expect a 3- to 4-week germination period. Germination percentages can vary greatly, but a good rate is 50 percent. These plants will spread, so space them 12 to 15 inches (30 to 38 centimeters) apart. Water lightly.

Sun/Soil: Full sun; soil that isn't too rich or moist.

Companion/Complementary Planting: Yerba de la negrita, horehound, and penstemons

Harvesting: Aerial parts may be cut with scissors or snips during mid- to late summer.

Market Potential: Low

Medicinal Benefits: Excellent for symptoms of winter illnesses, especially those of the throat, and also used for respiratory tract and digestive conditions

Parts Used: Aerial parts (preferably in flower), fresh or dried

Home Pharmacy Uses: Infusion, traditional tincture, cider vinegar tincture, syrup, elixir, lozenge, foot soak, sleep pillow, bath herb, infused oil, honey, liniment

Nepeta cataria

Catnip

Most people are familiar with catnip only for its intoxicating effect on cats, but it is a great herb for humans, too. Interestingly, catnip acts as a stimulant on cats but a sedative on people. 🌿

🌿 Catnip at a Glance

▸ **Plant Cycle:** Perennial

▸ **Type of Growth:** Herbaceous

▸ **Light Requirements:** Full sun, partial shade, shade

▸ **Water Requirements:** Light to moderate

▸ **Parts Used:** Aerial

▸ **Home Pharmacy Uses:** Infusion, traditional tincture, cider vinegar tincture, syrup, compress, poultice, elixir, medicinal food, ointment, salve, cream, balm, foot soak, bath herb, infused oil, honey, liniment, sleep pillow

Personality: Perennial; herbaceous (Zones 3–7)

Height: 15 to 24 inches (38 to 60 centimeters)

Bloom Traits: Spikes of small, white, purple-spotted, not especially showy flowers bloom on and off from summer to fall.

Likes/Dislikes: Catnip can be found growing in many different types of environments. It is likely to be discovered in disturbed areas, such as alongside streams, ponds, lakes, roadsides, and waste ground.

Propagation/Maintenance: Seeds will germinate at a higher percentage if they are stratified for a couple of weeks before sowing. Then sow directly outdoors into the garden soil in early to mid-spring, or start early indoors and transplant out in mid- to late spring. Germination is normally about 50 percent. Space plants 12 inches (30 centimeters) apart and provide low to moderate amounts of water. Catnip reseeds itself readily.

Sun/Soil: Full sun, partial shade, shade; no special soil needs

Companion/Complementary Planting: Oxeye daisy, black-eyed Susan, and sage

Harvesting: All of the aerial parts can be harvested at any time during the growing season. Use scissors or snips to cut the plant about 3 to 4 inches (7.5 to 10 centimeters) above the ground. Catnip can provide several harvests throughout the season.

Market Potential: Moderate; try the herbal pet products market, too

Medicinal Benefits: Catnip has many medicinal uses, including nervous system support, pain relief, and stress relief. It is also recommended for the digestive tract, cold and flu symptoms, and children's health concerns.

Parts Used: Aerial parts, fresh or dried

Home Pharmacy Uses: Infusion, traditional tincture, cider vinegar tincture, syrup, compress, poultice, elixir, medicinal food, ointment, salve, cream, balm, foot soak, bath herb, infused oil, honey, liniment, sleep pillow

Ocimum species
Basil

Everyone is familiar with basil as a delicious culinary herb. Historically, however, basil was considered a cure for sea dragon bites. It is a wonderful medicinal food that contributes to healthy digestive tract function.

Personality: Annual; herbaceous

Height: 15 inches (38 centimeters)

Bloom Traits: Flowers range from pink and purple to white.

Likes/Dislikes: Basil is considered a domestic plant. It will grow in most gardens, from tropical to temperate.

Propagation/Maintenance: Sow basil seeds indoors, in a warm and sunny location, 2 to 4 weeks before the final frost date in your area. Transplant them outdoors 12 inches (30 centimeters) apart in spring when all danger of frost has passed. The herb will grow in upright, bushy clumps if you pinch it regularly. Use a light to moderate amount of water. Basil will bloom in an effort to develop seed, but then the plant is spent. To prolong the life of your basil, keep the flowers pinched off.

Sun/Soil: Full sun; well-drained soil

Companion/Complementary Planting: Hot and sweet peppers and tomatoes are said to have enhanced flavor when planted next to basil.

Harvesting: Harvest the aerial parts throughout the growing season by hand-pinching or using a pair of scissors. You should be able to harvest basil about every 1 to 2 weeks.

Market Potential: Low in herbal products market; high in culinary-medicinal markets

Medicinal Benefits: Basil is an excellent digestive system support herb.

Parts Used: Aerial parts, fresh or dried

Home Pharmacy Uses: Medicinal food, infused oil, honey

Basil at a Glance

- ▸ **Plant Cycle:** Annual
- ▸ **Type of Growth:** Herbaceous
- ▸ **Light Requirements:** Full sun
- ▸ **Water Requirements:** Low to moderate
- ▸ **Parts Used:** Aerial
- ▸ **Home Pharmacy Uses:** Medicinal food, infused oil, honey

Oenothera biennis

Evening Primrose

This plant has delicate, lovely flowers that bloom at night. In the moonlight they appear to be glowing. Quite beautiful! The oil from evening primrose seeds is rich in essential fatty acids and is used both internally and externally to address a variety of ailments. 🌿

Personality: Biennial; herbaceous (Zones 4–8)

Height: 3 to 4 feet (.9–1.2 meters)

Bloom Traits: Yellow flowers bloom at dusk each day and fade by midmorning the next day. Flowers begin blooming from midsummer on.

Likes/Dislikes: Evening primrose can be found blooming alongside streams and rivers in disturbed soil. It also likes open fields and roadsides.

Propagation/Maintenance: Stratify seeds for several weeks and then sow directly in the soil outdoors in mid-spring. You can also start these indoors earlier in the spring, but it has been my experience that they do not do quite as well in an indoor environment. Germination percentage outdoors is usually very high, near 80 percent. Indoor germination is usually about 60 percent. A vigorous self-sowing herb, evening primrose should be spaced 10 to 12 inches (25 to 30 centimeters) apart. Water moderately.

Sun/Soil: Full sun, partial shade; prefers well-drained soil

Harvesting: Harvest aerial parts with snips while in flower or seed.

Market Potential: Low; the expressed seed oil is most sought after, and requires enormous amounts of plant material

Medicinal Benefits: Often recommended for women's health concerns and for skin and nail health

Parts Used: Aerial parts, fresh or dried

Home Pharmacy Uses: Infusion, traditional tincture, syrup

🌿 **Evening Primrose at a Glance**

- **Plant Cycle:** Biennial
- **Type of Growth:** Herbaceous
- **Light Requirements:** Full sun, partial shade
- **Water Requirements:** Moderate
- **Parts Used:** Aerial
- **Home Pharmacy Uses:** Infusion, traditional tincture, syrup

Opuntia species

Prickly Pear

Prickly pear is an important medicinal food among the cultures of Mexico and the southwestern United States. Adult-onset diabetes is a severe problem in these groups, and incorporating prickly pear into their diets is smart way to maintain blood sugar levels. 🌺

🌿 Prickly Pear at a Glance

- ▸ **Plant Cycle:** Perennial
- ▸ **Type of Growth:** Cactus
- ▸ **Light Requirements:** Full sun
- ▸ **Water Requirements:** Low
- ▸ **Parts Used:** Aerial
- ▸ **Home Pharmacy Uses:** Syrup, compress, ointment, medicinal food, salve, cream, balm, honey

Personality: Perennial; cactus (Zones 6–11, depending on species)

Height: 10 to 15 inches (25 to 38 centimeters)

Bloom Traits: Flowers bloom in pinks and yellows, depending upon species, from late spring into early summer.

Likes/Dislikes: Most prickly pears are desert plants that range from high mountain desert regions into the lower desert climates. They rely on spring rains to help sustain them through the dry summer.

Propagation/Maintenance: Simulate the desert environment by stratifying prickly pear seeds for 1 to 2 weeks. Just before sowing, soak seeds for 15 minutes in 3 percent hydrogen peroxide. Sow immediately in a loose soil mix and keep temperatures warm. Germination rates and time vary greatly from 10 to 70 percent, and 2 weeks to 3 or 4 months. Keep seeds evenly moist and be patient. Transplant outdoors when seedlings are 1 year old and well established. Water seedlings thoroughly and then wait a few days before watering again. Take care not to overwater. Depending on the species, some prickly pears will spread more aggressively than others. Space plants 12 to 15 inches (30 to 38 centimeters) apart. Water lightly when mature.

Sun/Soil: Full sun; prefers well-drained, sandy soil

Companion/Complementary Planting: White sage, California poppy, brickellia, and callirhoe

Harvesting: The pads, flowers, and fruits of prickly pear should be harvested carefully with snips while wearing gloves. Singe the spines off the harvested plants, using a campfire flame or even a butane lighter, then prepare the cactus for use.

Market Potential: Low to moderate; better in southwestern regions, where it is used as a medicinal food

Medicinal Benefits: Good for balancing blood sugar levels and for some gastrointestinal complaints, prickly pear is also useful as a skin herb.

Parts Used: Aerial parts, fresh

Home Pharmacy Uses: Syrup, compress, medicinal food, ointment, salve, cream, balm, honey

Origanum vulgare

Oregano

Oregano is usually thought of as a culinary herb, but it is also highly antiseptic. Consider preparing oregano as a topical remedy for cuts and scrapes. This herb has also been used to relieve nervousness, irritability, insomnia, tension, and anxiety. 🌿

Personality: Perennial; herbaceous (Zones 5–9)

Height: To 24 inches (60 centimeters)

Bloom Traits: Tiny lavender flowers grace oregano throughout the summer months.

Likes/Dislikes: Oregano is native to the Mediterranean regions of the world. It enjoys a hot, but not too wet, climate.

Propagation/Maintenance: Stratify seeds for 1 week and then sow them indoors. Germination is near 70 percent; seeds take a week or two to sprout. Transplant outside once spring weather is well settled. Oregano can also be propagated by tip cuttings; liquid rooting hormone will assist in the rooting process. Plants should be spaced 12 inches (30 centimeters) apart to allow for spreading. Water lightly to moderately.

Sun/Soil: Full sun, partial shade; well-drained soil

Harvesting: Harvest the aerial parts of oregano at any time during the growing season. Snips or scissors will work nicely for this task.

Market Potential: Low to moderate

Medicinal Benefits: A strong medicinal food, oregano is recommended during winter illnesses and to support healthy digestive system function. It is also strongly antiseptic for skin concerns.

Parts Used: Aerial parts, fresh or dried

Home Pharmacy Uses: Infusion, traditional tincture, medicinal food, ointment, salve, foot soak, bath herb, infused oil

🌿 Oregano at a Glance

- ▸ **Plant Cycle:** Perennial
- ▸ **Type of Growth:** Herbaceous
- ▸ **Light Requirements:** Full sun, partial shade
- ▸ **Water Requirements:** Low to moderate
- ▸ **Parts Used:** Aerial
- ▸ **Home Pharmacy Uses:** Infusion, traditional tincture, ointment, medicinal food, salve, foot soak, bath herb, infused oil

Passiflora incarnata

Passionflower

Passionflower is primarily wild-harvested to supply an ever-increasing demand from the natural products industry. I have spoken with brokers who are becoming more and more concerned about the stability of these wild populations as this demand increases. Because of the precarious situation, this is an excellent herb for certified organic growers to consider.

According to Richo Cech of Horizon Herbs seed company, seeds benefit from a fire treatment using a planted moistened flat that is then sprinkled heavily with pine needles and set on fire. He says the pine needles will burn out quickly, usually within a couple of minutes, but the moisture in the flat prevents the seeds from burning. Treated this way, the seeds will begin germinating in less than 2 weeks. 🌺

🌿 Passionflower at a Glance

- ▸ **Plant Cycle:** Perennial
- ▸ **Type of Growth:** Herbaceous
- ▸ **Light Requirements:** Shade, partial shade
- ▸ **Water Requirements:** High
- ▸ **Parts Used:** Aerial
- ▸ **Home Pharmacy Uses:** Infusion, traditional tincture, syrup, compress, elixir, foot soak, bath herb, honey

A.K.A.: Maypop

Personality: Perennial; herbaceous (Zones 6–9)

Height: 8 feet (2.39 meters) and much taller

Bloom Traits: Amazing, colorful, and very exotic white and lavender flowers bloom from mid-to late-summer.

Likes/Dislikes: Passionflower is native to the southeastern United States; it prefers moisture and humidity and will not tolerate a severe winter.

Sun/Soil: Shade, partial shade; prefers a rich humus soil

Companion/Complementary Planting: Passionflower is pollinated by bats, so plant it in an area that is accessible to these creatures, such as near bat houses or building eaves.

Propagation/Maintenance: Propagation from seed is very difficult. The most successful method is to stratify in moist peat moss in the refrigerator for 1 week, then sow seeds indoors in a very warm greenhouse. Seedlings usually appear in about 3 weeks. Germination is typically low, between 20 and 40 percent. Plant outdoors only after all danger of frost is past. I prefer growing passionflower from tip cuttings. I use a liquid rooting hormone and keep the cuttings warm and moist until rooting occurs, in about 2 weeks. I have good success growing it this way and keep a mother plant permanently on hand for this purpose. Space 24 inches (60 centimeters) apart and give these spreading, vining plants trellises at least 8 feet high to climb on. Water moderately to heavily.

Harvesting: Aerial parts of passionflower are harvested, including any flowers or fruits, at any point during the growing season. Use snips and a big basket (we use 30-gallon plastic tree baskets).

Market Potential: Very high

Medicinal Benefits: Passionflower is a strong sedative and nervine herb.

Parts Used: Aerial parts, fresh or dried

Home Pharmacy Uses: Infusion, traditional tincture, syrup, compress, elixir, foot soak, bath herb, honey

Penstemon species

Penstemon

Penstemons are glorious plants, native to many parts of the United States. Harvesting from the wild causes damage to other plants in fragile communities with them. Since penstemons can be grown with a little patience, there is no reason to wild-harvest them and risk damaging delicate ecosystems. 🌿

Penstemon at a Glance

▸ **Plant Cycle:** Perennial

▸ **Type of Growth:** Herbaceous

▸ **Light Requirements:** Full sun, partial shade

▸ **Water Requirements:** Low

▸ **Parts Used:** Flowers

▸ **Home Pharmacy Uses:** Compress, ointment, salve, cream, balm, foot soak, bath herb, infused oil, honey, butter, suppository

A.K.A.: Beardtongue

Personality: Perennial; herbaceous (Zones 4–11, depending on species)

Height: 8 to 36 inches (20 to 90 centimeters)

Bloom Traits: Pink, purple, red, salmon, white, or yellow flowers occur May through August.

Likes/Dislikes: Penstemons grow in a wide range of habitats, including prairies, alpine, cliffs, juniper forests, rocky areas, and disturbed soil.

Propagation/Maintenance: These are general guidelines, but the Penstemon Society (see Resources) can give you individual species requirements. Penstemons are propagated by seed or cuttings. Root divisions are sometimes difficult. Stratify seed for a minimum of 3 months. Some varieties will benefit from a 15- to 20-minute peroxide soak. Do not to soak longer or damage to the seed coat may occur. Germination is often sporadic, occurring anytime between 2 and 8 weeks, and ranges from 10 to 80 percent, depending on the species. Penstemons are ready for transplanting outdoors in mid- to late spring. Use care in watering; they easily rot in seed flats or pots if they are overwatered. Depending on the species, penstemon may grow in clumps or be sprawling in nature. Space plants 12 inches (30 centimeters) apart.

Sun/Soil: Full sun, partial shade; prefers poor to gravelly soil, but many species are tolerant of normal garden soil

Companion/Complementary Planting: Plant with cacti, yucca, *Stanleya*, maravilla, and *Agastache*.

Harvesting: Harvest in full bloom, as only the flowers are used. Flowers are handpicked.

Market Potential: Low

Medicinal Benefits: Topically used for a wide variety of skin conditions.

Parts Used: Flowers, fresh

Home Pharmacy Uses: Compress, cream, balm, foot soak, bath herb, honey, salve, infused oil, ointment, butter, suppository

Petroselinum crispum

Parsley

I plant a border of parsley around the perimeter of the garden to satisfy parsley-loving rabbits and deer. They do not seem to be inclined to venture farther into the garden, and the parsley does not mind the regular "trimming." 🌿

Personality: Biennial; herbaceous (Zones 5–8)

Height: 12 to 20 inches (30 to 50 centimeters)

Bloom Traits: In the second year, parsley will bloom with white flower umbels. Flowering usually occurs from early to midsummer.

Likes/Dislikes: Parsley is a Mediterranean plant by nature and will do best in a drier, hot climate.

Propagation/Maintenance: I stratify my seeds for at least 1 week. The day before sowing, I soak them in water for 12 to 24 hours. Parsley takes a long time to germinate, up to 4 weeks, but by stratifying and soaking it, I usually see germination in 2 weeks or less. Germination rate is usually in the neighborhood of 70 percent. Sow seeds indoors and transplant outside in mid- to late spring, or sow directly in the garden in early spring. This clump-growing herb should be spaced 12 inches (30 centimeters) apart. Water moderately.

Sun/Soil: Full sun, partial shade; no special soil needs

Harvesting: Aerial parts may be gathered at any point during the growing season. I prefer scissors, but snips will also work well. If you plan to use the roots, dig them in the fall of the first year or the spring of the second year. Use a garden fork or needle-nose spade.

Market Potential: Moderate

Medicinal Benefits: Parsley is a wonderful medicinal food and a strong antioxidant. It is beneficial to the digestive tract and is often recommended for urinary tract concerns.

Parts Used: Aerial parts and roots, fresh or dried

Home Pharmacy Uses: Infusion, decoction, traditional tincture, cider vinegar tincture, medicinal food

🌿 Parsley at a Glance

- ▸ **Plant Cycle:** Biennial
- ▸ **Type of Growth:** Herbaceous
- ▸ **Light Requirements:** Full sun, partial shade
- ▸ **Water Requirements:** Moderate
- ▸ **Parts Used:** Aerial, roots
- ▸ **Home Pharmacy Uses:** Infusion, decoction, traditional tincture, cider vinegar tincture, medicinal food

Plantago major, P. lanceolata, P. media

Plantain

If foot blisters become a problem when hiking, consider applying plantain. Place a leaf directly against the skin over the blister and secure with first-aid tape. Plantain leaf will soothe the irritation and promote healing of the affected tissue. 🌿

🌿 Plantain at a Glance

- ► **Plant Cycle:** Perennial
- ► **Type of Growth:** Herbaceous
- ► **Light Requirements:** Full sun, partial shade
- ► **Water Requirements:** Moderate
- ► **Parts Used:** Whole plant, roots, leaves, seeds
- ► **Home Pharmacy Uses:** Infusion, decoction, traditional tincture, cider vinegar tincture, compress, poultice, lozenge, ointment, medicinal food, salve, cream, balm, bath herb, infused oil, butter, suppository, insect repellent

Personality: Perennial; herbaceous (Zones 3–9)

Height: 8 to 20 inches (20 to 50 centimeters); *P. major* is short, *P. lanceolata* is taller

Bloom Traits: Tiny white flowers grace a stalk that later forms tan seeds.

Likes/Dislikes: Plantain is found in a wide variety of climates in disturbed soil. It is as common to find plantain growing intermixed with the grass at a local park as it is to see it alongside a mountain hiking trail.

Propagation/Maintenance: It is easy to grow plantain from seed. I prefer to stratify the seeds because it increases the germination rate to about 70 percent. Sprouting takes 1 to 2 weeks. Start directly outdoors in early to mid-spring, or start indoors in mid-spring to transplant out in late spring. Plantain grows in clumps and should be spaced 12 inches (30 centimeters) apart. Water moderately.

Sun/Soil: Full sun, partial shade; no special soil needs

Companion/Complementary Planting: Grow in community with self-heal, lady's-mantle, and hyssop.

Harvesting: Harvest the whole plant with a garden fork or needle-nose spade from spring through fall; choose a day when the soil is moist but not soggy. If you desire roots only, trim off the aerial parts with a pair of snips. Leaves may be handpicked or snipped at any point during the growing season. Harvest seeds upon maturity and then rub them between your hands to free them from the stalks and husks.

Market Potential: Moderate; seek out salve, cream, and ointment makers as buyers for plantain

Medicinal Benefits: Very good for gastrointestinal conditions, the urinary tract, skin problems, and children's health. *P. media* is also good for stopping minor bleeding and for relieving insect bites and stings.

Parts Used: Whole plant, roots, leaves, and seeds, fresh or dried

Home Pharmacy Uses: Infusion, decoction, traditional tincture, cider vinegar tincture, compress, poultice, lozenge, medicinal food, ointment, salve, cream, balm, bath herb, infused oil, butter, suppository, insect repellent

Balloon Flower at a Glance

- **Plant Cycle:** Perennial
- **Type of Growth:** Spreads
- **Light Requirements:** Sun, partial shade
- **Water Requirements:** Moderate
- **Parts Used:** Roots
- **Home Pharmacy Uses:** Decoction, traditional tincture, powder

Platycodon grandiflorus

Balloon Flower

Balloon flowers take their name from the way the blossoms form a puffy sack when they bloom. They are exquisitely beautiful. Balloon flowers are not used abundantly in Western herbalism. They are usually grown in North America as a perennial garden plant with little concern for their medicinal benefits. This is a wonderful medicinal herb that should become more well known for its uses.

Personality: Perennial; spreads (Zones 4–9)

Height: 12 to 15 inches (30 to 38 centimeters)

Bloom Traits: Varied; blue, pink, lilac, and white. Flowers often begin blooming in early summer and continue on and off throughout the summer months.

Likes/Dislikes: Mountain meadows are a good place to find balloon flowers. They prefer a moderately moist soil in open areas or those with dappled sunlight.

Propagation/Maintenance: Stratify seeds a minimum of 1 month before sowing; just before planting, soak seeds for 1 hour in warm water. They are best sown indoors and transplanted outside after frost danger has passed. Space 10 to 12 inches (25 to 30 centimeters) apart and water moderately. A single patch of balloon flowers will spread by multiplying its roots each year.

Sun/Soil: Sun, partial shade; gravelly, well-drained soil is best, but this herb is tolerant of many types of soil

Harvesting: The roots are harvested, preferably in the spring or fall, with a needle-nose spade or garden fork to prevent damaging the brittle root during the digging process.

Market Potential: Low

Medicinal Benefits: Balloon flower has traditionally been used to address gastrointestinal conditions, respiratory concerns, and skin health.

Parts Used: Roots, dried

Home Pharmacy Uses: Decoction, traditional tincture, powder

Potentilla species

Potentilla

Although potentillas are not used in great quantities by herbal products manufacturers, some companies do include them in their product lines. As with their cousins, wild geraniums, harvesting potentillas from the wild greatly impacts surrounding ecosystems. Organic cultivation, on a small scale, is needed for potentilla. 🌾

Potentilla at a Glance

▸ **Plant Cycle:** Perennial

▸ **Type of Growth:** Herbaceous, woody

▸ **Light Requirements:** Full sun, partial shade, shade

▸ **Water Requirements:** Moderate to high

▸ **Parts Used:** Aerial

▸ **Home Pharmacy Uses:** Infusion, decoction, traditional tincture, cider vinegar tincture, syrup, compress, poultice, elixir, lozenge, ointment, salve, cream, balm, foot soak, bath herb, honey, suppository, butter, liniment

A.K.A.: Five-fingers, cinquefoil

Personality: Perennial; herbaceous, woody (Zones 5–8)

Height: Herbaceous species, 6 to 20 inches (15 to 50 centimeters); woody shrubs, 2 to 4 feet (.6 to 1.2 meters)

Bloom Traits: Flowers appear all summer and are yellow, occasionally apricot or white.

Likes/Dislikes: Potentillas are found growing at higher elevations in more mountainous areas. They prefer meadows and pastures, with bushy varieties sometimes found along roadsides.

Propagation/Maintenance: It is nearly impossible to get viable seed; you must propagate by cuttings or by the more reliable root divisions or crown divisions. Cuttings may require several weeks to root. Once the root structure has developed, plant outdoors. If propagating by division, make sure that every division has some root attached to it, and plant in prepared garden space. Keep well watered until roots have a chance to establish themselves. Occasionally, a species of potentilla will have a spreading nature, but most often it grows in a clump. Space herbaceous species 10 to 15 inches (25 to 38 centimeters) apart; space shrub species 2 to 3 feet (.6 to .9 meter) apart. Provide moderate to heavy amounts of water.

Sun/Soil: Full sun, partial shade, shade, depending on species; prefers well-drained, somewhat sandy soil, but is very adaptable

Harvesting: Harvest aerial parts at any point during the growing season. Handpick or use snips or scissors.

Market Potential: Low

Medicinal Benefits: Potentilla is an astringent herb used for skin problems, some gastrointestinal conditions, and gum tissue health.

Parts Used: Aerial parts, fresh or dried

Home Pharmacy Uses: Infusion, decoction, traditional tincture, cider vinegar tincture, syrup, compress, poultice, elixir, lozenge, ointment, salve, cream, balm, foot soak, bath herb, honey, suppository, butter, liniment

Prunella vulgaris
Self-Heal

Self-heal is a beautiful perennial flower that acts in the garden as a well-behaved ground cover. It blooms generously for nearly 2 months in my garden. I plant it with irises because the foliage contrast is very appealing to the eye. 🌿

Personality: Perennial; herbaceous

Height: 8 to 10 inches (20 to 25 centimeters)

Bloom Traits: Flowers — varying in color from pinks and purples to white — will bloom in early and midsummer.

Likes/Dislikes: Self-heal is a common woodland and forest plant. It also grows in mountain meadows. It prefers to grow near streams and creeks, and will grow only in temperate climates.

Propagation/Maintenance: Stratify seeds for at least 1 month before sowing. Sow indoors and watch for germination within 3 weeks, at a rate of approximately 70 percent. Transplant outdoors in mid- to late spring. Space this spreader 10 to 12 inches (25 to 30 centimeters) apart and water moderately.

Sun/Soil: Full sun, partial shade; prefers a humus soil

Companion/Complementary Planting: Grow with betony and violets.

Harvesting: Harvest the aerial parts of self-heal with snips or scissors while it is in flower.

Market Potential: Moderate; seek companies that make topical preparations and flower essences

Medicinal Benefits: Self-heal is used for women's health concerns, the digestive tract, the throat, and skin conditions.

Parts Used: Flowering aerial parts, fresh

Home Pharmacy Uses: Infusion, traditional tincture, syrup, compress, poultice, elixir, ointment, salve, balm, cream, foot soak, bath herb, infused oil, honey

🌿 Self-Heal at a Glance

- ▸ **Plant Cycle:** Perennial
- ▸ **Type of Growth:** Herbaceous
- ▸ **Light Requirements:** Full sun, partial shade
- ▸ **Water Requirements:** Moderate
- ▸ **Parts Used:** Aerial
- ▸ **Home Pharmacy Uses:** Infusion, traditional tincture, syrup, compress, poultice, elixir, ointment, salve, cream, balm, foot soak, bath herb, infused oil, honey

Rosmarinus species

Rosemary

Rosemary is a traditional symbol of good health, fidelity, and remembrance. It is one of the best antioxidant herbs and is also excellent for enhancing circulation. Rosemary helps increase the oxygen supply to the brain, thus sharpening concentration and memory. 🌿

Rosemary at a Glance

- ▶ **Plant Cycle:** Tender perennial
- ▶ **Type of Growth:** Herbaceous
- ▶ **Light Requirements:** Full sun
- ▶ **Water Requirements:** Low to moderate
- ▶ **Parts Used:** Aerial

- ▶ **Home Pharmacy Uses:** Infusion, traditional tincture, cider vinegar tincture, syrup, compress, crystallized, elixir, lozenge, ointment, medicinal food, salve, cream, balm, foot soak, bath herb, infused oil, honey, liniment

Personality: Tender perennial; herbaceous (Zones 8–11)

Height: 12 to 36 inches (30 to 90 centimeters), although it can grow considerably taller

Bloom Traits: Blue flowers bloom profusely when the plants experience cooler nighttime temperatures (not below 38°F; 3°C) to set the flower buds.

Likes/Dislikes: Rosemary is from the Mediterranean region. It prefers hot temperatures and dry soil conditions, but it also enjoys extra humidity.

Propagation/Maintenance: Propagate rosemary from tip cuttings and use a liquid rooting hormone to encourage better root formation. Extra warmth and good air circulation are essential. Keep cuttings moist, but not soggy, until rooting structure is strong. Rosemary grows in clumps; plants should be spaced 12 to 15 inches (30 to 38 centimeters) apart. Water lightly to moderately.

Sun/Soil: Full sun; well-drained soil

Companion/Complementary Planting: Grows beautifully in community with lavender, hyssop, santolina, and California poppy

Harvesting: Aerial parts are harvested, using snips, at any time during the growing season. Multiple harvests will be possible if no more than 25 percent of the plant is taken at any one time.

Market Potential: Moderate to high; sell fresh as a medicinal food to chefs and at farmer's markets, and dried to makers of medicinal preparations

Medicinal Benefits: Rosemary is one of the best sources of antioxidants that we know of. It is beneficial for the immune system and for winter illnesses, and is often recommended for the digestive tract, the circulatory system, brain health, the respiratory system, and the skin. Crystallized rosemary flowers are not only beautiful and delicious, but they are therapeutic as well.

Parts Used: Aerial parts, fresh or dried

Home Pharmacy Uses: Infusion, traditional tincture, cider vinegar tincture, syrup, compress, crystallized, elixir, lozenge, medicinal food, ointment, salve, balm, cream, foot soak, bath herb, infused oil, liniment, honey

Rudbeckia hirta
Black-Eyed Susan

These sunny yellow flowers are so cheerful in the garden. In addition to having medicinal properties, black-eyed Susan was used by early American settlers to create a vibrant cloth dye. Depending on which mordant (color-fixing agent) is used, black-eyed Susan will yield up to eight different shades of gold, dark green, and deep brown. 🌸

Personality: Perennial; herbaceous (Zones 3–7)

Height: 2 to 3 feet (.6 to .9 meter)

Bloom Traits: Yellow coneflowers with chocolate brown centers bloom from early summer until late summer.

Likes/Dislikes: Often seen growing on the open prairie or in open grassy meadows, usually along streams or creeks

Propagation/Maintenance: Stratify seeds for a minimum of 4 weeks in the freezer or sow directly in the garden in the fall and let winter do the stratification for you. Sow early in spring outdoors, or indoors for later transplanting. Transplant outdoors 12 inches (30 centimeters) apart in mid- to late spring. Provide low to moderate amounts of water. Black-eyed Susan grows in clumps.

Sun/Soil: Full sun; no special soil needs

Companion/Complementary Planting: Repels insects when planted with feverfew, licorice, or hyssop. Black-eyed Susans attract birds of many kinds into the garden.

Harvesting: The roots may be dug in spring or fall. Leaves may be gathered by handpicking or with snips at any point during the growing season. Use a needlenose spade or a garden fork to lift the roots.

Market Potential: Low; used primarily by herbalists working hands-on with a client

Medicinal Benefits: Used mainly as an herbal diuretic. It is also used occasionally to support heart health and for women's health concerns.

Parts Used: Roots, leaves, fresh or dried

Home Pharmacy Uses: Infusion, traditional tincture

🌿 Black-Eyed Susan at a Glance

- **Plant Cycle:** Perennial
- **Type of Growth:** Herbaceous
- **Light Requirements:** Full sun
- **Water Requirements:** Low to moderate
- **Parts Used:** Roots, leaves
- **Home Pharmacy Uses:** Infusion, traditional tincture

Rumex acetosella

Sheep Sorrel

This herb is considered a strong ally of the immune and lymphatic systems. It is a traditional ingredient in Essiac, an herbal formula that is often used as a therapy for cancer patients. The leaves of Sheep Sorrel have been traditionally used as an edge for wool, producing a green/yellow color.

Personality: Perennial; herbaceous (Zones 3–9)

Height: 8 to 12 inches (20 to 30 centimeters)

Bloom Traits: Flower stalks are reddish purple and appear in mid- to late summer.

Likes/Dislikes: Sheep sorrel can be found in open grassy areas from the mountains to the prairie.

Propagation/Maintenance: Sow seeds indoors and transplant outside in mid- to late spring, or sow directly outdoors. Sheep sorrel is easy; seeds require no special treatments. Germination occurs in 7 to 10 days at a rate of about 70 percent. This herb will spread; space plants 12 inches (30 centimeters) apart. Water lightly to moderately.

Sun/Soil: Full sun; no special soil needs

Harvesting: Aerial parts are harvested with snips or scissors early in the summer season.

Market Potential: Moderate; this herb is a prominent ingredient in the famous Essiac cancer-treatment formula

Medicinal Benefits: Sheep sorrel is used for immune system and lymphatic system concerns.

Parts Used: Aerial parts, fresh or dried

Home Pharmacy Uses: Infusion, traditional tincture, cider vinegar tincture

Sheep Sorrel at a Glance

▸ **Plant Cycle:** Perennial

▸ **Type of Growth:** Herbaceous

▸ **Light Requirements:** Full sun

▸ **Water Requirements:** Light to moderate

▸ **Parts Used:** Aerial

▸ **Home Pharmacy Uses:** Infusion, traditional tincture, cider vingar tincture

Ruta graveolens

Rue

In the Latin American Catholic cultures, rue is considered a sacred herb. It is often referred to as herb o' grace, and is used in religious rituals. Rue is believed to offer protection for one's health and well-being.

Personality: Perennial; herbaceous (Zones 5–9)

Height: 12 to 15 inches (30 to 38 centimeters)

Bloom Traits: Flowers are yellow and bloom in mid- to late summer.

Likes/Dislikes: Rue likes to grow in both cool and hot climates. It will tolerate some wet environments as well as arid ones. It is originally native to the Mediterranean regions, where it prefers to grow in disturbed soil.

Propagation/Maintenance: Stratify seeds for 1 week before planting to encourage better germination percentages. Sow seeds indoors and expect about 50 percent germination in 7 to 10 days. Extra-warm temperatures (near 70°F; 21°C) help tremendously. Transplant outside when spring weather is well settled. Rue will grow in clumps; space 10 to 12 inches (25 to 30 centimeters) apart. Provide light to moderate amounts of water.

Sun/Soil: Full sun; no special soil needs

Companion/Complementary Planting: Rue helps deter pest insects in the garden. Plant it in areas where aphids, whiteflies, and thrips are present.

Harvesting: Aerial parts are harvested from mid- to late summer. Harvest the upper half of the plant using snips or scissors.

Market Potential: Low to moderate

Medicinal Benefits: Rue is used for women's health concerns and for ear ailments. It should not be used by pregnant women, however.

Parts Used: Aerial parts, dried

Home Pharmacy Uses: Infusion, traditional tincture

Rue at a Glance

▸ **Plant Cycle:** Perennial

▸ **Type of Growth:** Herbaceous

▸ **Light Requirements:** Full sun

▸ **Water Requirements:** Low to moderate

▸ **Parts Used:** Aerial

▸ **Home Pharmacy Uses:** Infusion, traditional tincture

Salvia apiana
White Sage

White sage has been greatly overharvested from the wild and is now nearly extinct in some regions. It is used to make ceremonial herbs and products that follow that theme. White sage is now on the United Plant Savers at-risk list, and we are hopeful that this plant will find its way into organic cultivation very soon. Certified organic growers are needed to relieve the burden on remaining populations of this herb. 🌱

Personality: Tender perennial; herbaceous (Zones 8–11)

Height: 12 to 24 inches (30 to 60 centimeters)

Bloom Traits: Flowers bloom pale blue in the late summer.

Likes/Dislikes: White sage is native to the southern California and northern Baja regions. It prefers a sunny area, having good tolerance for hot, dry, and windy conditions.

Propagation/Maintenance: Stratify seeds for 1 week and then sow indoors. Provide a warm nighttime temperature of 70°F (21°C) and hot daytime temperatures between 80 and 90°F (27 to 32°C). Germination is usually near 40 percent, and seeds take 2 to 3 weeks to sprout. Keep them evenly moist, but once seedlings are up, use care not to overwater. Transplant out in late spring. Space plants 12 inches (30 centimeters) apart; they will grow in clumps.

Sun/Soil: Full sun; well-drained soil

Harvesting: Harvest aerial parts with snips or scissors in late summer.

Market Potential: High

Medicinal Benefits: Useful for women's health concerns, digestive tract conditions, and throat and skin health, white sage is often recommended for winter illnesses and respiratory concerns. It is also a good insect repellent.

Parts Used: Aerial parts, fresh or dried

Home Pharmacy Uses: Traditional tincture, insect repellent

🌿 White Sage at a Glance

- **Plant Cycle:** Tender perennial
- **Type of Growth:** Herbaceous
- **Light Requirements:** Full sun
- **Water Requirements:** Low to moderate
- **Parts Used:** Aerial
- **Home Pharmacy Uses:** Traditional tincture, insect repellent

Salvia officinalis
Sage

Sage is a delicious culinary seasoning and a strong medicinal herb. This is one herb that is best avoided by nursing mothers. It will pass into the breast milk, and because most infants do not like the taste of sage, they will refuse to nurse. 🌿

Personality: Perennial; herbaceous (Zones 4–8)

Height: 24 inches (60 centimeters)

Bloom Traits: Purple flowers appear in mid- to late summer.

Likes/Dislikes: Sage is a Mediterranean plant by nature. It thrives in hot or cool, dry environments, often in disturbed soil.

Propagation/Maintenance: Stratify seeds for several weeks and then sow them indoors. Expect a germination rate of about 60 percent in 10 to 14 days. Transplant outside, 12 inches (30 centimeters) apart, in mid- to late spring. This clumping herb requires light to moderate watering.

Sun/Soil: Full sun; well-drained soil

Companion/Complementary Planting: Grow with pleurisy root, penstemon, and calendula.

Harvesting: Aerial parts are harvested at any point during the growing season using snips or scissors. Harvest only the upper half of the plant and it will regenerate more quickly, allowing for additional harvests during the same season.

Market Potential: Moderate; sage is becoming more popular as both an herbal product ingredient and a medicinal food

Medicinal Benefits: Used for winter illnesses, digestive tract and respiratory tract concerns, and throat conditions, sage is also important for skin and hair health, women's health, and as a medicinal food.

Parts Used: Aerial parts, fresh or dried

Home Pharmacy Uses: Infusion, traditional tincture, cider vinegar tincture, syrup, compress, poultice, elixir, lozenge, medicinal food, ointment, salve, cream, balm, foot soak, bath herb, infused oil, honey, liniment

🌿 Sage at a Glance

- ▶ **Plant Cycle:** Perennial
- ▶ **Type of Growth:** Herbaceous
- ▶ **Light Requirements:** Full sun
- ▶ **Water Requirements:** Moderate
- ▶ **Parts Used:** Aerial

- ▶ **Home Pharmacy Uses:** Infusion, traditional tincture, cider vinegar tincture, syrup, compress, poultice, elixir, lozenge, medicinal food, ointment, salve, cream, balm, foot soak, bath herb, infused oil, honey, liniment

Salvia sclarea

Clary Sage

Clary sage is known primarily as a highly esteemed essential oil. However, the plant should be used more than simply as an essential oil, since it contributes wonderful healing properties to women's health formulas. 🌿

Personality: Biennial or perennial; herbaceous (Zones 5–9)

Height: 3 feet (.9 meter)

Bloom Traits: Beautiful lavender, pink, and white flowers bloom from midsummer through late summer.

Likes/Dislikes: Clary sage is a Mediterranean plant that prefers a hot and dry climate.

Propagation/Maintenance: Sow seeds indoors for transplanting out in late spring, or sow directly outdoors in mid-spring. No special treatments are required. Expect 60 to 70 percent germination about 2 weeks after sowing. Clary sage gets quite large in circumference, so space plants 24 inches (60 centimeters) apart. Water moderately.

Sun/Soil: Full sun; prefers well-drained soil

Harvesting: Harvest aerial parts when in flower. Snips work best for this task. I wear gloves because the fragrance of the clary sage penetrates my skin and stays with me for many hours. Some people really like the smell, but I am not that fond of it.

Market Potential: Low; the market for clary sage essential oil is quite good, but other herbal products do not often contain this herb

Medicinal Benefits: Clary sage is used a great deal for women's health concerns. It is also popular as a fragrance fixative.

Parts Used: Aerial parts in flower, fresh or dried

Home Pharmacy Uses: Traditional tincture, compress, poultice, ointment, salve, cream, balm, foot soak, bath herb, sleep pillow, infused oil, honey, liniment

🌿 Clary Sage at a Glance

- ▸ **Plant Cycle:** Biennial or perennial
- ▸ **Type of Growth:** Herbaceous
- ▸ **Light Requirements:** Full sun
- ▸ **Water Requirements:** Moderate
- ▸ **Parts Used:** Aerial
- ▸ **Home Pharmacy Uses:** Traditional tincture, compress, poultice, ointment, salve, cream, balm, foot soak, bath herb, sleep pillow, infused oil, honey, liniment

Santolina species
Santolina

Santolina is an herb that does not burn very easily, and because of this it is often used in landscaping in areas where wildfires are common. Planted as a hedge, santolina not only is attractive, but can also act as a natural firebreak that will slow the progress of flames. 🌿

A.K.A.: Lavender cotton (*S. chamaecyparissus*)

Personality: Perennial; herbaceous (Zones 6–9)

Height: 12 to 24 inches (30 to 60 centimeters)

Bloom Traits: Gray santolina (*S. chamaecyparissus*) has yellow button flowers about the size of a dime. Green santolina (*S. rosmarinifolia*) has button flowers that are yellowish green in color. Both bloom in the early summer.

Likes/Dislikes: A warm-weather lover, santolina grows in hot, dry climates. It is originally from the Mediterranean region.

Propagation/Maintenance: Tip cuttings are the best way to propagate santolina. Use a liquid rooting hormone to further encourage rooting. Keep cuttings evenly moist but not overly wet. When cuttings have developed a strong rooting structure, transplant outdoors. Make sure that spring weather is fully settled before planting outside. Space plants 15 inches (38 centimeters) apart. The plants will grow in clumps and require light watering.

Sun/Soil: Full sun; well-drained soil

Companion/Complementary Planting: Santolinas repel insects, so they can be planted next to problematic plants to help prevent infestation.

Harvesting: Harvest the aerial parts of santolina at any time during the growing season. Use scissors or snips to get the task done easily.

Market Potential: Low

Medicinal Benefits: Santolina is an important component of herbal insect repellents.

Parts Used: Aerial parts, fresh or dried

Home Pharmacy Uses: Insect repellent

🌿 Santolina at a Glance

▸ **Plant Cycle:** Perennial

▸ **Type of Growth:** Herbaceous

▸ **Light Requirements:** Full sun

▸ **Water Requirements:** Low

▸ **Parts Used:** Aerial

▸ **Home Pharmacy Uses:** Insect repellent

Satureja hortensis

Summer Savory

Summer savory grows as a small, bushy plant. When it blooms the plant is covered with delicate, pale lavender flowers. This pretty herb seems to twinkle with so many tiny blooms. 🌿

Personality: Annual; herbaceous

Height: 12 to 20 inches (30 to 50 centimeters)

Bloom Traits: Flowers are pale lavender to white; blooming occurs throughout the summer months.

Likes/Dislikes: Summer savory is a Mediterranean plant by nature. It prefers a hot and somewhat dry climate.

Propagation/Maintenance: Sow seeds indoors and expect sprouting in about 2 weeks. No special seed treatments are required. Germination averages 60 percent. Transplant outside in late spring. Space this clumping plant 10 to 12 inches (25 to 30 centimeters) apart. Water lightly to moderately.

Sun/Soil: Full sun, partial shade; well-drained soil

Harvesting: Harvest aerial parts with snips or scissors throughout the summer months. I like to harvest my summer savory while it is in flower, but that is not absolutely necessary.

Market Potential: Low; restaurants and farmer's markets are the best customers for this herb

Medicinal Benefits: Primarily recommended for the digestive tract, respiratory tract, and urinary tract, summer savory is also considered a good astringent herb for throat conditions and for skin health.

Parts Used: Aerial parts, fresh or dried

Home Pharmacy Uses: Infusion, traditional tincture, cider vinegar tincture

🌿 **Summer Savory at a Glance**

- ▸ **Plant Cycle:** Annual
- ▸ **Type of Growth:** Herbaceous
- ▸ **Light Requirements:** Full sun, partial shade
- ▸ **Water Requirements:** Low to moderate
- ▸ **Parts Used:** Aerial
- ▸ **Home Pharmacy Uses:** Infusion, traditional tincture, cider vinegar tincture

Scutellaria species
Skullcap

Skullcap takes its name from its flowers, which resemble little skulls wearing hats. They are rather small flowers, but if you look closely, you're sure to see the resemblance. There are about 100 species of skullcap, including *Scutellaria lateriflora*, which is native to North America. Other species native to Europe and China have long histories of therapeutic use, as well. 🌿

Personality: Perennial; herbaceous (Zones 4–8)

Height: 8 to 24 inches (20 to 60 centimeters)

Bloom Traits: Skullcap blooms with light blue flowers from mid- to late summer.

Likes/Dislikes: Skullcap often grows in the mountains where there is a good amount of spring moisture. It will grow near streams and wash areas where water is flowing.

Propagation/Maintenance: Stratify seeds for a minimum of 1 week before sowing. Sow indoors and expect to see sprouting in approximatley 2 weeks or less. Germination rates are usually pretty good, near 75 or 80 percent. Transplant outside after all danger of frost is past. This herb grows in clumps; space 12 inches (30 centimeters) apart. Provide a moderate amount of water.

Sun/Soil: Full sun, partial shade; prefers well-drained, moist soil

Companion/Complementary Planting: Plant with feverfew, catnip, and chicory for a lovely effect.

Harvesting: Aerial parts are harvested when the herb is in full flower. I prefer to cut skullcap with scissors, but snips will also work. Harvest from about 3 inches above the ground.

Market Potential: High

Medicinal Benefits: Skullcap is an excellent nervine and sedative that relieves stress, anxiety, and pain while also nourishing the nervous system.

Parts Used: Flowering aerial parts, fresh

Home Pharmacy Uses: Traditional tincture, liniment

🌿 Skullcap at a Glance

- ▶ **Plant Cycle:** Perennial
- ▶ **Type of Growth:** Herbaceous
- ▶ **Light Requirements:** Full sun, partial shade
- ▶ **Water Requirements:** Moderate
- ▶ **Parts Used:** Aerial
- ▶ **Home Pharmacy Uses:** Traditional tincture, liniment

Sedum species

Sedum

Native-plant gardens in the United States frequently include sedum. There are many different color variations in both the foliage and flowers of sedum, but all varieties are stunning. This plant adds texture and interest to any garden design. 🌺

A.K.A.: Stonecrop

Personality: Perennial; herbaceous (Zones 3–11)

Height: 4 to 36 inches (10 to 90 centimeters)

Bloom Traits: Sedums bloom in a variety of colors — pinks, purples, and white — all through the summer months.

Likes/Dislikes: Habitat ranges widely from high mountain alpine environments to open grasslands.

Propagation/Maintenance: Root divisions can be done in the spring or fall. Cuttings are also very easy and can be accomplished any time the sedum is actively growing. Start cuttings indoors for transplanting out at any point that they are fully rooted. Sedum will spread, so space plants 10 to 15 inches (25 to 38 centimeters) apart. Water lightly to moderately.

Sun/Soil: Full sun to partial shady, depending on the species; well-drained soil

Harvesting: Aerial parts may be harvested from spring through fall. Use scissors or snips.

Market Potential: Low

Medicinal Benefits: Sedum is primarily used in food form to benefit the urinary tract and the digestive system.

Parts Used: Aerial parts, fresh

Home Pharmacy Uses: Medicinal food, cider vinegar tincture

🌿 Sedum at a Glance

▸ **Plant Cycle:** Perennial

▸ **Type of Growth:** Herbaceous

▸ **Light Requirements:** Full sun to partial shade

▸ **Water Requirements:** Low to moderate

▸ **Parts Used:** Aerial

▸ **Home Pharmacy Uses:** Medicinal food, cider vinegar tincture

Milk Thistle at a Glance

- **Plant Cycle:** Annual or biennial
- **Type of Growth:** Herbaceous
- **Light Requirements:** Full sun
- **Water Requirements:** Low
- **Parts Used:** Seeds
- **Home Pharmacy Uses:** Traditional tincture, cider vinegar tincture, medicinal food, powder

Silybum marianum

Milk Thistle

Certified organic milk thistle seed is in high demand. The difficulty is in the seed-cleaning process, which is extremely time-consuming. The ingenious person who comes up with an efficient and less laborious way to clean the seeds will have it made in this plant's market. 🐝

Personality: Annual or biennial; herbaceous (Zones 6–9)

Height: 2 to 3 feet (.6 to .9 meter)

Bloom Traits: Beautiful, spiny purple flowers bloom in late summer.

Likes/Dislikes: Milk thistle is a Mediterranean plant by nature. It prefers hot temperatures and not too much moisture.

Propagation/Maintenance: Sow milk thistle seeds directly outdoors when weather is fully settled, or start indoors and transplant out in late spring. Direct sowing works great for me and keeps me from having to handle prickly transplants. No special seed treatments are required and germination rates are usually excellent. Milk thistle grows in clumps and should be spaced 12 to 15 inches (30 to 38 centimeters) apart. Provide light amounts of water.

Sun/Soil: Full sun; no special soil needs

Harvesting: Harvest the seeds when they are a chocolate brown color — not before; the lighter colored seeds are not as medicinally potent. Harvesting must be done with gloves, as these are beastly plants. Snip off seed heads and place them in a shallow cardboard box. Then, with a glove, work to dislodge all the seeds from the pods and seed hairs. Screen out the seeds and discard the rest.

Market Potential: Very high

Medicinal Benefits: A well-recognized liver tonic herb, milk thistle has antioxidant action and also benefits the skin and nursing mothers.

Parts Used: Seeds, fresh or dried

Home Pharmacy Uses: Traditional tincture, cider vinegar tincture, medicinal food, powder

Solidago species

Goldenrod

The flowers and young shoots of this stunning herb are used to create beautiful yellow dyes for cotton and wool. Goldenrod is a late-summer flower that always signals the garden's transition to the next season. 🌿

Personality: Perennial; herbaceous (Zones 4–9)

Height: 2 to 4 feet (.6–.9 meter)

Bloom Traits: Large fans of golden yellow flowers bloom in the later months of summer.

Likes/Dislikes: Found in a variety of habitats, goldenrod grows in the prairie as well as in the mountains. It is commonly found growing near streams and lakes. It seems to prefer open spaces, and you'll see along mountain roadsides where it has the advantage of runoff water.

Propagation/Maintenance: Stratify seeds in moist peat moss or sand in the refrigerator for 7 to 10 days. This will give you very good germination, 90 percent or better. Sow indoors and transplant outside in mid- to late spring, or seeds can be sown directly out in the garden in early spring. Goldenrod grows in clumps and should be spaced 12 inches (30 centimeters) apart. Water lightly or moderately.

Sun/Soil: Full sun; no special soil needs

Companion/Complementary Planting: Grow in community with chicory, red clover, catnip, and potentilla.

Harvesting: Aerial parts, while in flower, are harvested in late summer with snips or scissors.

Market Potential: Moderate

Medicinal Benefits: Goldenrod is used primarily for conditions of the urinary tract and the respiratory tract. Traditionally, Native Americans have used this plant for toothaches, fevers, and coughs.

Parts Used: Aerial parts in flower, fresh or dried

Home Pharmacy Uses: Infusion, traditional tincture, syrup, foot soak, bath herb, honey

🌿 Goldenrod at a Glance

- **Plant Cycle:** Perennial
- **Type of Growth:** Herbaceous
- **Light Requirements:** Full sun
- **Water Requirements:** Low to moderate
- **Parts Used:** Aerial
- **Home Pharmacy Uses:** Infusion, traditional tincture, syrup, foot soak, bath herb, honey

Sphaeralcea coccinea
Yerba de la Negrita

In addition to using this herb medicinally, ethnic groups of the south-western United States prepare it as a shampoo. The leaves and flowers are both used to make hair grow strong and healthy. 🌿

A.K.A.: Globe mallow, cowboy's delight

Personality: Perennial; herbaceous (Zones 4–8)

Height: 10 to 12 inches (25 to 30 centimeters)

Bloom Traits: Spring brings wonderful apricot-colored flowers.

Likes/Dislikes: Yerba de la negrita is a high plains and mountain desert plant native to the southwestern parts of North America.

Propagation/Maintenance: Stratify seeds for at least 4 weeks. Just before sowing, scarify them and soak them in warm water for about 30 minutes. Sow indoors immediately and provide extra warmth to enhance germination. Germination is often sporadic, ranging from 30 to 50 percent. Sprouting may take up to 4 weeks; patience is a virtue with this plant. Transplant outdoors in mid- to late spring and expect good growth to begin in the second season. Yerba de la negrita is a spreading plant, and needs to be spaced 12 inches (30 centimeters) apart. Water lightly.

Sun/Soil: Full sun; well-drained soil

Companion/Complementary Planting: Yerba de la negrita is lovely planted with horehound, penstemon, and callirhoe.

Harvesting: The whole plant is harvested during the summer months. Use a garden fork or needle-nose spade to lift plants from the soil.

Market Potential: Low; used mostly in areas where it grows native

Medicinal Benefits: Yerba de la negrita is used primarily for the gastrointestinal tract and for skin conditions.

Parts Used: Whole plant, fresh or dried

Home Pharmacy Uses: Compress, ointment, salve, balm, infused oil

🌿 Yerba de la Negrita at a Glance

- ▸ **Plant Cycle:** Perennial
- ▸ **Type of Growth:** Herbaceous
- ▸ **Light Requirements:** Full sun
- ▸ **Water Requirements:** Low
- ▸ **Parts Used:** Whole plant
- ▸ **Home Pharmacy Uses:** Compress, ointment, salve, balm, infused oil

Spilanthes acmella (also known as *Acmella oleracea*)

Spilanthes

This herb is native to a number of tropical countries around the world, including Peru. In addition to its medicinal uses, spilanthes is also eaten as a spicy green salad. Expect to feel a pleasant tingle in your mouth whenever you eat this herb. 🌿

Spilanthes at a Glance

- **Plant Cycle:** Annual
- **Type of Growth:** Herbaceous
- **Light Requirements:** Full sun; partial shade
- **Water Requirements:** Moderate to high
- **Parts Used:** Aerial
- **Home Pharmacy Uses:** Infusion, traditional tincture, syrup, compress, elixir, lozenge, ointment, salve, cream, balm, foot soak, bath herb, honey, liniment

A.K.A.: Toothache plant

Personality: Annual; herbaceous

Height: 12 to 24 inches (30 to 60 centimeters)

Bloom Traits: The highly unusual, conical flowers of spilanthes are yellow on the outside with a perfectly round red dot on the very top. They bloom from summer until frost hits.

Likes/Dislikes: Spilanthes is a tropical plant. It prefers environments that are hot, with a good amount of moisture.

Propagation/Maintenance: Seed is easy and requires no special treatments. It should be started indoors and then transplanted outside only after all danger of frost is past. Germination rate is often 80 percent or so and seeds sprout in about 1 week. Space spilanthes 12 inches (30 centimeters) apart; it will grow in clumps. This herb requires moderate to high amounts of water.

Sun/Soil: Full sun, partial shade; prefers a soil rich in organic matter (4 to 5 percent) and fairly moist

Companion/Complementary Planting: Spilanthes grows well with gotu kola and stevia.

Harvesting: Aerial parts are harvested while in full flower. Cut anytime from mid- to late summer with snips or scissors.

Market Potential: Low to moderate; often used as a medicinal substitute for echinacea, spilanthes is experiencing increasing market demand

Medicinal Benefits: Useful for conditions associated with the immune system, respiratory tract, and winter illnesses, spilanthes is also recommended for oral gum health, the throat, and for gastrointestinal tract concerns.

Parts Used: Aerial parts in flower, fresh

Home Pharmacy Uses: Infusion, traditional tincture, syrup, compress, elixir, lozenge, ointment, salve, cream, balm, foot soak, bath herb, honey, liniment

Stevia rebaudiana
Stevia

The leaves and flowers of stevia have an intensely sweet flavor, making it an excellent sweetener for foods, beverages, and medicines. Stevia is also a good medicinal herb that supports digestion. 🌿

Personality: Annual; herbaceous

Height: 12 to 15 inches (30 to 38 centimeters)

Bloom Traits: Flowers are delicate and white, and they bloom on and off throughout the growing season.

Likes/Dislikes: A native of Paraguay and Brazil, stevia prefers an environment that is hot and humid.

Propagation/Maintenance: Cuttings may be taken of stevia fairly successfully. I use a liquid rooting hormone at a ratio of 1:8 (hormone to water) and supply a nighttime temperature of 70°F (21°C) and daytime temperatures in the 90-degree range (32°C) to encourage rooting. Seed propagation is also possible. Seeds should be kept moist and warm, and you will see about 30 percent germination over a 2- to 3-week period. Move plants outdoors only after weather is fully settled and very warm. Move back indoors before frost in the fall. Stevia may be grown outdoors in tropical regions all year long. A clumping plant, it should be spaced 10 to 12 inches (25 to 30 centimeters) apart. For best results, provide moderate to heavy amounts of water.

Sun/Soil: Full sun, partial shade, shade; grows best in a rich humus soil

Harvesting: Aerial parts may be harvested with scissors or snips at any point during the growing season.

Market Potential: Moderate

Medicinal Benefits: Stevia is considered an herbal sweetener, and it supports healthy digestive tract function.

Parts Used: Aerial parts, fresh or dried

Home Pharmacy Uses: Traditional tincture, powder

🌿 Stevia at a Glance

- ▶ **Plant Cycle:** Annual
- ▶ **Type of Growth:** Herbaceous
- ▶ **Light Requirements:** Full sun, partial shade, shade
- ▶ **Water Requirements:** Moderate to high
- ▶ **Parts Used:** Aerial
- ▶ **Home Pharmacy Uses:** Traditional tincture, powder

Symphytum × uplandicum
Comfrey

Much of the comfrey used in commerce is mislabeled as *Symphytum officinale*, when it is in fact *S. × uplandicum*. This is important because the research that has made everyone skeptical about comfrey's safety was apparently conducted using *S. officinale*. *S. × uplandicum* has considerably lower levels of pyrrolizidine alkaloids, a substance that can be toxic to the liver. It's actually quite safe for use in medicinal preparations.

A.K.A.: Russian comfrey

Personality: Perennial; herbaceous (Zones 3–9)

Height: 3 to 4 feet (.9 to 1.2 meters)

Bloom Traits: Lilac-rose flowers fade to purple or blue (*S. officinale* has purple, cream, mauve, or pink flowers)

Likes/Dislikes: Comfrey prefers to grow in a moist soil area near streams and ponds. It likes dappled sunlight.

Propagation/Maintenance: Comfrey is a sterile plant and must be propagated by root divisions. These will do best if divided outdoors in mid- to late spring. Space plants 24 inches (60 centimeters) apart. Comfrey will spread only if the root is dug up and divided or accidentally chopped up and dispersed in the soil (as might occur with a tiller or a plow). Water moderately.

Sun/Soil: Full sun, partial shade; prefers rich loamy or sandy soil but will grow in most soils

Harvesting: Harvest roots in the spring or fall, using a needle-nose spade or garden fork. The leaves may be harvested with snips or by handpicking at any time during the growing season.

Market Potential: Moderate

Medicinal Benefits: Well known for its benefits to the muscles and bones, and also for healing topical wounds, comfrey is also used internally for digestive tract concerns.

Parts Used: Roots and aerial parts, fresh or dried

Home Pharmacy Uses: Infusion, decoction, traditional tincture, cider vinegar tincture, syrup, compress, poultice, medicinal food, ointment, salve, cream, balm, foot soak, bath herb, infused oil, liniment

Comfrey at a Glance

- ▶ **Plant Cycle:** Perennial
- ▶ **Type of Growth:** Herbaceous
- ▶ **Light Requirements:** Full sun, partial shade
- ▶ **Water Requirements:** Moderate
- ▶ **Parts Used:** Roots and aerial
- ▶ **Home Pharmacy Uses:** Infusion, decoction, traditional tincture, cider vinegar tincture, syrup, compress, poultice, medicinal food, ointment, salve, cream, balm, foot soak, bath herb, infused, liniment

Tanacetum parthenium

Feverfew

Feverfew is recognized mainly as a headache remedy. In Europe, people take their daily dose of feverfew leaves as a sandwich. If you'd like to try this remedy, butter two pieces of bread, add two fresh feverfew leaves and some cucumber and tomato slices, and enjoy.

Feverfew at a Glance

- **Plant Cycle:** Perennial
- **Type of Growth:** Herbaceous to semi-woody
- **Light Requirements:** Full sun, partial shade
- **Water Requirements:** Moderate
- **Water Requirements:** Moderate
- **Parts Used:** Leaves and aerial
- **Home Pharmacy Uses:** Infusion, traditional tincture, cider vinegar tincture, syrup, medicinal food, balm

Personality: Perennial; herbaceous to semi-woody (Zones 4–9)

Height: 24 inches (60 centimeters)

Bloom Traits: Small, white, daisylike flowers begin blooming in midsummer and usually continue through the end of the season.

Likes/Dislikes: Feverfew is now considered only a garden plant that will grow in most temperate climates. It is native to southeast Europe, but has become naturalized in many places in the world.

Propagation/Maintenance: For best results, stratify seeds for at least 1 week before sowing. Sow indoors and transplant out in late spring, or sow directly outdoors in mid-spring. Typically, feverfew germinates at 65 to 70 percent and takes approximately 2 weeks to sprout. A vigorous self-sowing herb, plants should be spaced 12 inches (30 centimeters) apart. Water moderately.

Sun/Soil: Full sun, partial shade; prefers a richer loamy soil, but is tolerant of most soils

Companion/Complementary Planting: Plant in community with anise hyssop, licorice, and monarda. It also seems to deter insects from the garden.

Harvesting: Harvesting can include leaf only or flowering aerial parts, depending on your personal preference. Herbalists tend to go back and forth between the two. Most of the research was completed on feverfew leaf, so I like to use the leafy parts. Scissors or snips will work nicely for this harvesting job.

Market Potential: Moderate to high, although there are a lot of growers farming this herb

Medicinal Benefits: Feverfew is used primarily to treat headaches, especially migraines.

Parts Used: Leaves and flowering aerial parts, fresh or dried

Home Pharmacy Uses: Infusion, traditional tincture, cider vinegar tincture, syrup, medicinal food, balm

Taraxacum officinale

Dandelion

In some places dandelions are finally gaining the respect they deserve. They are finding favor among chefs and are drawing a good price at farmer's markets and some groceries. Medicinal manufacturers commonly use dandelion in their products. The best news yet is that Aspen and Carbondale, two upscale mountain communities in Colorado, have declared it illegal to spray herbicides to eradicate dandelions. They are suggesting that people eat the health-giving plants instead. 🌺

Dandelion at a Glance

- ▶ **Plant Cycle:** Perennial
- ▶ **Type of Growth:** Herbaceous
- ▶ **Light Requirements:** Full sun, partial shade
- ▶ **Water Requirements:** Low to moderate
- ▶ **Parts Used:** Whole plant
- ▶ **Home Pharmacy Uses:** Infusion, decoction, traditional tincture, cider vinegar tincture, syrup, elixir, medicinal food, infused oil, honey

Personality: Perennial; herbaceous (Zones 3–9)

Height: 8 to 10 inches (20 to 25 centimeters)

Bloom Traits: Sunny yellow flowers bloom throughout the growing season.

Likes/Dislikes: Where do dandelions *not* grow in the temperate and subtropical parts of the world? Dandelions are equally at home in mountain meadows, along streams or roadsides, and in big grassy prairies. They usually find their home in disturbed soil and they prefer a bit of sun. They are terrific for attracting bees for pollination.

Propagation/Maintenance: Dandelion is easy to grow from seeds. The seeds will germinate well with no special treatments, but stratifying them for even 1 week will bring the germination rate up to about 90 percent. They can be sown directly into the garden soil or you can start them indoors and then plant out the seedlings in mid- to late spring. Dandelions grow in clumps and self-sow vigorously; space 10 to 12 inches (25 to 30 centimeters) apart. Light to moderate watering is all that's needed.

Sun/Soil: Full sun, partial shade; no special soil needs

Companion/Complementary Planting: Dandelions grow well with just about every other plant.

Harvesting: All portions of the dandelion are used medicinally. Harvest the whole plant or the roots by using a garden fork. Roots are best harvested in early spring or late fall, whereas the whole plant may be harvested at any time during the growing season. Trim leaves with scissors or handpick, and harvest at any time. The flowers are handpicked from spring through fall.

Market Potential: High to very high

Medicinal Benefits: Dandelion is considered a whole-body tonic and has medicinal action in nearly every body system. It is especially recognized for its benefits to the liver, urinary tract, and skin.

Parts Used: Whole plant, fresh or dried

Home Pharmacy Uses: Infusion, decoction, traditional tincture, cider vinegar tincture, syrup, elixir, medicinal food, infused oil, honey

Thymus vulgaris

Thyme

During the Middle Ages in Europe, thyme was given much symbolic value. It was believed to give protection from harm, and soldiers bathed in thyme water to heighten their bravery. ❦

Thyme at a Glance

- **Plant Cycle:** Perennial
- **Type of Growth:** Herbaceous
- **Light Requirements:** Full sun, partial shade
- **Water Requirements:** Low to moderate
- **Parts Used:** Aerial
- **Parts Used:** Aerial
- **Home Pharmacy Uses:** Infusion, traditional tincture, cider vinegar tincture, syrup, compress, poultice, elixir, lozenge, ointment, salve, cream, balm, foot soak, bath herb, infused oil, honey, butter, liniment

Personality: Perennial; herbaceous (Zones 5–9)

Height: 12 to 15 inches (30 to 38 centimeters)

Bloom Traits: Flowers vary and can be purple, pink, or white. Blooming will occur on and off throughout the summer months.

Likes/Dislikes: Native to the Mediterranean regions of Europe, it prefers hot, dry climates and soils that are not too rich.

Propagation/Maintenance: There are three good ways to propagate thyme; my favorite is by seed. Seed is easy and can be sown indoors for transplanting outside in late spring. Germination rates are 60 to 70 percent; sprouting takes place in about a week. Thyme can also be grown from cuttings, dipped in liquid rooting hormone for enhanced rooting, and from root divisions. Regardless of the method you choose, you should have good success rates. Space this spreading herb 10 to 12 inches (25 to 30 centimeters) apart. It requires light to moderate water.

Sun/Soil: Full sun, partial shade; well-drained and somewhat dry soil is best

Companion/Complementary Planting: Grow in community with oxeye daisy, catnip, horehound, and goldenrod.

Harvesting: Harvest the aerial parts with snips or scissors at any point during the summer months.

Market Potential: Moderate; both fresh and dried are favored for antibacterial and antiseptic properties

Medicinal Benefits: Thyme is beneficial for winter illnesses and immune system support. It is often recommended for digestive and respiratory concerns, sore muscles, throat conditions, nervous system support, and skin health.

Parts Used: Aerial parts, fresh or dried

Home Pharmacy Uses: Infusion, traditional tincture, cider vinegar tincture, syrup, compress, poultice, elixir, lozenge, ointment, salve, cream, balm, foot soak, bath herb, infused oil, honey, butter, liniment

Thymus × citriodorus
Lemon Thyme

This is such a lovely herb to use when preparing "tummy" formulas for children. Lemon thyme tastes delicious and sweet, and will calm an upset stomach very nicely. ✿

Personality: Perennial; herbaceous (Zones 5–9)

Height: 12 to 15 inches (30 to 38 centimeters)

Bloom Traits: Pale lavender flowers bloom throughout the summer months.

Likes/Dislikes: Lemon thyme is a garden plant only.

Propagation/Maintenance: Lemon thyme must be grown from cuttings; they are best started indoors and transplanted outside when they have an established root structure and the weather is reasonably well settled. Liquid or powder rooting hormone can increase the speed of rooting, but I often root cuttings without it. Lemon thyme will spread; plants should be spaced 12 inches (30 centimeters) apart. Water lightly to moderately.

Sun/Soil: Sun, partial shade; well-drained soil is preferred

Companion/Complementary Planting: Grow with other thymes, rosemary, and lavender.

Harvesting: Harvest the aerial parts of lemon thyme at any point during the growing season. Use scissors or snips for easy harvesting.

Market Potential: Moderate

Medicinal Benefits: Lemon thyme is a wonderful herb for children's health concerns and for supporting good digestive function.

Parts Used: Aerial parts, fresh or dried

Home Pharmacy Uses: Infusion, traditional tincture, cider vinegar tincture, syrup, elixir, lozenge, ointment, salve, cream, balm, foot soak, sleep pillow, bath herb, infused oil, honey

✂ Lemon Thyme at a Glance

▸ **Plant Cycle:** Perennial

▸ **Type of Growth:** Herbaceous

▸ **Light Requirements:** Sun, partial shade

▸ **Water Requirements:** Low to moderate

▸ **Parts Used:** Aerial

▸ **Home Pharmacy Uses:** Infusion, traditional tincture, cider vinegar tincture, syrup, elixir, lozenge, ointment, salve, cream, balm, foot soak, sleep pillow, bath herb, infused oil, honey

Trifolium pratense
Red Clover

Properly picked red clover is in good demand. Many companies prefer to buy it dried, and will not want leafy portions of the stem included. Picking red clover is very labor- and time-intensive, but the market for high-quality blossoms exceeds the supply. ❧

Personality: Perennial; herbaceous (Zones 5–9)

Height: 12 to 15 inches (30 to 38 centimeters)

Bloom Traits: Large, bright pink blossoms appear throughout the summer months.

Likes/Dislikes: Red clover is found growing in many different disturbed areas, but it is especially fond of mountain meadows and the banks of rivers and streams. It is often seen along mountain roadsides where moisture runoff gathers.

Propagation/Maintenance: Stratify seeds for several weeks and then sow directly outdoors. Germination will occur in 7 to 10 days at a rate of 75 percent or so. Space these clumping plants 12 inches (30 centimeters) apart. Water moderately.

Sun/Soil: Full sun, partial shade; no special soil needs

Harvesting: Harvest the flower blossoms only. They should be picked carefully by hand. This is time-consuming, but necessary for sale to most herb buyers. To dry this herb properly, pick in the early morning while the dew is still on the blossoms. Handle them gently; they bruise easily. Lay flowers on a screen in a single layer and allow to dry. They will have a deep purplish red color when fully dried. Store in a glass jar or paper bag, out of direct light and heat, until ready for use.

Market Potential: High, especially for good-quality blossoms

Medicinal Benefits: A tonic and medicinal food herb, red clover is often suggested for women's and children's health concerns, winter illnesses, and immune system support.

Parts Used: Flowers, fresh or dried

Home Pharmacy Uses: Infusion, traditional tincture, cider vinegar tincture, syrup, elixir, lozenge, medicinal food, ointment, salve, cream, balm, honey

❦ Red Clover at a Glance

▸ **Plant Cycle:** Perennial

▸ **Type of Growth:** Herbaceous

▸ **Light Requirements:** Full sun, partial shade

▸ **Water Requirements:** Moderate

▸ **Parts Used:** Flowers

▸ **Home Pharmacy Uses:** Infusion, traditional tincture, cider vinegar tincture, syrup, elixir, lozenge, medicinal food, ointment, salve, cream, balm, honey

Urtica dioica
Nettle

The nettle plant has gotten an undeserved bad reputation from the childhood memories most people hold of getting stung by a patch of them. The stinging sensation, which feels like a bad sunburn and may be accompanied by small blisters, is caused by formic acid, and occurs only when the plant is touched in its fresh state. Cooked, processed, or dried nettles will no longer cause stinging. If you do get stung by nettles, the discomfort will be gone in an hour or so. Wearing protective clothing and gloves is a good idea when working with this herb. It is also wise to plant nettles in a part of the garden away from paths and out of the reach of young children. 🌿

Nettle at a Glance

- **Plant Cycle:** Perennial
- **Type of Growth:** Herbaceous
- **Light Requirements:** Full sun, partial shade, shade
- **Water Requirements:** Moderate to heavy
- **Parts Used:** Aerial
- **Home Pharmacy Uses:** Infusion, traditional tincture, cider vinegar tincture, elixir, medicinal food, ointment, cream, salve, balm, foot soak, bath herb, infused oil, honey, liniment

Personality: Perennial; herbaceous (Zones 5–9)

Height: 2 to 4 feet (.6 to 1.2 meters)

Bloom Traits: Tiny, cream-colored, pearl-like flowers bloom from early to late summer.

Likes/Dislikes: Nettles grow around the world. This species is native to Eurasia and is now naturalized in North America. It grows wherever there is good moisture: near streams, rivers, ponds, or lakes. It usually is found in a disturbed area.

Propagation/Maintenance: Stratify seeds and sow them directly in the garden, or sow indoors and transplant out in late spring. About half of the seeds sown will germinate. Propagation by root divisions is best done in early spring. Wear gloves when working with seedlings or when dividing plants. This plant spreads, so space it about 12 inches (30 centimeters) apart. Provide moderate to heavy amounts of water.

Sun/Soil: Full sun, partial shade, shade; prefers a soil high in organic matter (4 to 5 percent)

Companion/Complementary Planting: Plant with sunflowers and fennel.

Harvesting: Harvest the aerial parts at any point during the growing season, except when flowering. Wear heavy gloves and use snips or scissors. If you are preparing the leaves fresh, keep your gloves on. Dried, nettles won't cause stinging.

Market Potential: Moderate

Medicinal Benefits: Nettles are definitely a whole-body tonic, rich in vitamins and minerals, and are a fabulous medicinal food. Valuable for male and female reproductive health, respiratory and urinary tract concerns, immune health, and allergy relief, they are great for the skin and hair and appropriate for childhood ailments.

Parts Used: Aerial parts, fresh or dried

Home Pharmacy Uses: Infusion, traditional tincture, cider vinegar tincture, elixir, medicinal food, ointment, cream, salve, balm, foot soak, bath herb, infused oil, honey, liniment

Valeriana officinalis
Valerian

Valerian root is recognized for its very strong, unpleasant fragrance. Interestingly, beautifully scented flowers bloom on this pungent plant in the spring. It is an excellent medicinal herb that is widely valued. ❦

Personality: Perennial; herbaceous (Zones 4–7)

Height: 3 to 4 feet (.9 to 1.2 meters)

Bloom Traits: Valerian flowers are intensely fragrant and white with just the palest touch of pink. They bloom in late spring and early summer.

Likes/Dislikes: A woodland plant by nature, valerian prefers to grow near streams, lakes, and ponds. It thrives in conditions from sun to shade providing it grows in moist soil.

Propagation/Maintenance: Seeds germinate well at 60 to 70 percent with no special treatments. Sprouting takes place in 7 to 14 days. Transplant outdoors in late spring. Seed may also be sown directly into the garden soil in early spring. Space plants 12 to 15 inches (30 to 38 centimeters) apart; they will grow in clumps. Moderate to heavy watering is necessary.

Sun/Soil: Full sun, partial shade (preferred), shade; prefers a humus soil

Harvesting: The roots are harvested in the fall of the first year or the spring of the second year. Valerian is a perennial plant, but the roots follow the behavior of biennial roots and begin to deteriorate in quality by the fall of the second year. For easiest harvest, use a garden fork or needle-nose spade, and dig on a day when the soil is consistently moist but not overly wet.

Market Potential: High

Medicinal Benefits: Valerian is used as a strong sedative and pain-reliever.

Parts Used: Roots, fresh or dried

Home Pharmacy Uses: Decoction, traditional tincture

❧ Valerian at a Glance

- ▸ **Plant Cycle:** Perennial
- ▸ **Type of Growth:** Herbaceous
- ▸ **Light Requirements:** Full sun, partial shade, shade
- ▸ **Water Requirements:** Moderate to heavy
- ▸ **Parts Used:** Roots
- ▸ **Home Pharmacy Uses:** Decoction, traditional tincture

Verbascum thapsus

Mullein

Mullein is a great indicator of soil contamination. If the soil is high in heavy metals or chemical contaminants, mullein's normally straight stalk will often grow twisted and distorted. Do not harvest from such plants; they likely will not be safe for use.

Occasionally the mullein stalks will be forked but still growing relatively straight. This simply indicates that the stalk was broken off somehow and responded by sending up multiple stalks from that point. 🌿

🌿 Mullein at a Glance

- ▸ **Plant Cycle:** Biennial
- ▸ **Type of Growth:** Herbaceous
- ▸ **Light Requirements:** Full sun
- ▸ **Water Requirements:** Low to moderate
- ▸ **Parts Used:** Roots, leaves, flowers
- ▸ **Home Pharmacy Uses:** Infusion, decoction, traditional tincture, cider vinegar tincture, syrup, ointment, salve, cream, balm, infused oil

Personality: Biennial; herbaceous (Zones 3–9)

Height: 5 to 6 feet (1.5 to 1.8 meters)

Bloom Traits: In the second year, a stalk of individual yellow flowers emerges. Blooming begins at the bottom and continues up to the tip over the course of a couple of weeks in mid- to late summer.

Likes/Dislikes: Grows in mountain meadows, open grasslands, and along streams and rivers. Prefers a disturbed area with dry, well-drained soil. Mullein does not grow in tropical regions; it likes a more arid climate.

Propagation/Maintenance: Seeds are easy. Sow directly outdoors or indoors for transplanting in mid- to late spring will improve germination to 75 to 80 percent. It takes about 2 weeks to sprout. Reseeds vigorously and grows in clumps. Space plants 15 inches (38 centimeters) apart and water lightly to moderately.

Sun/Soil: Full sun; well-drained soil

Companion/Complementary Planting: Grow with oxeye daisy, mugwort, feverfew, and echinacea.

Harvesting: The whole plant is used but the different parts are harvested at different times. Harvest roots with a needle-nose spade or garden fork in the fall of the first year's growth or in the spring of the second. Handpick leaves at any time during the growing season; I prefer late spring or early summer. Handpick flowers during blooming time. To harvest the flowering tops, snip off the upper 3 to 6 inches (7 to 15 centimeters) of stalk, when it is heavily flowering and full of buds just about to pop. Lay out the plant material for several hours in a shady location to give weevils a chance to exit the plant parts.

Market Potential: Moderate (roots, leaves) to high (flowers). Ask if your buyer will accept flowers only or flowering stalks; flowers take much longer to harvest.

Medicinal Benefits: Roots are considered specific for the urinary tract; leaves and flowers are used for the respiratory tract, the skin, and the ears.

Parts Used: Roots, leaves, and flowers, fresh or dried

Home Pharmacy Uses: Infusion, decoction, traditional tincture, cider vinegar tincture, syrup, ointment, salve, cream, balm, infused oil

Verbena hastata
Blue Vervain

When blue vervain flowers, the blooms begin at the bottom of the green spikelet and circle their way toward the top. Gradually, over a period of several weeks, this herb will finish growing its delicate lavender flowers at the tip of the spikelet. They remind me of fairy garden flowers. 🌿

Personality: Perennial; herbaceous (Zones 3–7)

Height: 3 to 5 feet (.9 to 1.5 meters)

Bloom Traits: Blue to purple flower spikes that stretch from spike base to tip bloom from mid- to late summer.

Likes/Dislikes: Blue vervain most often grows in open grassy prairies, although it also enjoys moist locations. Its purple flowers are easily visible from some distance as it grows among native grasses and other wildflowers.

Propagation/Maintenance: Stratify the seeds for at least 2 weeks and then sow indoors. Transplant out by mid- to late spring. Space 12 inches (30 centimeters) apart; a clump of blue vervain may easily grow four to six stalks on one plant. Water moderately.

Sun/Soil: Sun, partial shade; well-drained soil that is reasonably high in organic matter

Harvesting: It is preferable to harvest the aerial parts while the plant is blooming. I harvest the upper half of the plant at this time with snips or scissors.

Market Potential: Moderate; many manufacturers prefer certified organic blue vervain over wild-harvested plants

Medicinal Benefits: Blue vervain relieves a variety of cold and flu symptoms, and is considered a stress-relief herb.

Parts Used: Flowering aerial parts, fresh or dried

Home Pharmacy Uses: Infusion, traditional tincture, cider vinegar tincture, syrup, elixir, lozenge, ointment, salve, cream, balm, foot soak, bath herb, honey

🌾 Blue Vervain at a Glance

▸ **Plant Cycle:** Perennial

▸ **Type of Growth:** Herbaceous

▸ **Light Requirements:** Sun, partial shade

▸ **Water Requirements:** Moderate

▸ **Parts Used:** Aerial

▸ **Home Pharmacy Uses:** Infusion, traditional tincture, cider vinegar tincture, syrup, elixir, lozenge, ointment, salve, cream, balm, foot soak, bath herb, honey

Verbena officinalis
Vervain

Keep vervain nearby for those stressful days. Pluck a sprig and prepare yourself a cup of vervain tea. The herb will help settle your nerves, allowing you to proceed with your day in a calmer fashion. 🌿

Personality: Perennial; herbaceous (Zones 5–9)

Height: 12 to 36 inches (30 to 90 centimeters)

Bloom Traits: Flowers are pale purple, blooming from mid- to late summer.

Likes/Dislikes: Vervain, native to the mountains of the Mediterranean, grows best in disturbed soils.

Propagation/Maintenance: Stratify seeds for 1 to 2 weeks and then sow indoors. Germination takes 3 to 4 weeks, with a success rate of less than 50 percent. Transplant outside in late spring. Vervain will root wherever a stem lies against the ground. This causes the plant to slowly spread across a given area. Space plants 10 to 12 inches (25 to 30 centimeters) apart, and provide low to moderate amounts of water.

Sun/Soil: Full sun, partial shade; well-drained soil

Companion/Complementary Planting: Vervain is great planted in community with horehound, thyme, and California poppy.

Harvesting: Flowering aerial parts can be harvested with snips or scissors from mid- to late summer.

Market Potential: Low; blue vervain (*Verbena hastata*) is a much more popular herb in the natural products industry

Medicinal Benefits: Used for winter illnesses, respiratory concerns, digestive tract conditions, achy muscles, and to aid in stress relief, vervain is also an excellent herb for children.

Parts Used: Flowering aerial parts, fresh or dried

Home Pharmacy Uses: Infusion, traditional tincture, syrup, elixir, lozenge, foot soak, bath herb, infused oil, honey

🌺 Vervain at a Glance

- ▸ **Plant Cycle:** Perennial
- ▸ **Type of Growth:** Herbaceous
- ▸ **Light Requirements:** Full sun, partial shade
- ▸ **Water Requirements:** Low to moderate
- ▸ **Parts Used:** Aerial
- ▸ **Home Pharmacy Uses:** Infusion, traditional tincture, syrup, elixir, lozenge, foot soak, bath herb, infused oil, honey

Vinca minor, V. major
Periwinkle

This plant has much lore associated with it. Once called the sorcerer's violet, periwinkle was thought to possess magical powers. It was used in many different potions, and was even worn as a protection against witches. Europeans believed the flowers brought immortality and held aphrodisiac properties. In England, brides wore periwinkle in their garters to ensure a fertile marriage. It is thought that the "blue" in the traditional wedding rhyme "something old, something new/something borrowed, something blue" is an allusion to this bright flower.

Periwinkle often graces our landscape as a rambling ground cover. It is a vigorous plant and easy to grow in the garden. From looking at the bright blue flowers, no one would guess what a fantastic skin antiseptic periwinkle is. 🌿

Personality: Perennial; herbaceous (Zones 4–9 for *V. minor*, Zones 7–11 for *V. major*)

Height: 10 to 12 inches (25 to 30 centimeters)

Bloom Traits: Periwinkle blue flowers appear throughout the growing season.

Likes/Dislikes: A woodland and forest plant, it prefers the shady and moist environment of a tree canopy. This herb is native to Europe and is naturalized in eastern North America.

Propagation/Maintenance: Root divisions in the spring or fall will work nicely. Propagation by cuttings, using a liquid rooting hormone, is also very successful. Space these spreading plants 15 to 20 inches (38 to 50 centimeters) apart and water lightly to moderately. *V. minor* is an aggressive ground cover, so monitor its spreading.

Sun/Soil: Full sun, partial shade (preferred), shade; no special soil requirements

Harvesting: Harvest the aerial parts with snips at any time during the growing season.

Market Potential: Low

Medicinal Benefits: Periwinkle is a strong astringent herb for skin health.

Parts Used: Aerial parts, fresh or dried

Home Pharmacy Uses: Infusion, traditional tincture, foot soak

---

🌿 **Periwinkle at a Glance**

- ▸ **Plant Cycle:** Perennial
- ▸ **Type of Growth:** Herbaceous
- ▸ **Light Requirements:** Full sun, partial shade, shade
- ▸ **Water Requirements:** Low to moderate
- ▸ **Parts Used:** Aerial
- ▸ **Home Pharmacy Uses:** Infusion, traditional tincture, foot soak

Viola species

Violet

Violets are an old-fashioned, wonderful addition to any herb garden. When they bloom in spring and early summer, the air is filled with the most lovely fragrance — amazing for such tiny flowers. 🌺

Violet at a Glance

▸ **Plant Cycle:** Perennial

▸ **Type of Growth:** Herbaceous

▸ **Light Requirements:** Full sun, partial shade, shade

▸ **Water Requirements:** Moderate to heavy

▸ **Parts Used:** Leaves, flowers

▸ **Home Pharmacy Uses:** Infusion, traditional tincture, cider vinegar tincture, syrup, compress, poultice, crystallized, elixir, lozenge, ointment, medicinal food, salve, cream, balm, foot soak, bath herb, infused oil, honey, liniment

A.K.A.: Heartsease (*V. tricolor*)

Personality: Perennial; herbaceous (Zones 2–11, depending on species)

Height: 4 to 8 inches (10 to 20 centimeters)

Bloom Traits: Most people are familiar with the purple flower, but violets also come in yellow, pink, and white. It usually blooms in the spring.

Likes/Dislikes: Many violets are woodland plants that prefer a shady and moist growing environment. However, some species grow in a variety of habitats.

Propagation/Maintenance: Stratify seed for a minimum of 3 months. Sow in early spring indoors. Seed prefers dark conditions to germinate. Germination is sporadic over several weeks; expect between 30 and 40 percent overall germination. Transplant outdoors in mid- to late spring. These clumping plants reseed vigorously. Space violets 6 to 8 inches (15 to 20 centimeters) apart and water moderately to heavily.

Sun/Soil: Full sun, partial shade, shade (depending on species); prefers a soil high in organic matter (4 to 5 percent)

Harvesting: Leaves may be handpicked at any time during the growing season. Flowers are picked in spring, but leave some for seed production.

Market Potential: Low

Medicinal Benefits: Often used for heart health, digestive tract and respiratory tract concerns, skin conditions, and throat ailments, violets are also helpful for women's and children's health, stress relief, and nervous system support.

Parts Used: Leaves and flowers, fresh or dried

Home Pharmacy Uses: Infusion, traditional tincture, cider vinegar tincture, syrup, compress, poultice, crystallized, elixir, lozenge, medicinal food, ointment, salve, cream, balm, foot soak, bath herb, infused oil, liniment, honey

Vitex agnus-castus
Chaste Berry

In the Middle Ages, chaste berry was called monk's pepper. Monks used to grind the herb and use it as a substitute for the similar-tasting black pepper. These clergymen believed that the plant would suppress libido, but, in fact, it does not.

Chaste Berry at a Glance

- **Plant Cycle:** Perennial
- **Type of Growth:** Woody
- **Light Requirements:** Full sun, partial shade
- **Water Requirements:** Moderate
- **Parts Used:** Leaves, flowers, berries
- **Home Pharmacy Uses:** Decoction, traditional tincture, cider vinegar tincture, syrup, elixir, medicinal food

Personality: Perennial; woody (Zones 6–9)

Height: 2 to 10 feet (.6 to 3.0 meters)

Bloom Traits: Gorgeous lavender-colored spikes of flowers bloom in mid- to late summer beginning in the second year. In the colder parts of its range, chaste berry may not flower or form fruit.

Likes/Dislikes: Chaste berry is from the Mediterranean region of the world. It likes growing in hot temperatures and appreciates some humidity.

Propagation/Maintenance: Stratify seeds for 3 to 4 weeks, then scarify them and soak them in warm water for 30 minutes before sowing. Sow immediately indoors. Seeds may take up to 4 weeks to germinate. The germination rate is 50 to 60 percent, although I have sometimes gotten better results. Transplant outdoors, 12 to 24 inches (30 to 60 centimeters) apart, in late spring when the weather is well settled. This herb grows in clumps and requires moderate watering.

Sun/Soil: Full sun, partial shade; well-drained soil

Harvesting: The leaves and tender stem growth of the upper 4 inches (10 centimeters), along with the flowers and ripening seeds, may be harvested for medicinal purposes. (Most buyers will prefer only the ripened berries, without the leafy and flowering portions.) Use snips to harvest leafy portions; if only berries are desired, gently rub the berries loose from the stems and then screen them out of the leafy and flowering parts. I prefer to make my remedies using the leafy, flowering portions along with the berries.

Market Potential: High to very high, particularly for dried

Medicinal Benefits: Considered a tonic herb for both the male and female reproductive systems.

Parts Used: Leaves, flowers, and berries, fresh or dried

Home Pharmacy Uses: Decoction, traditional tincture, cider vinegar tincture, syrup, elixir, medicinal food

Yucca species

Yucca

Yucca is a plant that is used in an amazing number of ways. The root is the medicinal part, but the leaves can also be used to make fabric, mats, baskets, and twine. The flowers are delicious. 🌿

Personality: Perennial; herbaceous (Zones 5–10)

Height: 15 inches (38 centimeters) and taller

Bloom Traits: Large, beautiful, cream-colored blooms appear in late spring and early summer.

Likes/Dislikes: Most yuccas grow in arid regions of the world but they will thrive in moist areas. They prefer wide open, sunny places where the soil is well drained. They are common in disturbed areas.

Propagation/Maintenance: Stratify seed for 3 months in the freezer or for 2 weeks in moist sand in the refrigerator. Sow seed indoors and supply extra heat for optimum germination and growth. Germination percentages are usually good for treated seed, often in the neighborhood of 60 to 70 percent. Germination time is sporadic and can take up to 4 weeks, so be patient. Transplant outside, 15 inches (38 centimeters) apart, in late spring or early summer. Yucca grows in clumps and requires light watering.

Sun/Soil: Full sun; well-drained soil

Harvesting: Harvest yucca roots in the fall of the second year's growth. Use a garden fork or needle-nose spade — or both — to dig roots. Leaves may be harvested in the late spring or throughout the summer using a sharp pair of snips. Wear gloves when working with these plants; they tend to poke the skin. Flowers are handpicked in the spring.

Market Potential: Moderate

Medicinal Benefits: The root is considered beneficial for joint conditions and men's health concerns.

Parts Used: Roots, leaves, and flowers, fresh or dried

Home Pharmacy Uses: Decoction, traditional tincture, cider vinegar tincture, syrup, compress, poultice, ointment, salve, cream, balm, foot soak, bath herb, infused oil, liniment

🌿 Yucca at a Glance

- ▶ **Plant Cycle:** Perennial
- ▶ **Type of Growth:** Herbaceous
- ▶ **Light Requirements:** Full sun
- ▶ **Water Requirements:** Low

- ▶ **Parts Used:** Roots, leaves, flowers
- ▶ **Home Pharmacy Uses:** Decoction, traditional tincture, cider vinegar tincture, syrup, compress, poultice, ointment, salve, cream, balm, foot soak, bath herb, infused oil, liniment

Personality: Perennial; herbaceous (Zones 9–11)

Height: 3 to 4 feet (.9 to 1.2 meters)

Bloom Traits: Spikes of waxy, yellowish green flowers with some purple on the lip. It rarely flowers under cultivation.

Likes/Dislikes: A shade-loving plant, ginger grows in hot, moist, tropical regions of the world.

Propagation/Maintenance: Propagate by planting the rhizomes. They grow in "sections" that can be broken apart easily at the joints. Look for buds, called eyes, on each section; plant the rhizome with the eyes facing up toward the soil surface. Plant rhizomes 1 to 2 inches (2.5 to 5 centimeters) below the surface of the soil, about 15 inches (38 centimeters) apart. Ginger rarely produces seeds, and when seeds do form they are sterile. Ginger grows mainly in a clump and spreads slowly by rhizomes. It requires a great amount of water.

Sun/Soil: Shade to partial shade; prefers a rich, loamy, and well-worked soil that is kept evenly moist

Harvesting: A garden fork is ideal. Harvesting times depend on how ginger is to be used. For fresh preparations, harvest rhizomes between 4 and 7 months of age. The older (7 to 9 months), more pungent and less fleshy rhizomes are harvested for dried preparations. According to Paul Schulick (author of *Ginger: Common Spice & Wonder Drug*), research shows peak constituent levels at 265 days.

Market Potential: Very high

Medicinal Benefits: Ginger is a warming herb, often used for the circulatory and digestive systems. It is a well-known antioxidant and has anti-inflammatory properties. Ginger is used for fevers, nausea, dizziness, headaches, as a heart tonic, and to support male and female reproductive systems.

Parts Used: Rhizome, fresh or dried

Home Pharmacy Uses: Infusion, traditional tincture, cider vinegar tincture, syrup, elixir, crystallized, medicinal food, compress, poultice, lozenge, ointment, salve, cream, balm, foot soak, bath herb, infused oil, honey, butter, liniment

Zingiber officinale

Ginger

Although the yield for organically grown ginger is roughly half of nonorganically grown plants, the market value for organic ginger can be 5 or 6 times greater.

Ginger at a Glance

- ▸ **Plant Cycle:** Perennial
- ▸ **Type of Growth:** Herbaceous
- ▸ **Light Requirements:** Partial shade, shade
- ▸ **Water Requirements:** Heavy
- ▸ **Parts Used:** Rhizome

- ▸ **Home Pharmacy Uses:** Infusion, traditional tincture, cider vinegar tincture, syrup, elixir, crystallized, medicinal food, compress, poultice, lozenge, ointment, salve, cream, balm, foot soak, bath herb, infused oil, honey, butter, liniment

Recommended Reading

Ableman, Michael. *From the Good Earth: A Celebration of Growing Food Around the World.* New York: Harry N. Abrams, Inc., 1993.

————. *On Good Land: The Autobiography of an Urban Farm.* San Francisco: Chronicle Books, 1998.

American Herbal Products Association. *Botanical Safety Handbook.* Boca Raton, FL: CRC Press, 1997.

Cowan, Eliot. *Plant Spirit Medicine.* Newberg, OR: Swan, Raven & Company, 1995.

Ellis, Barbara W., and Fern Marshall Bradley. *The Organic Gardener's Handbook of Natural Insect and Disease Control.* Emmaus, PA: Rodale Press, 1996.

Findhorn Community. *The Findhorn Garden.* New York: Harper & Row, Publishers, 1975.

Foster, Steven, and James A. Duke. *Peterson Field Guide: Eastern/Central Medicinal Plants.* New York: Houghton Mifflin Company, 1990.

Garland, Sarah. *The Herb Garden.* New York: Penguin Books, 1984.

Green, James. *The Herbal Medicine-Maker's Handbook.* Forestville, CA: Simplers Botanical Company, 1990.

Grieve, Maud. *A Modern Herbal, Volumes I and II.* New York: Dover Publications, Inc., 1981.

Kains, M. G. *Five Acres and Independence: A Handbook for Small Farm Management.* New York: Dover Publications, 1973.

Kalmbacher, George. *The Color Dictionary of Flowers and Plants for Home and Garden.* New York: Crown Publishers, 1969.

Kindscher, Kelly. *Medicinal Wild Plants of the Prairie.* Lawrence, KS: University Press of Kansas, 1992.

McCullag, James C. *The Solar Greenhouse Book.* Emmaus, PA: Rodale Press, 1978.

Miller, Amy Bess. *Shaker Medicinal Herbs.* Pownal, VT: Storey Books, 1998.

Mollison, Bill. *Permaculture: A Designers' Manual.* Tyalgum, Australia: Tagari Publications, 1988.

Moore, Michael. *Medicinal Plants of the Desert and Canyon West.* Santa Fe, NM: Museum of New Mexico Press, 1989.

————. *Medicinal Plants of the Mountain West.* Santa Fe, NM: Museum of New Mexico Press, 1979.

————. *Medicinal Plants of the Pacific West.* Santa Fe, NM: Red Crane Books, 1993.

Murray, Elizabeth. *Cultivating Sacred Space: Gardening for the Soul.* San Francisco: Pomegranate, 1997.

Phillips, Roger. *Wild Food.* Boston: Little, Brown and Company, 1986.

Pleasant, Barbara. *The Gardener's Bug Book: Earth-Safe Insect Control.* Pownal, VT: Storey Books, 1994.

————. *The Gardener's Guide to Plant Diseases: Earth-Safe Remedies.* Pownal, VT: Storey Books, 1995.

————. *The Gardener's Weed Book: Earth-Safe Controls.* Pownal, VT: Storey Books, 1996.

Proctor, Rob, and David Macke. *Herbs in the Garden.* Loveland, CO: Interweave Press, 1997.

Romain, Effie, and Sue Hawkey. *Herbal Remedies in Pots.* New York: DK Publishing, 1996.

Silverman, Maida. *A City Herbal.* Woodstock, NY: Ash Tree Publishing, 1997.

Sturdivant, Lee, and Tim Blakely. *Medicinal Herbs in the Garden, Field and Marketplace.* Friday Harbor, WA: San Juan Naturals, 1999.

Tilford, Gregory L. *Edible and Medicinal Plants of the West.* Missoula, MT: Mountain Press Publishing Company, 1997.

————. *From Earth to Herbalist: An Earth-Conscious Guide to Medicinal Plants.* Missoula, MT: Mountain Press Publishing Company, 1998.

Weed, Susun S. *Healing Wise.* Woodstock, NY: Ash Tree Publishing, 1989.

Wren, R. C. *Potter's New Cyclopaedia of Botanical Drugs and Preparations.* Essex, England: The C. W. Daniel Company Limited, 1988.

Resources

Seeds and Plants

High Country Gardens
2902 Rufina Street
Santa Fe, NM 87505
(800) 925-9387
Plants only

Horizon Herbs
P.O. Box 69
Williams, OR 97544
(541) 846-6704
Seeds and bare roots

J. L. Hudson, Seedman
Star Route 2, Box 337
La Honda, CA 94020
Seeds only

Johnny's Selected Seeds
1 Foss Hill Road
RR 1, Box 2580
Albion, ME 04910
(207) 437-4395
Seeds

Lawyer Nursery, Inc.
950 Highway 200 West
Plains, MT 59859
(406) 826-3881
Seeds and plants

Native Seeds/SEARCH
526 North Fourth Avenue
Tucson, AZ 85705
(520) 622-5561
Seeds

Plants of the Southwest
Aqua Fria
Route 6, Box 11A
Santa Fe, NM 87501
(505) 471-2212
Seeds

Western Native Seed
P.O. Box 1463
Salida, CO 81201
(719) 539-1071
Seeds

Gardening Supplies

Ward's Nursery and Garden Center
600 South Main Street, Route 7
Great Barrington, MA 01230
(413) 528-0166
Plants, tools, and other gardening supplies

Organic Growing Supplies

Gardens Alive!
5100 Schenley Place
Lawrenceburg, IN 47025
(812) 537-8651
Pest and insect controls, fertilizer

Peaceful Valley Farm Supply
P.O. Box 2209
Grass Valley, CA 95945
(888) 784-1722 or (530) 272-4769
Pest and insect controls, fertilizers, tools, seeds, irrigation and greenhouse supplies

Beneficial Insect Suppliers

Green Spot, Ltd.
93 Priest Road
Nottingham, NH 03290
(603) 942-8925

M & R Durango
P.O. Box 886
Bayfield, CO 81122
(800) 526-4075 or (303) 259-3521

Testing Services

For soil testing and insect and disease identification, contact the county extension service in your area.

Seed Testing of America
630 South Sunset Street
Longmont, CO 80501
(303) 651-6417
Tests seed viability and germination percentages

Educational and Networking Resources

American Herbal Products Association (AHPA)
4733 Bethesda Avenue, #B345
Bethesda, MD 20814
(301) 951-3204
E-mail: AHPA@ix.netcom.com

American Penstemon Society
1569 South Holland Court
Lakewood, CO 80232

Food and Drug Administration (FDA)
Center for Food Safety and Applied Nutrition Dietary Supplements
200 C Street SW
Washington, DC 20204
(202) 205-4168 or (888) 293-6498
Web site: www.FDA.gov and www.nara.gov/fedreg.com

Herb Research Foundation
1007 Pearl Street, Suite 200
Boulder, CO 80302
(303) 449-2265
All types of medicinal herb information

National Center for the Preservation of Medicinal Herbs
33560 Beech Grove Road
Rutland, OH 45775
(740) 742-4407

National Nutritional Foods
Association (NNFA)
3931 MacArthur Boulevard, Suite 101
Newport Beach, CA 92660
(949) 662-6272
Web site: www.nnfa.org

United Plant Savers
P.O. Box 98
East Barre, VT 05649
(802) 479-9825

U.S. Small Business Administration
P.O. Box 0660
Denver, CO 80201
(303) 844-3985

Organic Certification Information

The county extension service in your area should have certification information for your state. Information is also available from the following organizations.

Organic Growers and Buyers Association
7362 University Avenue NE, Suite 208
Fridley, MN 55432
(615) 572-1967
Information and certification service

Organic Trade Association
P.O. Box 1078
Greenfield, MA 01302
(413) 774-7511
Information service

Quality Assurance International
12526 High Bluff Drive, Suite 300
San Diego, CA 92130
(619) 792-3531
Certification service

Remedy-Making Supplies

Apothecary Products
11531 Rupp Drive
Burnsville, MN 55337
(612) 890-1940
Suppository molds, graduated cylinders

Industrial Containers
3572 West 1820 South
Salt Lake City, UT 84126
(800) 748-4250
Bottles and jars, droppers, caps

Mountain Rose Herbs
20818 High Street
North San Juan, CA 95960
(800) 879-3337
Excellent selection of medicine-making supplies, bottles, beeswax, oils, etc.

Scent Jewels
327 East Fremont Drive
Tempe, AZ 85282
(800) 838-5226 or (602) 838-5226
Essential-oil supplies

StarWest Botanicals
11253 Trade Center Drive
Rancho Cordova, CA 95742
(916) 853-9354
Bottles, jars, oils

Index

Page numbers in *italics* indicate photos. Page numbers in **boldface** indicate charts.